The New Minority

The New Minority

White Working Class Politics in an Age
of Immigration and Inequality

JUSTIN GEST

OXFORD
UNIVERSITY PRESS

OXFORD
UNIVERSITY PRESS

Oxford University Press is a department of the University of Oxford. It furthers
the University's objective of excellence in research, scholarship, and education
by publishing worldwide. Oxford is a registered trade mark of Oxford University
Press in the UK and certain other countries.

Published in the United States of America by Oxford University Press
198 Madison Avenue, New York, NY 10016, United States of America.

Library of Congress Cataloging-in-Publication Data
Names: Gest, Justin, author.
Title: The new minority : white working class politics in an age of immigration and inequality / Justin Gest.
Description: New York, NY : Oxford University Press, 2016. |
Includes bibliographical references and index.
Identifiers: LCCN 2016010130 (print) | LCCN 2016022736 (ebook) |
ISBN 9780190632540 (hardcover : alk. paper) | ISBN 9780190632557 (pbk. : alk. paper) |
ISBN 9780190632564 (Updf) | ISBN 9780190632571 (Epub)
Subjects: LCSH: Working class—Political activity—Great Britain. | Working class—Political activity—
United States. | Whites—Great Britain—Politics and government. | Whites—United States—Politics and
government. | Whites—Great Britain—Social conditions. | Whites—United States—Social conditions. |
Right wing extremists—Great Britain. | Right wing extremists—United States.
Classification: LCC HD8395 .G47 2016 (print) | LCC HD8395 (ebook) | DDC 324.086/230941—dc23
LC record available at https://lccn.loc.gov/2016010130

9 8 7 6 5 4

Paperback printed by Webcom Inc., Canada
Hardback printed by Bridgeport National Bindery, Inc., United States of America

CONTENTS

PREFACE

The Radicalized Middle

Cockneys are pretty much extinct. I'm an Englishman without England. What does it mean to be English anymore? We've been invaded without any blood being spilled. All I hear are foreign languages and it makes me feel like I'm in a foreign country. I feel like other people should have the same opportunities as us, but that we should come first. We should be in the center, but I feel like I'm on the outside, as far from the center as possible.
—Ollie Marks, age 30
Dagenham, East London

The middle has fallen out of American and European politics.

Across the Atlantic, political movements increasingly appeal to the extreme left and right, reflecting the polarization of political constituencies. Rebel representatives and violent activists employ tactics to stall government, hinder coalition building, and communicate their agendas through antidemocratic means. Opinion polls suggest that the public, despite expressing a preference for compromise, is increasingly uncompromising in its preferences.

This polarization and brinkmanship can be explained in multiple, overlapping ways. Some observers note that campaign financing and publicity incentivize confrontation and disagreement among elected officials. Other observers blame the news media's voracious appetite for drama and its focus on ratings at the expense of accuracy and equilibrium. Still others blame electoral and governing institutions that provide fringe groups with an outsized ability to obstruct the predominant prerogatives of those at the middle of the political spectrum.

In this book, I suggest that these trends intensify an underlying demographic phenomenon: the communities of white working class people[1] who once occupied the political middle have decreased in size and moved to the fringes, and

American and European societies are scrambling to recalibrate how they might rebuild the centrist coalitions that engender progress.

It was not so long ago that the white working class occupied the middle of British and American societies. During the mid-twentieth century, the vast majority of white people lacked university credentials and worked in manual or non-managerial labor, often in the manufacturing industry (US Census Bureau 2015a; Skidelsky 2013; Pierce and Schott 2012; Sveinsson 2009; Abramowitz and Teixeira 2009: 395). The middle class was made up of people without university degrees, and the wage gap between those with and without university educations was relatively small (US Census Bureau 2015b; Abramowitz and Teixeira 2009: 392). Many industrial sectors were unionized (UK Department for Business, Innovation and Skills 2015; Bureau of Labor Statistics 2015). The diffuse confederation of white working class voters was the bellwether that backed presidents Franklin Roosevelt and then Dwight Eisenhower; and prime ministers Winston Churchill and then Clement Attlee. Later, many supported Lyndon Johnson and then Richard Nixon; and in the United Kingdom, Harold Macmillan and then Harold Wilson.

Today, members of the same demographic sometimes resort to violence and intimidation to achieve a fraction of the political influence they once wielded as a powerful voting bloc (Dancygier 2010). Estranged from the middle, they feel silenced and ignored by mainstream political parties and therefore, in the United States and the United Kingdom, have created their own.

In the United States' constrained two-party system, the Tea Party emerged as a rebellious faction within the Republican Party after the election of President Barack Obama in 2008. In each subsequent congressional election, this movement expanded their share of the Republican caucus and deposed a number of establishment candidates, including House Majority Leader Eric Cantor in November 2014 and eventually Speaker John Boehner, who was pressured to resign in October 2015. Tea Party members along with many white working class people elevated the unexpected presidential candidacy of real-estate mogul Donald Trump to international prominence and the Republican nomination in 2016. Simultaneously on the left, a separate faction has sought the reorientation of American capitalism. Embodied by the Occupy Wall Street movement during the financial crisis, this group has pulled Democrats to more populist and protectionist economic stances. Among white working class Americans, many denounce global trade deals and censure the collusion between Washington lawmakers and K Street's business lobbyists, and then, in the same sentence, go on to revile undocumented immigrants, demand cuts to welfare programs, and scoff at ongoing movements for racial justice.

In Europe since 2010, far-right parties have scored victories across national and European Parliamentary elections. The Swiss People's Party, the

Danis People's Party, and the National Front took more than a quarter of their most recent national votes in Switzerland, Denmark, and France respectively (European Parliament 2015). In Britain, the United Kingdom Independent Party (UKIP) collected 27% of the British vote in the 2014 European elections, 12% in the 2015 Parliamentary election (BBC News 2015), and soon displaced Prime Minister David Cameron when the 'Leave' campaign they backed won the referendum on Britain's EU membership in June 2016. Amid multiple losses, the British Labour Party panicked, appointed far-left socialist Jeremy Corbyn, and then endured a leadership vacuum of their own, without any clear policy platform or electoral strategy in sight. Among white working class Britons, many seek greater unionization and the expansion of social services while simultaneously supporting the dissolution of the European Union, backing the mass deportation of immigrants, and condemning Islam.

At this juncture, most mainstream political parties have eschewed the full endorsement of the most extreme viewpoints, despite their obvious traction among many white working class people. The way a ringmaster gingerly approaches a tiger, parties cautiously navigate around these viewpoints—often acknowledging their legitimacy without engaging their policy implications for fear of alienating more moderate supporters. Both left and right moderates are reluctant to embrace white working class xenophobia and the economic protectionism that will turn off growing ethnic minority voting blocs and the neoliberal business lobby, respectively. Barack Obama won both the 2008 and 2012 presidential elections despite double-digit defeats among white voters without university degrees (Levison 2013). David Cameron was also re-elected in 2015 without the white working class vote (Ford 2015). White working class people have become at best a destabilizing force on attempts to assemble broad, centrist coalitions and at worst, a diminishing, enigmatic afterthought.

How did we get here? How does a group of people synonymous with Middle Britain and Middle America—the heart, soul, and backbone of their respective countries—drift to marginality? What drives their emerging radicalism? What transformations lead a group with such enduring numerical power to, in many instances, consider themselves a "minority" in the countries they once defined?

ACKNOWLEDGMENTS

Upon our first encounter, Chicago community organizer Josh Hoyt said to me, "I don't talk to no one no one sent." (In other words, he required a personal reference before partnering or really even opening up to someone he didn't already know.) This sentiment extends to so many white working class people and their communities, if not so overtly or explicitly. In their pubs and neighborhoods, our credentials are not achievements or affiliations, but rather the people we know who vouch for our credibility and character. For a scholar of immigration politics extending his work to immigrants' primary antagonists, I needed to build these credentials one relationship at a time. And despite the distrust that characterizes the white working class communities I studied in Youngstown and East London, so many people were kind enough to hear me out and welcome me into their homes. Many I am now proud to call my friends.

In Youngstown, Phil Kidd holds the keys to all doors. His knowledge of people and politics is vast in the city he adopted and now loves more than any native. I am also very grateful to Alyssa Lenhoff, Tim Francisco, and John Russo who facilitated my visiting scholarship at Youngstown State University. It was also a luxury to return each day to the home of Bobby Hagan and Michele Lepore-Hagan, my wise and hospitable landlords. Thank you to Mike Shaffer for hosting me at Youngstown's YMCA, and to the founders of Greyland (Rocco Sait, Melanie Buonavolonta, Paul Burgess, and Hannah Woodroofe), my hangout.

In East London, I thank the responsive civil servants at the Barking and Dagenham Council for their guidance and assistance. Mark Adams was always there when I had a question, and I was also aided by Nicki Lane, Paul Hodson, John Dawe, and Darren Rodwell. I learned the most from Wayne Tuckfield, who went out of his way to integrate me into East London's daily life. Most essentially, and across both cities, I appreciate the honesty and candidness of my many respondents, from whom I learned so much about struggle and dignity, and dignity in struggle.

The book would not have been possible without research grants from the Horowitz Foundation for Social Policy, Harvard University's Center for European Studies, Harvard University's Institute for Quantitative Social Science, and George Mason University's School of Policy, Government, and International Affairs. These grants supported my fieldwork, but also an extraordinary team of research assistants over the years—Sheyda Aboii, Francesca Annichiarico, Andrew Bush, Robert Dagger, Aubrey Grant, Brendan Kopp, and Aaron Roper. You were each so diligent, and have such bright futures ahead.

My quantitative data analysis is thanks to my partnership with Rob Ford, who generously placed my series of questions on his broader YouGov survey in the United Kingdom. I am also deeply indebted to Jerry Mayer, for his support of the American survey and my scholarship more generally, and to Tyler Reny, who was always prepared to share his statistical acumen and sharp analytical skills.

At multiple junctures, I profited from critical feedback from a number of friends and colleagues, who were kind enough to take time from their schedules to read my work and provide their suggestions and encouragement. Thank you to Anna Boucher, Nick Carnes, Noam Gidron, Sean Gray, Zoli Hajnal, Peter Hall, Jennifer Hochschild, Kay Schlozman, Kris-Stella Trump, and Jennifer Victor. And thank you to Nancy DiTomaso, Jack Goldstone, Eric Kaufmann, Michele Lamont, Monica McDermott, Kimberly Morgan, Dan Rasmussen, John Russo, Danny Schlozman, and Jessica Streib, who participated in my book workshop or volunteered to review the entire manuscript.

I am also very grateful to Niko Pfund, Dave McBride, Anne Rusinak, and especially Angela Chnapko at Oxford University Press for their thorough editorship and belief in my work.

The book's impetus emerged during the defense of my doctoral research on European Muslim political behavior at the London School of Economics, when Steve Vertovec challenged me to apply my ideas to white working class people. The idea was subsequently nourished by my various mentors—Terri Givens, David Held, Henrietta Moore, and Sid Verba. Thank you so much for your unconditional support, thoughtful guidance, and never-ending enthusiasm for my ideas.

At Harvard University, my profound thanks to David Ager, Mary Brinton, Tim Colton, Steve Levitsky, Judy and Sean Palfrey, Mary Waters, and Cheryl Welch for supporting my fellowship and lectureship. I also very much appreciate the assistance provided by Nancy Branco, Frankie Hoff, Sharon Jackson, Karen Kaletka, Joanna Lindh, Dotty Lukas, Suzanne Ogungbadero, Laura Thomas, and Diana Wojcik. At George Mason University, I am grateful to David Hart, Naoru Koizumi, Mark Rozell, and Roger Stough for facilitating my research and welcoming me to the university. I also very much appreciate the assistance provided by Chris Anclien, Bill Coester, Michelle Ely, Barb Hill, Susan McClure, and Ryan Pryke.

Controversial and current, my subject matter frequently came up in conversations with my friends, who supported me and shared their perspectives. My sincerest thanks to Lynn Armitt, Matt Bai, Gideon Bresler, Nick Broadway, Belinda Broido, Kat and Sarah Burgess, Andrew Butters, Matt Cipolla, Joana Cruz, Jeremy Ferwerda, Ole Frahm, Justin Fraterman, Marian Gamboa, David and Kira Gest, Kathy and Ted Gest, Catherine Giguère, Irem Güney, Debra Hauer, Christina Helden, Janet Hiebert, Sharon Howell, Xandra Kayden, Laura Kelly, Chris Kyriacou, Ralph Mamiya, Sona Narula, Jessica Purmort, Eric Rachlin, Will Rasmussen, Parisa Roshan, Katrina Rouse, Erik Sand, Arthur Schilling, Bill Schneider, Desireh Sedaghat, Amish Shah, Patricia Shour, Alexandra Sicotte-Levesque, Stephen Noble Smith, Jack St. Martin, Shai Steinberger, Susan Wilen, Amanda Weingarten, Jeffrey Weingarten, Sara Whitaker, and Nader Yermian for their sustained interest and support.

Finally, I would like to acknowledge the love I received from my family members over the course of writing this book. For backing my every endeavor, thank you to my parents Gail and Max Gest, my brother Darren, my sister-in-law Rebecca, my parents-in-law Tatjana and György Hargitai, my brother-in-law Gyuri, my nephew Ádám, my adopted grandparents Ann and Matt VandeWydeven, my grandmother Jeannette Litt, my late grandfather Alvin Litt, and to my most precious wife Monika and our daughter Valentina, who have given me unending joy and inspiration.

Hell's Kitchen, New York City
JUSTIN GEST
June 2016

The New Minority

1

Introduction

The snake which cannot cast its skin has to die. As well the minds which are prevented from changing their opinions; they cease to be mind.
—Friedrich Nietzsche

White working class people are perplexing.

They are subject to the pressures of intensifying inequality across much of the developed world, and yet inherit the advantages of language and integration. They live in societies that are subject to significant demographic change, but not in such a way that the predominance of white people is in question. They are so frustrated politically that they would rather start their own movements than submit to the compromises required by mainstream coalitions. Some have become quite rebellious. Has ever a group so purportedly marginalized possessed such power?

In this book, I contend that this tension—between the vestiges of white working class power and its perceived loss—produces the phenomenon of their radicalization. I use multiple research methods to examine white working class people's attitudes and clarify these paradoxes, in order to improve our understanding of white working class people's political behavior—which can be extreme and, thanks to their numbers, remains meaningful in North American and European societies.

Multiple Narratives of Decline

A key reason that white working class people perplex observers is that multiple narratives depict their plight and attempt to explain their political behavior in the United States and the United Kingdom.

According to an *economic narrative*, Western countries' reorientation toward more service-oriented, high technology, globalized economies since the Second World War required the outsourcing of light manufacturing and basic services to developing nations with minimal labor standards. This economic transformation undermined the social and political strength of white working class communities by diminishing their ranks, loosening associational life, and jettisoning state-sponsored welfare support systems which had been in place in the postwar era. The white working class individuals who adapted to these changes have since joined a reconsolidated social majority of white people and ethnically diverse immigrants who constitute globalization's winners (and losers who are at least acquiescent).

Those slower to adapt are commonly understood as the dispersed, unorganized holdouts of an earlier era without access to the benefits of a globalized economy. Over the course of the twentieth century in the United Kingdom, the proportion of the working population employed as "manual workers" fell from 75% to 38%, while the proportion of professionals and managers rose from 8% to 34% (Sveinsson 2009). In 1940 in the United States, 74% of employed workers were white and did not hold professional or managerial jobs. By 2006, that percentage plummeted to 43% (Abramowitz and Teixeira 2009: 394–395). In 1940, 86% of adults 25 years old and over were white and without a four-year college degree. By 2007, that percentage declined to 48% (ibid.). In 1947, 86% of American families were white families with less than $60,000 in income (in 2005 dollars). In contrast, that percentage declined to 33% by 2005 (ibid.).

The postindustrial middle classes have therefore swelled with various European-origin, white communities and upwardly mobile immigrant-origin people who are increasingly integrating into a largely inclusive capitalist meritocracy that has elevated standards of living and altered social solidarities. This transformation not only shrunk the community of those understanding themselves as white working class; it also splintered the broader working class into an aspirational immigrant stratum, and the enduring remainder of poor white natives. For the poor, chances of upward mobility remain low. The United States and the United Kingdom feature the least economic mobility among OECD countries (OECD 2010; Corak 2013); parental income remains highly determinant of lifelong economic status. This conclusion has been elaborated in great detail in research on the United States, where mobility has stalled for over a generation (Chetty et al. 2014).

Advocates of this resource-oriented perspective argue that while ethnic, gender, and cultural backgrounds are factors in explaining a person's life prospects and behavior, it is the social class into which one is born that is still most determinant (National Equality Panel 2010). In this depiction, the outmoded white working class is juxtaposed with a white middle class and upper class that both expanded with economic development in the twentieth century and have since created economic—along with cultural—space between themselves and those who failed to make this socioeconomic leap. Such resource disadvantages have been shown to consistently lead to disengaged political behavior (see Verba and Nie 1972; Verba, Nie, and Kim 1978; Verba, Schlozman, and Brady 1995; Schlozman, Verba, and Brady 2013).[1] The widening gap is indeed frequently justified on meritocratic grounds that subtly insinuate cultural differences. Nevertheless, resource-oriented explanations of white working class marginalization argue that the social stigma ascribed to that demographic is merely the residue of severe inequality.

A *moral narrative* characterizes poor white people as antagonists clinging to the unfair advantages of an earlier time. Resistant to progressive change in order to maintain power over ethnocultural minorities, poor white people are conventionally portrayed as the last vestige of the most forgettable era in twentieth-century social history—what Usherwood (2007) described as the "amoral and apolitical section in society who are neither deserving nor poor. It is a group that is against learning, anti-intellectual, and comprised of individuals who—in the words of one commentator—'despise browns and blacks' (especially if they are making something of their lives) and also education, enlightenment and internationalism" (Alibhai-Brown 2007). Accordingly, poor white people represent an antagonist to other, often equally poor, ethnocultural minority groups—groups that have worked to gain equal footing through efforts like the continuing civil rights movement.

More subtly, white elites, whose antecedents may have once supported policies of exclusion and rose to elite status through prejudiced systems of education and promotion, vilify poor whites (see Jones 2011; Wray 2006). In the drive to counterbalance historical discrimination, both white elites and minority groups often distance themselves from poor white people to account for their success in these systems—systems that working class white people had a lesser hand in building.

Specifically, white members of the "underclass" have been singled out as behaviorally or morally inferior. In the United Kingdom, they are associated with "backwardness" and stereotypes condemning "unclean" and "lazy benefit-hunting mother[s] of several children" (Jones 2011; Wray 2006), even while white people are also able to claim a rhetorical high ground as their country's "heart and soul"—the people that historically spilled blood and perspired for a continuing national existence.

Charles Murray (2012) describes the white underclass, and its deviant norms in the United States, thusly: "In the years after 1960, America developed something new: a white lower class that did not consist of a fringe, but of a substantial part of what was formerly the working class population." Murray goes on to describe the deviant characteristics of this new white underclass at length. First, he contends that the members of this white underclass violate the traditional American norm of industriousness. More and more of these white individuals are claiming disability benefits or are employed in "less-than-full-time work"; Murray (2012: 171, 176) notes that this is especially true among less-educated white males.

Furthermore, the labor force participation rate has decreased considerably in the white underclass, again with less-educated white males leaving the labor force in much greater numbers (Murray 2012: 172–173). According to Murray, these trends cannot simply be explained away by citing macroeconomic conditions because the overall economy grew well enough from 1960 to the present day. Instead, Murray argues that these trends are a sign that the American norm of industriousness "has softened" in the white underclass: "White males of the 2000s were less industrious than they had been twenty, thirty, or fifty years ago," he wrote, "and . . . the decay in the industriousness occurred overwhelmingly [among the least educated]" (181).

Beyond work habits, Murray cites the deterioration of American norms with regard to religiosity and marriage. He writes that, "White America as a whole became more secular between 1960 and 2010, especially from the beginning of the 1990s. Despite the common belief that the working class is the most religious group in white American society, the drift from religiosity was far greater in [working class America]" (200; see Wilcox 2010: 48–49 for further supporting evidence). Since church-going is a major source of social capital, Murray argues that the decline in religiosity directly impacts the environmental tools available to members of the white underclass, and therefore has serious implications for individual prospects in social mobility. Similarly, Murray and others have pointed to a deterioration of the institution of marriage within the white underclass. Lower status whites are much more likely to get divorced within 10 years of marriage, have children out of wedlock, and report unhappiness with their current marriage (see Douthat and Salam 2008; Wilcox 2010). To put the scale of these trends into perspective, the extramarital birth rate among white American women with a college degree has remained nearly constant at 5% since the 1960s. Meanwhile, the rate of extramarital births among white American women without a high school diploma is now 60% (Murray 2012: 161–162; see also Douthat and Salam 2008: 134).

In a recent column lamenting white working class support for Donald Trump's presidential candidacy, the *National Review*'s Kevin Williamson (2016) wrote:

> "[If] you take an honest look at the welfare dependency, the drug and alcohol addiction, the family anarchy—which is to say, the whelping of human children with all the respect and wisdom of a stray dog—you will

come to an awful realization. It wasn't Beijing. It wasn't Washington, as bad as Washington can be. It wasn't immigrants from Mexico, excessive and problematic as our current immigration levels are. It wasn't any of that.

Nothing happened to them. There wasn't some awful disaster. There wasn't a war or famine or a plague or a foreign occupation. Even the economic changes of the past few decades do very little too explain the dysfunction and negligence—and the incomprehensible malice—of poor white America. So the gypsum business in Garbutt ain't what it used to be. There is more to life in the 21st century than wallboard and cheap sentimentality about how the Man closed factories down.

The truth about these dysfunctional, downscale communities is that they deserve to die. Economically, they are negative assets. Morally, they are indefensible. Forget all your cheap theatrical Bruce Springsteen crap. Forget your sanctimony about struggling Rust Belt factory towns and your conspiracy theories about the wily Orientals stealing our jobs. Forget your goddamned gypsum. . ... The white American underclass is in thrall to a vicious, selfish culture whose main products are misery and used heroin needles."

Williamson, Murray, and other commentators who have highlighted the deviant norms of lower-status whites may do so primarily as a way to draw boundaries that are meant to justify working class whites' lower social position. And yet, at the same time, other accounts focus on deteriorating mores in an attempt to signal a brewing crisis within the white working class itself. It is often difficult to distinguish between these two agendas. Independent of the underlying objective, however, it is consequential that more attention is being paid to the cultural norms of a white underclass (Murray 2012; Jones 2011), in a manner similar to treatment of poor racial and ethnoreligious minority groups.

This moral account contends that white working class political behavior is a product of cultural habits that diverge from other groups of white people and an essentialized understanding of "white culture" (see Demie and Lewis 2010 for examples; and see reviews in Jones 2011). It juxtaposes the ostensible complacency, ignorance, and backwardness of white working class people with the industry, naïveté, and resourcefulness of immigrants and minority groups who push forward despite adversity and structural disadvantage, but also with the way the primarily East and West Coast bourgeoisie have adapted to the economic transformations that they had a hand in driving. However, the ubiquity of this culturalist account appears to be institutionalizing itself. It acts as a sort of structural hindrance to the advancement of white working class individuals, who have trouble shaking off this stigma, and therefore improving their economic well-being and making political claims effectively. As this book shows, white working class people conventionally value hard work and use it—for better or worse—as a mark of moral distinction and as a means of identification to separate themselves from non-white working class countrymen.

This dichotomous moral narrative obscures an important *demographic narrative*. Before the Second World War, many industrialized societies were largely racially homogenous, and mainstream social divisions were grounded in differences of religious sect or white ethnicity (native nationals, along with people of Jewish, Irish, Mediterranean, Levantine, and Eastern European origin). Indeed, from the founding of the nation through 2004, a majority of Americans were white and had concluded their education before obtaining a four-year college degree (Brownstein 2011). Even as late as the 1990 census, whites without a college degree represented more than three-fifths of American adults. However, with the steady influx of immigrants, attenuating native fertility rates, and an increasingly global economy, the fault lines of sociopolitical relations shifted (see Kaufmann 2004c; Abrajano and Hajnal 2014).

With the end of the Second World War, an amalgam of ethnic white groups emerged as an expanding middle class. They occupied the industrial working classes of the United States and parts of Western Europe and were boosted by dual-income families, elevated life expectancies, and steady economic growth. Over time, immigrants from disparate countries of origin, spanning Latin America and East Asia in the United States, South Asia in the United Kingdom, North Africa in Western Europe, and Turkey in Central Europe, replaced these ethnic whites. Since 2004 in the United Kingdom, the minority population has almost doubled, and minority groups account for 80% of the country's population growth (Sunak and Rajeswaran 2014: 6). The nonwhite population represented 37% of the United States population in 2015, and it is expected to grow as the American population under age 5 is over 50% nonwhite (US Census Bureau 2015c). The United States' foreign-born population grew from 9.6 million (4.7%) in 1970 to 40 million (12.9%) in 2010—the highest share since 1920 (Singer 2013).

Ever since the earliest waves of immigration to Western industrialized democracies, these societies have grappled with the challenge of socially, politically, and economically integrating diverse peoples into economies and societies organized around equal rights. Accordingly, social hierarchies metamorphosed. Whether white people's working class status is defined according to education-, occupation-, or income-based standards, a 30% to 50% decline in the relative size of this group from the World War II era to today in the United States has transpired (Abramowitz and Teixeira 2009: 395). Recent research (Case and Deaton 2015) suggests that these trends may be intensified by an extraordinary 22% rise in the mortality rate of white working class people since 1999—which has taken place in an era during which the death rates among all other groups decline.

Even with the decline of the British and American manufacturing industries and the countries' ongoing demographic changes, white working class people still compose a significant sector of the voting public. They represent at least one-third of the American population as of 2005, depending on how working class status is understood:

- 36% of Americans are white people without college degrees holding non-salaried jobs (Jones and Cox 2012);
- 33% of American families are white households earning less than $60,000 per year (Abramowitz and Teixeira 2009);
- 43% of Americans are white people without professional or managerial jobs (ibid.);
- 48% of Americans are white people without a four-year college degree (ibid.).

As a result, this subset of the American electorate can still affect electoral outcomes, but nevertheless remains misunderstood and under-mobilized. Even though nearly 50% of the US population is white and without a college degree, this group made up only 39% of voters in 2008 and 35% of voters in the 2010 election (CNN 2008; 2010). This is true despite the fact that white Americans are disproportionately of voting age vis-à-vis non-white Americans. The British white working class is even larger. According to the 2011 census, white British people make up 80.5% of all Britons, and unlike Americans, the British working class has shown a propensity to identify as "working class" even when employed in middle-class occupations, some of which require some higher education.

Post-Traumatic Cities

The setting for these countervailing narratives is not uniform, but they are prominent in what I call "post-traumatic" cities. Post-traumatic cities are exurbs and urban communities that lost signature industries in the mid- to late-twentieth century and never really recovered. Examples include Blackburn, Bolton, Hartlepool, Hull, Wolverhampton, and East London in the United Kingdom, and Erie, Flint, Gary, Kenosha, Michigan City, Toledo, and Youngstown in the Rust Belt of the United States. At the peak of Western states' manufacturing economies, particular companies or industries employed enough people for a long enough duration that they could single-handedly support these cities' economies and dominate their politics. Today, such cities endure as shells of their former splendor.

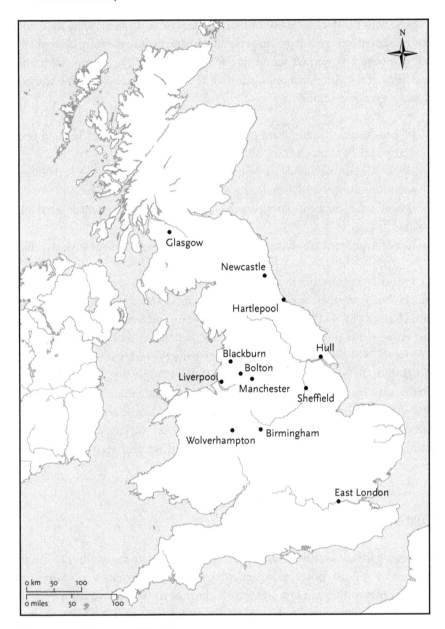

Map 1 Map of the United Kingdom.

East London was planned as a "Garden City," to be anchored by major manufacturers that would lure white working class East Enders away from London's
congested inner city after it became crowded with Eastern European Jewish
(and later, South Asian) immigrants. In 1922, May & Baker's chemical plant
relocated to Dagenham from Wandsworth. In 1925, the Barking Power House

electric station was established in Creekmouth. And in 1931, the Ford Motor Company built what would become an enormous factory on several square miles of Dagenham's riverfront (Hudson 2009). These employers provided dependable jobs for the residents of the new estate. The population of Dagenham soared from 9,000 to 90,000 between 1921 and 1931, and the combined populations of Barking and Dagenham increased another 50% before 1951.

However, after the mid-1970s, East London's economy went the way of the Ford factory, which endured massive downsizings. As that market declined, unions weakened, labor laws liberalized, and industrial jobs followed a more global move offshore. Britain's postindustrial economy had little use for Barking and Dagenham's white working class tradesmen, as it shifted to high technology and a broader service sector.

Alongside the economic changes, the borough's demographics also altered. A new generation of residents moved in to take advantage of mortgages and rentals that were a fraction of those in inner London. While some purchased homes, many new immigrants were assigned to public housing in council-owned rowhouses and tower blocks. There were sub-Saharan Africans, Lithuanians, Bosnians, Poles, and South Asian Muslims in each of the borough's wards. By

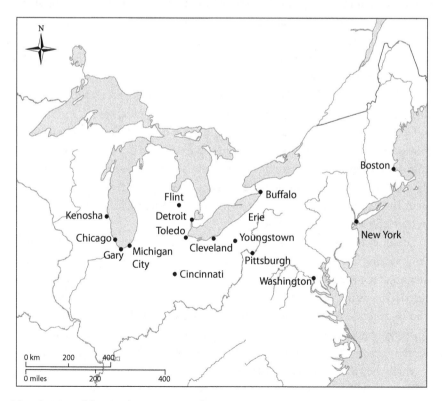

Map 2 Map of the Northeastern United States.

the 2000s, these immigrant groups composed about half the population of East London, as an extension of London's globalizing metropolis.

Youngstown, Ohio was once known as "Steeltown USA." For years, the foundries and furnaces of about a half-dozen companies provided not only jobs, but also housing, loans, supporting industries, philanthropy, and sites for political organization and social life. Throughout the late 1800s and early 1900s, a 30-mile-long stretch of mills developed along the Mahoning River. Rapid population growth fueled the city's meteoric industrialization, thanks to the arrival of working class immigrants from every corner of Europe. By 1930, nearly half the city's population owned their homes, and by the 1940s, Youngstown's population reached 170,000—about 90% of which was white (Linkon and Russo 2002: 38; Buss and Redburn 1983: 2).

These circumstances ended with the swift collapse of Youngstown's steel industry in the late 1970s and early 1980s. In a matter of six years, Ohio State Employment Services estimates that 50,000 jobs were lost in basic steel and related industries, costing Youngstown's working class $1.3 billion in annual manufacturing wages (ibid.). Unemployment climbed to a staggering 24.9% in 1983 and a wave of personal bankruptcies and foreclosures resulted (ibid.). The city spiraled into a tailspin characterized by domestic abuse, substance abuse, divorce, suicide, murder, and ultimately, the mass departure of its population. Today, Youngstown has barely a third of its 1970 population, and about half of its citizens are now black or Latino—groups who simply did not flee as quickly as their white neighbors.

East London and Youngstown are but two examples of a class of cities that have experienced this trauma of a simultaneous economic, social, and political collapse. They are also characteristic of the more industrialized neighborhoods of larger cities. There and elsewhere, the white working class populations I consider are consumed by a nostalgia that expresses bitter resentment toward the big companies that abandoned their city, a government that did little to stop them from leaving, and a growing share of visible minorities who are altering their neighborhoods' complexion.

Other cities and regions have undergone economic and social decline. However, few have experienced such a decline so universally and so immediately after enjoying the zenith of prosperity and influence that once characterized industrial towns in the mid-twentieth century. Post-traumatic cities were often so wholly dependent on a single company or sector that their sudden closure or downsizing undercut an entire social, political, and economic infrastructure— depriving their vast communities of the sense of stability, power, and centrality to which they had become accustomed.

The sprawling factories, towering smokestacks, and vast warehouses that once pumped and percolated with the booming business of an era now sit still in the center of cities that remain physically oriented around their lost productivity. Residents maneuver around the crumbling, rusty relics of industrialism much like the way today's Greeks and Italians maneuver around the roped-off ruins of Ancient Athens and Rome. They simultaneously taunt inhabitants with memories of better days, and render false hope that they are one big break from returning to glory.

This determinism of the built environment and pervasive nostalgia corrodes innovation and paralyzes the evolution of these communities. And as a result, the characteristic politics of these cities is often backward facing. Rather than adapt to the post-traumatic future, people seek to reinstate the pre-traumatic past—which is an impossibility. Small programs have begun to shrink some cities, returning outlying land to nature and clearing the amassed tangle of deserted railroad tracks, electrical lines, and auxiliary piping. But as with urban planning, the politics of modernization are laced with resentment.

Most of us witness the politics of resentment at the national level, where it is detached from its origins in post-traumatic environments. Headlines depict the xenophobic platforms of nativist political movements rising to power. Election results show exit polls touting white working class support for candidates vowing to limit social programs. Satellite news channels beam images of unions and working class white people protesting global trade deals or demanding the maintenance of outdated subsidies. Police mobilize against hate crimes and forms of political violence.

However, such events are exceptional, and they distract from the diversity of white working class political behavior. Many white working class people engage in peaceful democratic processes. A large group is simply too busy to advocate, given the demands and pressures of daily life. Still others quietly withdraw to the fringes. How can we understand these political choices and the attitudes that underpin them? How can we understand white working class marginality?

A Theory of Marginality

Much of our knowledge of political behavior links the intensity of citizens' political participation with their resources, in the form of income, education, and skills. Yet among similarly under-resourced communities of white working class people, what leads some individuals to engage in the democratic political system to create reform, and others to circumvent the political system by rebelling or withdrawing from it? This is not a question of intensity, but rather one that inquires about the nature—the orientation—of individuals' political activism.

In earlier research, I addressed this question as it relates to communities of Muslims in Western Europe—highly politicized people who have largely demonstrated their inclination to robust democratic engagement, but also their vulnerability to insularity and violent extremism (Gest 2010). In many ways, and especially in Europe, white working class people represent Western Muslims' primary antagonist. In Britain, nativists have frequently clashed in the streets with Muslims protesting for the establishment of shariah (Islamic law). In the United States, white working class vigilantes have sought to harm random Muslim citizens in retaliation for equally random attacks pursued by extremists in the name of Islam. Indeed, many of the claims that each community makes of the political system is in reaction to the other. Working class white people often seek to restrict immigrants' access to welfare, abolish affirmative action policies, and receive priority in public housing. Muslims often want more muscular anti-discrimination provisions, reduced pressure to assimilate, and increased accommodation of cultural and religious difference.

By examining white working class politics in parallel with the (far more expansive) scrutiny of Muslim politics, I hope to develop a broader understanding of political marginality—in terms of both rebellion and withdrawal—in the context of democratic engagement. My earlier research on Western Muslims found that senses of deprivation—the discrepancy between individuals' expectations and their perceptions of reality—drive political choices. More specifically, I found that Muslim respondents whose expectations of political power and social rights were greatly disappointed were more likely to join radical, antidemocratic organizations. Correspondingly, I found that Muslim respondents whose expectations were more fulfilled were more likely to engage in democratic political participation or be complacent.

Can we speak of a broader theory of political marginality? These earlier conclusions would be strengthened if they were supported by evidence from multiple communities subject to disadvantage. White working class communities provide a powerful test because they represent a most different case study—a most unlikely counterpoint to the plight of Muslims and other visible minorities in Western democracies. While it is unreasonable to expect Muslims and white working class people to report the same sources of dissatisfaction, I ask whether their dissatisfaction is structured in a similar manner and similarly driving their political choices. Can we speak of a broader theory of alienated and engaged political behavior?

How Do You Measure Marginality?

The great challenge in studying marginality is its typical form as a nonevent. Social scientists conventionally measure the observable (political participation, political organizations, government decisions, etc.), so marginality is often only evident in the absence of observable action (withdrawal or proscribed rebellion). And naturally, those who are withdrawn or rebellious are less likely to be visible to researchers' eyes. The withdrawn are less likely to be a part of a survey sample, because they are less likely to be accessed in the first place. The rebellious are less likely to acknowledge their violent or radical behavior for fear of incrimination or concerns about palatability. I therefore pursue my investigation in ways that allow for greater sensitivity to withdrawal and rebellion, in a manner that makes subjects feel comfortable sharing their views and activities.

I begin with ethnographies of East London and Youngstown to develop the vernacular of people's marginality and map the full diversity of their political behavior. East London and Youngstown do not represent cases that enable the examination of a peculiar trend. Rather, they exemplify the British and American postindustrial story that takes place in the manufacturing sectors of many cities and towns. They are two prominent cases among many in their respective countries.[2] Their trajectories take place in historically stable democracies with postindustrial economies that were severely affected by global financial crises. Each group is conventionally thought to be the core ethnoreligious constituency of their respective countries, despite an era of increasing demographic diversification and low native birth rates. Each group occupies a similar social position within their social milieu, which is characterized by marginality and, simultaneously, cultural authenticity. However, the United Kingdom and the United States have different approaches to social programs, local governance, and immigration (see Appendix A). This cross-national lens permits a broader discussion of white working class political behavior, and correspondingly, an opportunity to build broader hypotheses about it.

I spent three months in each community and carried out in-depth, unstructured interviews with 120 people to understand daily life and political culture— the interaction between respondents' "personal narratives" and surrounding social developments (Maynes, Pierce, and Laslett 2008). I supplemented this with archival research about the communities in an effort to further trace the formation of political beliefs expressed by interviewees.

I also analyzed survey data about white working class people's attitudes and behavior to test these ideas. To render respondents a greater sense of privacy and to access people less available by phone or in person, I relied upon Internet-based, nationally representative polling—a YouGov survey administered to nearly 5,000 British respondents, and an SSI poll of just over 1,000 American respondents. The survey questions were based on the ideas derived from my ethnographies and allowed me to consider the conclusions drawn from them with a much larger sample. (A fuller discussion of my research methods may be found in this book's appendix.)

In both my fieldwork and quantitative analysis, I emphasize three lines of inquiry. First, I pursue a more reflexive understanding of white, working class

American and British identity. In order to do so I sought to assess how participants understand their personal and social position vis-à-vis other reference groups in society, such as blacks, immigrants, or educated bourgeois whites. This reflects an enduring scholarship about structures of identity as a matter of group position, and more specifically, how white Americans react to perceived threats to the organization of social hierarchies (see Blumer 1958; Hofstadter 1967; Roediger 1991; Olson 2008; Parker and Barreto 2013; Masaoka and Junn 2013). As Cheryl Harris (1993: 1713) writes about the course of American history, "the set of assumptions, privileges, and benefits that accompany the status of being white have become a valuable asset that whites sought to protect." As these settled expectations have become so embedded, white people understand them to be "a natural order of things that cannot legitimately be disturbed" (Harris 1993: 1778). How are these relationships reconciled and reflected in political choices? How are these relationships reconciled and reflected in political choices? In this way, I engage individuals' senses of social, economic, and political positionality.

Second, I encouraged participants to think visually and elaborate about their ideals of American and British democracy, their visions of the future, and their characterization of present sociopolitical circumstances. I expect this will most clearly illuminate individuals' sense of place, their nostalgia, and the lost landscapes of their past. Do these utopian imaginaries exist? What are individuals' perceptions of change, their personal and collective future, and the trajectory of their society? In this way, my investigation reveals the discrepancies between their ideals and their perceived realities.

Third, I attempted to understand how similar people under similar circumstances hold divergent attitudes about their positions and divergent ideas about how (and whether) to make claims of the political system. I solicited the personal histories and ideational background of the people I interviewed to trace the process of their attitude formation. What are the attitudes behind a sense of estrangement and a sense of engagement? How are these attitudes connected to and informed by perceptions of socioeconomic position and trajectory? How do these individuals propose to best reconcile social, economic, and political inequities? What courses of action are available to those who feel marginalized, and how are such courses understood and pursued?

Pressing Questions and Findings

This book's investigation of the motivations behind white working class political choices plugs into a series of pressing, public questions discussed by researchers and other observers.

IS WHITE WORKING CLASS MARGINALITY AND POLARIZATION A TRANSATLANTIC PHENOMENON?

It is tempting to perceive a convergence of Western European and North American politics toward a shared narrative. Both continents are undergoing fundamental shifts in the structure of their societies. Their economies have largely completed the sweeping deindustrialization and denationalization that began in the early 1980s. As part of this shift and the realities of demographic aging, their societies have admitted millions of ethnically diverse immigrants to address skill shortages, reunify with family, and rescue refugees. And their political spectra have been altered by the weakening position of labor movements and the integration of expanding urban bourgeoisies and these immigrant-origin groups into the left. In this spirit, white working class politics possess a transatlantic dimension.

However, the two continents diverge in the way these trends are understood and approached. The United States and Canada are settler states where nearly all citizens have traceable origins as immigrants themselves, while Europeans can still speak of (constructed) national identities forged in blood and historical sacrifice. In particular, the American economy features fewer safety nets and a more open marketplace that its citizens (often blindly) understand to be ultimately more meritocratic. And the American political spectrum is constrained by the expediencies of a two-party system that suppresses the potential emergence of breakaway movements responding to fleeting senses of urgency or perceived rigidity in the mainstream parties. These convergences and divergences inform and contextualize the politics of white working class people I observed in each venue. They make the dynamics of white working class political behavior quite different across the two contexts.

Still, from my research, there emerges a transatlantic politics of white working class people defined by their senses of economic obsolescence and social relegation. This is not to say that white working class people have all gotten poorer, although many have. My respondents exhibit a resilience to financial difficulty, to which many have become accustomed. Rather, this is to say that—across the postindustrial regions of Western Europe and North America—white working class people sense that they have been demoted from the center of their country's consciousness to its fringe. And many feel powerless in their attempts to do something about it.

IS WHITE WORKING CLASS ANGST MERELY RACISM?

Prejudice and discrimination span generations and certainly play a role in white working class politics. However, the resentment that white working class communities express through their rhetoric and political choices is not as simple as their discomfort with the proximity of ethnic minorities in their neighborhoods (e.g., Newman 2012a; Abrajano and Hajnal 2014). Rather, the individuals I surveyed and interviewed as part of my ethnographic fieldwork believe ethnic minorities have been given social advantages at the expense of white working class people. My respondents perceive a society that (they acknowledge) once rendered white people an inherent advantage, but now overcompensates for these missteps. In short, many white working class people feel like the victims of discrimination.

Politically, white working class people face a catch-22: should they complain about the promotion of ethnic minorities at their expense, they are labeled racists. Should they blame an economic model featuring expanding inequality and increasingly unstable employment, they are deemed to be lazy. Consequently, the politics of race and demographic change is fought indirectly, and often in coded terms. In Britain, debates linger over public housing priorities, and whether and when immigrants deserve access to welfare. In the United States, white working class people—often dependent on social programs themselves—perceive ethnic minorities as exploitative of welfare and vote to reduce its scope. In Britain, the right is tugging the political center to cut ties with the European Union and curtail the admission of immigrants, including those who possess the highest skills. In the United States, the criminalization of approximately 12 million undocumented immigrants has overshadowed the politics of a system that has settled nearly 60 million newcomers over the last two generations. These issues related to the status of ethnic minorities are actually proxies for issues related to the changing status of native-born white people in the societies they once defined.

WHAT DRIVES SOME WHITE WORKING CLASS PEOPLE TO RADICAL POLITICAL BEHAVIOR?

People seem to be more frustrated by that which they have lost, than that which they never possessed. In this book, I find that white working class people's rebellion is driven by a sense of deprivation—the discrepancy between individuals' expectations of power and social centrality, and their perceptions of fulfillment. More specifically, white working class people are consumed by their loss of social and political status in social hierarchies, particularly in relation to immigrant and minority reference groups. Their politics are motivated and pervaded by a nostalgia that reveres, and seeks to reinstate, a bygone era.

While this finding emerges from my ethnographic fieldwork, it is corroborated by the data from my nationally representative survey data. I find that political deprivation—as measured by perceived loss of power—creates a form of political capital that is channeled into not only protest activism, but also support for the violence and xenophobia of radical right groups. The data suggest that while the wealthier, the educated, and the older opt for peaceful means of protest, younger white working class men are more likely to pursue acts of rebellion. Driving this radicalism is not merely a measurable sense of political deprivation and economic obsolescence, but according to the data and controlling for other factors, a profound sense of social deprivation—a shift to the periphery of their society.

Outline of the Book

The challenge of this book is to explain the divergent individual political behavior of white working class people in response to their marginality. This marginality is contested, for good reason, by observers who point to the residual advantages that even poor white people continue to enjoy in the United Kingdom and the United States. However, there is reason to—at a minimum—consider their self-assertion that they represent a new minority. The next chapter explores this contention.

By putting into conversation diverse literatures addressing socioeconomic inequality, minority politics, and political behavior, Chapter 2 exhibits how systemic, psychological, and rhetorical forces interact to institutionalize the marginalized social position of white working class people in the United States and United Kingdom. I consider the challenges such circumstances and self-assertions pose for the external observer. I then consider the ways individuals have been observed to respond to these circumstances in their political behavior. In the end, we are confronted with a puzzle: why do white working class political actors in similar positions of systemic, psychological, and economic entrenchment respond with variable forms of political behavior?

Chapters 3 and 4 investigate the roots of this variation by undertaking ethnographies of two communities of working class white people situated at the fault lines of the last half-century's social transformation: East London, England (Chapter 3) and Youngstown, Ohio (Chapter 4). Based on interviews with 120 people—35 of whom are elites—and observations during six months of immersion across the two venues, my interview and ethnographic data exhibit two communities characterized by drastic economic transformation and demographic change, which has left many people consumed by their collective and individual falls from grace. Unable to cope with the trauma resulting from the twin collapses of commercial and social life, the populations examined are also subject to governments disconnected from their preferences, and their incapacity to do much about it. I closely examine the social, political, and economic circumstances that contextualize important trends: the observed disconnection between citizens and their government, individuals' poignant nostalgia and sometimes aggressive nativism, the rise of anti-system political organizations like the British National Party in London, and the extent of political corruption in Youngstown. I seek a more rigorous understanding of white working class culture, social boundaries, and their experiences with various forms of deprivation—all in order to better explain the political choices they subsequently make.

In Chapter 5, I explore the aforementioned economic narrative as it relates to inequalities in the political institutions that structure white working class civic engagement. After laying out the observable variation in respondents' political behavior, I describe three key institutional factors that enable the problematic trends in democratic politics across the cases: (1) the single-party landscape of both political constituencies; (2) the different institutional rules governing local government; and (3) the weak infrastructure of social capital left by Youngstown's and East London's union histories. Institutional explanations set the context for white working class people's political marginality in postindustrial environments, but they struggle to explain individual-level differences among the populations this book considers.

Chapter 6 considers the aforementioned moral or cultural narrative, which implies that white working class people establish political identities in opposition to ethnic and racial minorities who might otherwise unite with white people as part of an impactful proletariat constituency. I begin this chapter by discussing the reinvigoration of class as a defining social division in Youngstown and East London. I contend that the white working class people I study draw more conventionally understood ethno-racial boundaries on top of contemporaneous class boundaries, which are frequently muted by socioeconomic circumstances. I then observe that class divisions are more salient than ethno-racial divisions for white working class respondents who live in neighborhoods that are predominantly composed of ethnic minority residents. Ultimately, I argue that it is more accurate to think of white working class political divisions as a matter of social status, which integrates the overlapping divisions of race and class and converts them into narratives that structure people's experiences in the market, society, and the political sphere.

Chapter 7 seeks to build more sophisticated understandings by linking individuals' political behavior to their understanding of local social hierarchies. I find that while respondents in East London interpret their predicament through the prism of nativity and its entitlements, those from Youngstown view their economic decline through the prism of a dubious American meritocracy. I argue that subjects use these constructed repertoires to rationalize their plight and inform their political behavior. In the remainder of the chapter, I argue that the choice to withdraw or rebel is based on individuals' expectations about their system's responsiveness, their expectations of their own power, and their perceptions of whether or not these expectations are fulfilled in practice. More simply, I hypothesize that radical political behavior is underpinned by a discrepancy between subjects' expectations of how government and society ought to be, and how they perceive it to be. Conventionally known as "subjective status deprivation," the discrepancy of expectations and perceived fulfillment pertains to economic status, and more relevantly here, respondents' different symbolic repertoires of their local social hierarchies.

Chapter 8 applies the arguments developed in my fieldwork to a much broader sample than qualitative research permits. Since the early twenty-first century, the United Kingdom and United States have each featured a well-known, far right flank. The British National Party, English Defence League, and English National Alliance are anti-system groups that pursue xenophobic agendas with often violent tactics. While notorious, their prominence and palatability in British public discussion permits survey research about people's inclination toward anti-system forms of behavior without much concern that respondents may be reluctant to reveal their affiliation or favor. In the United States, I exploit the rise of the Tea Party and the presidential campaign of Donald Trump. I find that while political deprivation is correlated with protest activism among wealthier, older, and more educated white people, it is correlated with radicalism among younger, working class white people. Less ambiguously, the data show that radicalism is also driven by individuals' sense of social deprivation—that is, their sense of their own movement to their society's periphery.

Chapter 9 applies the findings of earlier chapters to white working class electoral politics and their implications for campaigns and mobilization efforts. While white working class voters make up a major portion of the electorate, especially in Rust Belt regions, mainstream parties on the right and left alike are baffled about how to reach them—or at least how to do so in a modern economy without alienating other crucial segments of their respective electoral coalitions. This chapter traces how history has shaped this voting bloc's viewpoints of the parties and of politics, explores how its priorities and allegiances have evolved in the early twenty-first century, and provides insights for any political organization that might want to make an affirmative attempt to bring the white working class back into the political fold. It identifies and explains prominent public opinion paradoxes and party failures. In the end, this chapter provides insights and strategies for how to promote the greater political engagement of the white working class and appeal to one of Europe and North America's most mystifying electoral communities.

2

The New Minority

A COUNTER-NARRATIVE AND ITS POLITICS

We are people who are used to being represented as problematic. We are the long-term, benefit-claiming, working class poor, living through another period of cultural contempt. We are losers, no hopers, low life scroungers. Our culture is yob culture. The importance of welfare provisions to our lives has been denigrated and turned against us; we are welfare dependent and our problems won't be solved by giving us higher benefits. We are perverse in our failure to succeed, dragging our feet over social change, wanting the old jobs back, still having babies instead of careers, stuck in outdated class and gender moulds. We are the challenge that stands out above all others, the greatest social crisis of our times.
—Peter Mandelson, Labour Minister[1]

This book's polemical title suggests that white working class people may be understood as a minority. I do not introduce this counter-narrative in the interest of reappropriating victim status or competing with the claims of ethnocultural minorities, whom I have previously studied at length. Rather, it is to demonstrate that marginalization and minoritization may be experienced in different ways, and simultaneously, by different people. It is to explore how disparate experiences of marginalization are not necessarily mutually exclusive. It is to consider what connects the marginalization of ethnocultural minority and majority communities. And it is to examine the extent to which the white working class can control their fate, and to what extent it is determined by the severity of their circumstances.

The conceptualization of any group of white people in the United Kingdom or the United States as a "minority" is questionable, to be modest. Less modestly, such a conceptualization stands in the face of 50 years of progress achieved by civil rights struggles, community cohesion agendas, and affirmative action policies. At their inception, such efforts acknowledged—and indeed were mobilized against—the privileged status of white people.

White people benefit from a political and social system of their own creation. They are advantaged by a history of structural discrimination in their favor, a trajectory unfettered by the legacies of slavery or the exploitation of colonialism. They boast an acquaintance with what are widely perceived to be norms of national culture and language, which enable their effortless integration into circles of belonging and recognition. White males in particular assume the "privileged role of universal subject" (Kennedy 1996: 88). They enjoy the intangible sense of affinity with predominantly white leaders in business and politics. They are unhindered by the pressures of adaptation. Some describe the situation in harsher terms, going so far as to argue that whites exploit "unearned advantages" as a means to "improve or maintain their social position" (Olson 2002: 388). Earned or unearned, it is assumed that these advantages make white individuals, in short, the incumbents.

And yet, among white working class people, there is an emerging sense of displacement and disempowerment. From my ethnographic research in East London and Youngstown, I find that claims of minority status range from the subtle to the blatant, but nearly all pertain to three phenomena:

Outnumbering : White working class people recognize the steady deterioration of their numbers. Increasing proportions of all population groups are attaining higher levels of education, and white people comprise a decreasing share of national populations in the United States and the United Kingdom (Kaufmann 2004c; Dench et al. 2009). By 2040, the US census estimates that white people will number less than 50% of the American population. However, this is more conventionally a local matter, when demographic change alters the share of white working class people in neighborhoods and cities. Such change is attributable to fertility rates, foreigners' immigration, and native emigration to other parts of a region or country.

In my interview with activist Nancy Pemberton in Thamesview, East London, she would stop me if I referred to immigrant groups as "minorities." "It's a fact that we are a minority," she asserts. "There's not a school in the borough that's not 80% ethnic. Nobody English moves into this borough. They only move out. It's gotten to the stage where, even queuing for the loo, it's a novelty when you meet an English person to speak to. [. . .] I won't allow myself to feel on the outside of my society. But a lot of other people are scared. They feel intimidated." Nancy's statements reflect a generally monolithic view of nonwhite, non-English people that is shared by many in her neighborhood.

Externality : White working class people are sensitive to their exclusion from consultation and representation—not only in bodies of representative government, but also more generally in popular entertainment, public institutions, and employment. They are wary that the same principles of equal access and representation that compensate for other groups' disadvantages do not apply to them. Congresspeople who have previously belonged to the working class comprise only 2% of Congress (Carnes 2012). The *Washington Post* reports that between 1984 and 2009, the median net worth of a member of the House of Representatives grew from $280,000 to $725,000 in inflation-adjusted dollars, while the wealth of an American family slightly declined from $20,600 to $20,500 (Whoriskey 2011). As a result, government and business feel distant, clubby, and unwelcoming.

In Youngstown, 29-year-old chef Paul Podolsky says disempowerment extends to the workplace. "Whites are the minority now," he says. "Sometimes, it gives [black people] greater power because it's the higher group. So they can get their way. My uncle works at a plant where everybody is scared to tell the black people what to do because they're worried about retaliation. The managers are outnumbered and they don't have a backbone. [. . .] White people are held to a different standard. In history books, whites were always above the blacks. But we desegregated to change the world. It's been 100 years and they still want more." Paradoxically, Paul implies that black people are privileged, while simultaneously acknowledging that white people continue to occupy most positions of authority.

Subjection to prejudice : Many white working class people believe they are frequently subject to conscious or unconscious prejudgment by members of ethnic minorities, as well as by middle- and upper-class white people. They believe that such prejudice affects their ability to get hired for jobs, receive equal treatment by officials and businesses, and access government benefits like housing or welfare. Sometimes, this is also a matter of the special treatment white working class people believe members of nonwhite minorities receive—such as scholarships, employment, exemptions or leniencies, and government contracting.

"I fought for this country," lamented pensioner Harriet Johnson from Dagenham, East London, "and it ain't even our country anymore. You're not the priority. We've got everything here. Gays, lesbians—what do you call them?—bisexuals, prostitutes, pedophiles. This place is like [the soap operas] 'Coronation Street' meets 'East Enders' and 'Holly Oaks' all at once." In Youngstown, electrician Iggy Nagy says, "White people have become the minority itself. [. . .] People have freaked out on me for things I've said, because I can't say anything [about black people] because of slavery and their historical oppression. People aren't looking for equality; they're looking for retaliation." While Harriet refers to her relegation in priority beneath people she finds deviant, Iggy does not mind relegation so long as it promotes actual equality. However, many white working-class individuals view the struggle for equal treatment as a personal loss of status—a campaign to demote white people, rather than to promote others.

This indeed turns the tables of racial politics. And yet, this book's closer examination suggests that, in powerful ways, the tables have been turned on white working class people in their countries' post-traumatic regions.

The next section of this chapter exhibits how (1) systemic, (2) psychological and rhetorical, and (3) political forces compound to institutionalize the marginalized social position of white working class people in the United Kingdom and the United States. As a foundation for my examination of what explains white working class political behavior and marginality, I also discuss how their disempowerment poses challenges to external observers who study this group. Finally, I consider the variable ways individuals respond to these circumstances of disempowerment with political behavior. In the end, we are confronted with a puzzle: why do white working class political actors in similar positions of disempowerment respond so differently?

Multiple Means of Disempowerment

White working class people's disempowerment is entrenched in three primary ways: (1) by systemic forces; (2) by rhetorical and psychological forces; and (3) by political forces. By identifying each of these, we see how they compound to reinforce white working class marginality.

(1) SYSTEMIC ENTRENCHMENT

A review of recent scholarship about inequality in the United Kingdom and the United States exhibits how socioeconomic conditions (among both white and nonwhite communities) may be entrenched by key processual dynamics and structures of the political system. These conditions exist from the highest echelons of power down to individual preferences. Gilens presents evidence of what he describes as an "elite-led democracy" where, consistently, government policy is more strongly related to the preferences of higher income voters (2005: 788–789). However, even if democratic governing bodies better reflected the interests of both the poor and the rich, economic inequality could still prove to be self-reinforcing. Kelly and Enns (2010: 856) conclude that this is the case, due to how the preferences of both the rich and the poor respond to changes in income inequality. They find a distinct tendency in the American populace to oppose redistribution in the face of rising inequality with a significant negative correlation between economic inequality and public opinion favoring redistribution. Surprisingly, this relationship holds for individuals in both the top and the bottom quintiles of income. Taken together, such trends enable political agenda-setting by elites—a mechanism of control defined by Gaventa as "the second dimension of power" (1980: 9–11). Agenda setting allows elites to exclude grievances or issues from the relevant decision-making arenas by "controlling the rules of the game," considered by Gaventa to be a set of predominant values, beliefs, rituals, and institutional procedures. These act as barriers preventing the dominated group from even participating in the decision-making process.

When they have a say about economic assistance from the government, white working class communities are prone to "welfare chauvinism," whereby xenophobia distracts or derails redistributive agendas that would otherwise benefit them. Studies find that more ethnically heterogeneous societies display lower levels of support for redistributive welfare (Freeman 2009: 2–5).[2]

While the phenomenon of welfare chauvinism reflects the salience of income-oriented political divisions, this fault line is complicated by emerging cultural divisions. Gelman (2009) shows that where income is not an accurate predictor of American electoral behavior, we see voters (especially those in richer states) voting against their economic interests to support social or culturally aligned agendas. Under these circumstances cultural considerations can be so important that income and voter choice has no correlation (Gelman 2009: 18). However, this has been shown to be less true outside the American South, where many poorer voters are attracted to the sociocultural agendas of Republican policymakers, who simultaneously oppose further wealth redistribution (see Bartels 2008; Gelman 2009: 83; and Inglehart and Welzel 2005: 3).

Explaining such trends, Saffran (1977: 10) contends that because working class people tend to be predominantly liberal on economic issues and predominantly conservative on most social issues, an increase in the salience of social issues will encourage these individuals to vote against their own economic self-interest. Using the concept of "assortative migration," Bishop argues that internal migration in the United States serves as a mechanism for Americans to sort themselves into more homogeneous "tribes," a process that generates segregation. Critically, this sorting process leads to segregation (by income, belief system, political affiliation, etc.), and entrenchment inevitably results.

The effects of this sorting and resulting segregation are profound. In terms of opinions and beliefs (political, social, religious, etc.) the grouping of like-minded people may act as a positive feedback loop. Indeed, research in social psychology suggests that "as people [hear] their beliefs reflected and amplified, they . . . become more extreme in their thinking" (Bishop 2008: 6). This in turn leads to more intense polarization, and a lack of common ground that makes (sometimes violent) anti-system political behavior more likely (20–21; see Gest 2010). Perhaps more specifically relevant to our discussion of socioeconomic entrenchment is the fact that the American population is simultaneously being sorted along socioeconomic lines.

While a certain level of segregation by income and education has always been present in American society, Bishop and others now warn that this trend is accelerating beyond any historical precedent—in part, as a result of modern transportation, social insurance programs, and a more efficient "college sorting machine" (Bishop 2008: 11). Murray also cites the dramatic rise of "superZips," ZIP codes in which residents earn on average in the 95th to 99th percentile of household income. At the same time, the lower status groups are also re-sorting themselves geographically along class lines (Bishop 2008: 135). Over time, this self-segregation results in further socioeconomic entrenchment, in part because the chances for social mobility that are created by the mixing of different types of people are diminished, and perhaps also because society is also being divided by cognitive ability, as Charles Murray more controversially suggests (61).

While Bishop, Murray, and others have highlighted many important effects (political, economic, social, etc.) of internal migration and population "sorting," their preliminary investigations leave important gaps unexplained. For instance, how do these migration trends influence political behavior on the individual level? As previously noted, Bishop suggests that the decreased common ground and increased extremism associated with segregation along ideological lines may increase the likelihood that individuals turn to active, anti-system behavior. Current scholarship does not provide a model for how such demographic trends might alter political behavior. And yet, if resource-oriented understandings of political behavior are correct, such transformations hold serious implications for the psychological orientations that promote civic engagement (and disengagement).

(2) PSYCHOLOGICAL AND RHETORICAL ENTRENCHMENT

Given the growing inequality in developed states, recent scholarship demonstrates a set of paradoxical tendencies among actors that reinforce immobility. A sociological and psychological literature on "system justification theory" traces people's tendency to support and justify the status quo, particularly inequality and social hierarchies. Jost and Hunyady (2005: 263–264) argue that most people, from both advantaged and disadvantaged groups, possess at least some motivation to see the social, economic, and political arrangements around them as fair and legitimate. This tendency to "justify" the current social system is driven by people's desire to reduce uncertainty and threat by maintaining what is familiar, thereby providing psychological benefits such as increased satisfaction at the individual level (Jost and Hunyady 2005: 262). The mechanism by which people engage in system justification consists in forming stereotypes that rationalize social and economic status differences between groups. These stereotypes come about by attributing more moral worth to the advantaged than to the disadvantaged (Jost et al. 2004: 894, 912).

However, even if white working class constituencies were to develop a sense of collective grievance and a desire to organize, they lack an acknowledged identity around which they may mobilize. Poorer white people are subject to the same elite classism that subordinates poorer ethnocultural minorities, but due to their status as an in-group, poorer whites exist without widespread recognition of the structural circumstances that entrench their deprivation. This "invisibility" of the white working class position affects how these individuals make political claims and socially define themselves. As Zweig (2000: 61) argues, "when society fails to acknowledge the existence and experience of working people it robs them of an articulate sense of themselves and their place in society." And unlike ethnocultural minority members of the working class, poor whites are largely deficient of the local social cohesion and compensatory governance mechanisms that attempt to mitigate the effect of marginality on visible minority groups (Fenton et al. 2010).[3]

The importance of a strong identity around which to organize is highlighted by the experiences of African Americans in the United States as described by Dawson (1995). He attributes much of the unity of African-American political behavior to their "linked fate." According to this logic, where prospects of success were deemed to be determined by one's race, that which is good for the racial community is also good for the individual (Dawson 1995: 81). Similarly, Lamont (2000: 20–21) argues that black working class individuals exhibit a more "collectivist" morality than their white counterparts, a unity formed around black "cultural resources" such as the shared experience of "fighting together against racial segregation and discrimination." White workers who do not have access to these same collective cultural resources and subsequently tend to embrace a more individualistic moral code.

It has also been shown that communities at the bottom of social hierarchies may be further disincentivized to act politically because of certain psychological tendencies. Laurin et al. (2010) have shown how beliefs in the fairness of sociopolitical conditions impact people's motivation to pursue and willingness to invest resources in long-term goals, which are recognized as being fundamental to psychological and physical well being. Fairness beliefs, they find, are more important in the motivation of members of disadvantaged groups when pursuing long-term goals, because their chances of success are more likely to be determined by fairness of opportunity (Laurin et al. 2010: 165).

Such perceptions also connect with psychological research on individuals' "locus of control," their understanding of the extent to which they can control events that affect their life (see Rotter 1990). A sense of powerlessness, in turn, may encourage withdrawal from the political sphere, which then further diminishes the power of that group. Indeed, Zweig notes that feeling powerless within the political sphere results in the belief that politics is a waste of energy (2000: 166)—a belief that may derive from a number of different sources, including perceptions about the influence of corporations or wealthy individuals, impressions of government corruption or incompetence, or even broader feelings about the efficacy of the political system. As I previously suggest, these beliefs may be reinforced or amplified in communities where like-minded working class individuals reside. Table 2.1 summarizes different demographics' perceptions of their political power, based on this book's original surveys of Britons. We see that perceptions of politics power are weakest among those without university educations, the working class, and those who are middle-aged. However,

Table 2.1 **Perceived Political Power**

	United Kingdom Mean	*United States Mean*
Education		
University Education	3.88	4.46
No University Education	3.53	3.38
Age		
18–24	3.99	3.97
25–39	3.78	4.27
40–59	3.54	3.31
60 +	3.73	3.47
Self-reported Social Class		
Upper	4.02	6.07
Middle	3.71	4.28
Lower Middle	3.54	N/A*
Working	3.25	2.81
Gender		
Male	3.79	3.86
Female	3.60	3.58

British respondents were asked to report to what extent "people like me have political power" on a scale from 0 to 10. 10 indicates that the respondent thinks that "people like me have a lot of political power" and 0 indicates that "people like me don't have any political power." White working class here is defined as white and having no college education. * In the United Kingdom, class is measured using the British NRS social grade scale. There is no equivalent in US surveys.

the range of perceptions is much wider between the rich and poor in the United States. (See Appendix A for a discussion of survey methods.)

White working class communities' tendency to self-segregate or justify their disadvantage is reinforced—or perhaps inspired—by similar trends in social discourse that crystallize class tensions. In deconstructing the rhetorical treatment of white people, Wray (2006) details how over time the most disadvantaged "white people" have been cognitively categorized as an out-group. Terms such as "white trash" are evidence of the symbolic distancing and social exclusion of the lowest-status white citizens (Wray 2006: 134). This symbolic boundary can, with enough social power, become institutionalized and therefore lead to unequal opportunities for those stigmatized by the stereotype. If we again consider psychological research, there is a tendency for people to fulfill the characteristics of a stereotype more than they otherwise would if the stereotype did not exist (Steele 1997).

These findings about boundary-making and white people's exclusion from working class cultural resources suggest a subtle racial dimension to white working class entrenchment. While stigma against them may be less intense, it is more socially accepted in light of the other advantages white people enjoy. And while white people remain a numerical majority nationally, they are constrained from forming organizations based on a sense of group consciousness. Finally, as Chapter 6 discusses, even if they were to form such organizations, the basis for white working class identity is weak and incoherent.

(3) POLITICAL ENTRENCHMENT

With a set of structural conditions that hardens social hierarchies and a set of perceptive tendencies that inhibit dissent and activism, white working-class communities possess limited resources and even fewer outlets for political engagement. Indeed, the extant circumstances reinforce each other and combine to exert downward pressure. In his comprehensive consideration of political opinion, Zaller (1992) reveals the dynamics of marginalized communities' dismissal by political opinion leaders. His model suggests that individuals with low political awareness are less likely to change their attitudes over political issues, primarily because of the low probability of political communication filtering through to them. Political parties consequently tend to divert their efforts to citizens with higher levels of reception to their outreach, typically those in the middle classes and above. The implication of this trend is that marginalized communities are ignored. Conversely, Goodwin (2011) reveals that many poor white British voters experienced more face-to-face contact with extremist party campaigners than those from mainstream parties, who lack an active and visible presence in poor white communities.

Such findings hold true for the marginalized independent of their ethnocultural identity. In his consideration of African Americans, Dawson (1995) shows how the poor may be funneled into political organizations that do not accurately represent their interests or views due to a deficiency of group-specific outlets for political expression. Despite finding class-based differences in African-American public opinion, he notes that isolation on the left of the political spectrum could mask important political cleavages within the black community (Dawson 1995: 181). While the Democratic Party is the only viable mainstream partisan outlet for African Americans, poor white Britons are perhaps even more restricted today. During thirteen years of Labour Government from 1996 to 2010, little attention was paid to the plight of the white working class—the party's one-time base—and the United Kingdom's inequality gap expanded. However, options became limited with the unlikely coalition of Conservatives—long viewed as averse to working class agendas—and Liberal Democrats—who have a mixed relationship with poor whites anyway, given the party's views on European integration and immigration. Such circumstances relate to the earlier argument advanced by Templeton (1966: 256) that the traditional two-party political system does not allow a significant proportion of the electorate to express their political views with their vote. Given the trends discussed above, it is reasonable to expect poor white people to be among the least represented.

Because people are thinking beyond the paradigms provided by political parties today, individuals are increasingly able to define their political views separately from organized agendas (Inglehart and Welzel 2005). In order to pursue alternative agendas, activists are engaging in largely informal means including Internet-based petitions, demonstrations, boycotts, and blogging rather than party campaigning, associational membership, and letters to policymakers. While Inglehart and Welzel argue that these shifting means of political activism should placate fears of widespread civic disengagement and a "crisis of democracy" (2005: 117), it is questionable how much access under-resourced communities have to such efforts. The under-resourced tend to lack a sense of internal and external political efficacy, lack access to new tools of self-expression, and lack the disposable time and energy of middle-class citizens. At the same time, as previously noted, individuals of lower socioeconomic status feel a deficiency of influence because of the notion that the government is controlled by rich campaign donors and "corporate influence" (Zweig 2000, 166). Table 2.2 summarizes different demographics' perceptions of politicians' care for their interests, based on this book's original surveys of Britons.

We see that perceptions of politicians' care are lowest among the working class, those without university educations, and those who are middle-aged. And again, the range of perceptions is much wider between the rich and poor in the United States.

Since the beginning of the twenty-first century, we have subsequently witnessed the rising salience and support of radical right and populist political parties in Europe and similar movements in the United States. Ford and Goodwin

Table 2.2 **Perceived Politicians' Care**

	United Kingdom Mean	United States Mean
Education		
University Education	3.93	4.38
No University Education	3.49	3.46
Age		
18–24	4.11	3.99
25–39	3.66	4.38
40–59	3.42	3.47
60+	3.93	3.24
Self-reported Social Class		
Upper	4.12	5.32
Middle	3.75	4.08
Lower Middle	3.47	N/A*
Working	3.14	2.94
Gender		
Male	3.64	3.89
Female	3.74	3.61

British respondents were asked to report to what extent "politicians care a lot about people like me" on a scale from 0 to 10. 10 indicates that the respondent thinks that "people like me have a lot of political power" and 0 indicates that "politicians don't care about people like me." Working class here is defined as having no college education. * In the United Kingdom, class is measured using the British NRS social grade scale. There is no equivalent in US surveys.

(2010: 3) recognize rising support for the British National Party among white working class voters in the United Kingdom. Similarly, Sniderman, Hagendoorn, and Prior (2004) show how the growth of ethnic minorities in Western European countries has, in several countries, driven increased support for extreme right-wing parties. Despite this support, Givens (2005) argues that the success of radical right parties across countries is largely determined by differences in these countries' electoral systems. Proportional-representation electoral systems, and conditions where two main parties form coalition governments, both reduce strategic voting among radical rightists, who instead may feel incentivized to back a fringe candidate (Givens 2005: 100). However, in first-past-the-post (i.e., winner-take-all) electoral systems like those of the United States and the United Kingdom, the relative difficulty of supporting such parties and movements (and their subsequent lack of success) has led significant numbers of individuals to disengage from the political process completely.

Challenges for the External Observer

The circumstances I describe here, and elaborate on in the pages ahead, pose two primary challenges for observers' consideration of white working class politics and social affairs. First, the state of white working class people's politics and social affairs challenges conventional considerations of minority groups. The general public has typically equated minority status with smaller numbers and persistent legacies of disadvantage, rather than self-assertion of said status (Joppke 2010: 50). In particular, social scientists have followed Wirth's early definition of a minority as "a group of people who, because of their physical or cultural characteristics, are singled out from the others in the society in which they live for differential and unequal treatment, and who therefore regard themselves as objects of collective discrimination" (Wirth 1940: 347). These approaches disqualify any claims of minority status by white people, whose physical characteristics have allowed them to evade such discrimination and instead employ it to their advantage. Going one step further, Waters (1990: 156) has distinguished the claims of European-origin immigrants in the United States as those of an "ethnic group"—rather than those of an "ethnic minority" that has endured the "real and often hurtful" effects of being black, Latino, or Asian. However, are poor white people subject to the same empowerment enjoyed by wealthy white people?

White working class people lead us to question whether minoritization is—alongside socioeconomic disadvantage, histories of disempowerment, sociocultural discrimination, and situated demography—also a matter of race. If the concept of a "minority" cannot apply to white people, this suggests the limitation of its use as a universal concept—for how useful is a concept that cannot be applied across populations? Alternatively, if minority status is not necessarily a matter of race, it demands the consideration of alternative claims of minority status from a group that similarly experiences disempowerment and forms of disadvantage. It demands sober consideration when they claim to be "minoritized."

Second, the objective study of white working class people demands that the observer reasonably consider claims of disadvantage. While we are obligated to contextualize and even vet the claims made by the people with whom I speak, we are also obligated to resist the immediate dismissal of these claims on grounds of moral judgment. Scholars and observers of minority politics and social affairs generally maintain a sense of empathy (or at least common understanding) that heightens their sensitivity to subjects' disadvantage and their perceptions, despite their subjects' demonstrated flaws. The challenge is to sustain this empathy for the primary antagonist of the minority subjects we are accustomed to examining.

Indeed, white working class people complicate conventional understandings about marginality because the social and political system is one that they believe they helped build, and one that rendered them a structural advantage for centuries. This remains true even though working class white people are subject to alternative forms of disadvantage. In response to a perceived loss of social, economic, and political status, the last decade has witnessed white working class communities' efforts to reclaim the high ground of cultural politics. The British National Party and UKIP developed footholds in several English constituencies and boroughs, leading to the election of numerous municipal councilors, a Member of Parliament, and Members of European Parliament in the United Kingdom. In the United States, white working class constituencies have swayed several national and congressional election campaigns in the "swing states" that determine presidential campaigns. Simultaneously, white working class communities have engaged in political violence through organizations like the English Defence League in the United Kingdom and "sovereign citizen" or "survivalist" groups across the American countryside. There has also been extensive disillusionment from the democratic political arena, leading to lower civic participation levels and organizational apathy. These trends represent white working class responses to their disempowerment, and it is imperative that we understand them more clearly.

Political Responses to Disempowerment

In light of the disempowerment that white working class people perceive and experience, I am particularly concerned with individuals who decide that the best course of action is:

(A) to deliberately withdraw from the political sphere of their society; or
(B) to pro-actively disrupt the political sphere by engaging in coercive or circumventive activities to achieve their political preferences.

I refer to these political choices as anti-system political behavior, and I argue that they embody a political expression of marginality (see Gest 2015.)

Beyond Voice and Loyalty

Democracies depend on a citizenry that is confident in the government's capacity to govern without constant reinforcement. Indeed, democracies make myriad daily decisions without public consultation. To make this form of self-governance function effectively, then, the system simultaneously depends on citizens' generally passive vigilance of government action and, when needed, citizens' active intervention to express dissatisfaction. While voting in elections represents an appointed opportunity for intervention, most other forms of voluntary participation are subject to the impulsive or calculated desire of citizens to advocate. In this spirit, passivity with the readiness to act and participation within democratic channels can be thought to support such a political system.

Albert Hirschman (1970: 32) refers to this as "an alternation of involvement and withdrawal" (see also Schudson 1999). Hirschman argues that democracy benefits from a mix of "alert" and "inert" citizens—a situation in which political participation is somewhere between "permanent activism" and "total apathy." A critical weakness of Hirschman's model is that he focuses almost exclusively on actions within the political system. That is, Hirschman considers "exit" in the sense that an individual may leave an association or political party in order to switch to a new group, simply changing affiliations. However, he—and most other scholars of political behavior—does not address the possibility that the same individual might just as easily rebel against the political system or exit the political system entirely, and certainly not with the intention of doing so indefinitely. Anti-system political behavior exists in contraposition to the political system, outside the boundaries of its procedures of consultation.

Contrapositions

As indicated above, one such contraposition exists among individuals who have a potential cause to advocate but who nevertheless choose to refrain from making any claims of the system—a conscious withdrawal. In this case, passivity is not a conscious "step back" taken with the intention to return when feasible or more motivated. Instead, it represents a conscious commitment to inactivity, the removal of oneself as a stakeholder in the political system, regardless of their desire for reform. I will refer to this as passive anti-system behavior, or more simply, withdrawal.

A second such contraposition exists among political advocates who act to impose their preferences on the political system by employing tactics that circumvent the system's established channels for influence and, in doing so, undermine its capacity to reflect popular will. Such activities may include violence, bribery, exclusivist hate groups, intimidation, or campaigning for civic abstention. I will refer to this as active anti-system behavior, or more simply, rebellion. Both withdrawal and rebellion represent political choices (see Figures 2.1 and 2.2).

PRO-SYSTEM	ANTI-SYSTEM
I. **Active**: Activity that impairs, disrupts circumvents or overthrows the system. Examples: a. Violence for political purpose b. Membership in an exclusivist organization c. Revolutionary action d. Clandestine activity	II. **Active**: Activity that engages the institutions and channels of the democratic system. Examples: a. Voting, parties, holding office b. Commune, union, cooperative c. Association or NGO membership d. Civil disobedience, protest e. Volunteer or community work
III. **Passive**: State of inactivity within the system. Examples: a. Complacent, satisfied b. Ignorant, disinterested c. Otherwise occupied	IV. **Passive**: Committed inactivity and withdrawal from the system. Examples: a. Rejection b. Withdrawal

Figure 2.1 VARIATION IN POLITICAL BEHAVIOR. The four quadrants model the observable behavior of individuals who are anti-system or engaged, passively or actively. (See Gest 2015.)

	PRO-SYSTEM	ANTI-SYSTEM
ACTIVE	ENGAGEMENT	REBELLION
PASSIVE	SITTING OUT	WITHDRAWAL

Figure 2.2 VARIATION IN POLITICAL BEHAVIOR. This is a shorthand edition of the four quadrants modeling observable political behavior (Gest 2015).

The passive anti-system individual does not voluntarily participate in democratic political life. He or she is withdrawn. As previously discussed, apathy in the form of non-participation does not necessarily mean a person is alienated; rather, he or she may be satisfied, complacent, ignorant, or lack the resources to participate. So passive anti-system behavior encompasses individuals' conscious removal from the political system. Unlike active anti-system behavior, this passive variant neither intentionally weakens the democratic system, nor intentionally hinders or overrides other citizens' capacity to make claims. Instead, it allows disagreeable governance to continue, under circumstances in which citizens believe they have a legitimate grievance. Withdrawal leaves a lack of government accountability, a less representative political system, and a widening social rift between those citizens who make claims of the system and those who do not.

Whereas active anti-system behavior circumvents democracy's mechanisms and impairs the capacity of other citizens to make claims of the system, passive anti-system behavior atrophies democratic mechanisms and mutes the claims of the alienated themselves.

The active anti-system individual is committed to behavior that undermines or attempts to topple the democratic system. He or she may engage in clubs, organizations, and other political efforts that become substitutes for the democratic political system or are detrimental to it. His or her form of protest is not intended to reform the system, but rather to undermine or defeat it. An example might be someone espousing or practicing political violence as part of the British National Party, English National Alliance, or an American "sovereign citizen" group, but also exclusive or racist political movements. This definition excludes strong critics of the democratic political system who see struggles against "powers-that-be" as a struggle for improving democracy in a system that they perceive to have become less democratic.

As long as such a movement attempts to improve the democracy in noncoercive ways that do not infringe on others' capacity to dissent, there is no reason to think of them as anti-system. Indeed, such movements attempt to improve the system using the mechanisms of the system.

Based on these definitions, Table 2.3 and Table 2.4 assemble self-reported political behavior data from this book's original surveys of white Britons and white Americans, respectively. The results show that over 8% of white Britons say they have participated or would participate in the violent racism of groups like the British National Party or the English Defence League. Another 13% have abstained or would deliberately abstain from any political engagement in light of their frustration. A further 37% would strongly consider voting for UKIP. In the United States, over 60% of white people would favor a third party that mirrored the British National Party's platform and 17% have or would abstain from any political engagement. This is a significant segment of the electorate, about whom we lack a strong understanding. This book addresses this void.

Prospectus

Until now, contemporary understandings of social marginality and political alienation have been primarily informed by examinations of ethno-religious minorities (e.g., see Bourdieu and Passeron 1977; Wilson 1987; Wacquant 2008; Gest 2010). These understandings leverage the externality of the group from the social and political system that excludes them (or the system from which the group has excluded itself). Indeed, my earlier research contends that people who are actively or passively alienated are likely to perceive

Table 2.3 **Demographics of Anti-System Behavior in the United Kingdom**

	Favor Radical Right	*Favor Withdrawal*	*Support any RR*
Education			
University Education	.05	.14	.29
No University Education	.10	.11	.46
Age			
18–24	.07	.08	.31
25–39	.10	.13	.35
40–59	.08	.16	.42
60+	.05	.10	.42
Self-reported Social Class			
Upper	.06	.14	.33
Middle	.06	.13	.36
Lower Middle	.10	.13	.45
Working	.10	.10	.44
Gender			
Male	.08	.13	.42
Female	.07	.13	.36
Working Class			
White Working Class	.09	.11	.46
All Other Whites	.05	.15	.39
Full Sample	**.08**	**.13**	**.39**

Cells indicate the proportion of British respondents for each demographic category that indicated that it had engaged or expressed willingness support the Radical Right. This includes people who have voted or expressed willingness to vote for the British National Party, or took part or expressed willingness to take part in English Defence League or English National Alliance protest or demonstration. The "withdrawn" are those who have purposefully abstained from voting in the last 12 months.

a political system that does not work for their interests and is not going to change (Gest 2010).

White working class communities are structurally disadvantaged in ways that differ greatly from the deprivation endured by ethno-religious minorities. Divorced by upwardly mobile white co-ethnics and relegated to an increasingly entrenched economic underclass where they are segregated from the solidarities of ethno-religious affinities, white working class communities are disempowered

Table 2.4 **Demographics of Anti-System Behavior in the United States**

	Trump	Tea Party	Third Party	Withdrawal
Education				
University Education	.29	.31	.58	.13
No University Education	.41	.36	.67	.18
Age				
18–24	.26	.34	.58	.22
25–39	.41	.37	.66	.21
40–59	.38	.34	.66	.15
60 +	.41	.34	.65	.10
Social Class				
Upper	.35	.18	.56	.05
Middle	.30	.36	.56	.15
Working	.30	.36	.64	.25
Gender				
Male	.42	.41	.65	.16
Female	.33	.30	.64	.18
Full Sample	.37	.35	**.64**	**.17**

Cells indicate the proportion of American respondents for each demographic category that indicated they support the presidential candidacy of Donald Trump, the Tea Party, or a hypothetical third party that advocated for "stopping mass immigration, providing American jobs for American workers, preserving America's Christian heritage, and stopping the threat of Islam." I classify each of these as support for the radical right.

in a very unconventional sense. Summarizing the review I undertook earlier in this chapter, white working class individuals in the United States and the United Kingdom tend to be:

- subject to economic pressures that widen socioeconomic inequality;
- raising children that are unlikely to experience much social mobility in future years;
- pessimistic about their chances of improving their general well-being or political clout;
- subject to political parties that are disinclined to solicit their electoral support or views;
- situated at the fringe of sprawling cities or in declining factory towns;
- complacent or averse to altering these social and political conditions;

- unconfident in their ability to enact political change or agenda-setting;
- and in many cases, unsupportive of redistributive agendas anyway.

This book seeks to explain why white working class political actors in similar positions of systemic, psychological, and economic entrenchment respond politically in divergent ways. In other words, given the same structural circumstances, why are not all white working class people in one box—or even on one side—of the political behavior diagram? What leads some to maintain faith in the democratic channels of participation? What leads others to rebel, and still others to deliberately withdraw?

3

Peripheral Visions

*There is a harshness about Barking . . . Here a native population seems to have
maintained its presence, with a kind of bleakness or hardness of attitude . . .
It remains a strangely isolated or self-commuting neighbourhood, where the
London accent seems particularly thick.*
—Peter Ackroyd

This chapter examines white working class political behavior and its context in
Barking and Dagenham, East London. Based on interviews with 55 people—15
of whom are elites—and ethnographic observation during three months of immersion, it undertakes an analysis of subjects' attitudes and actions. I begin with
a discussion of Barking and Dagenham's history and its narratives of memory
amid dramatic demographic change. I then explore the externality of the state
government and the legacies of class and social hierarchies that condition observed political behavior. I conclude by outlining the nature of white working
class subjects' marginality.

History Told

The story of Barking and Dagenham gets told countless times, every day of
every week, in every house and meeting place in the borough. From a nan to
her grandson, from a mum to her daughter, from a barmaid to her regular, from
one man smoking cigarettes in front of a betting shop to the passerby. Each
time it is told, it changes ever so slightly. The storyteller is that much more
distant from the account he recites, that much more moved by what she wit-
nesses today, that much more influenced by the nuances of the same stories as
heard from others.

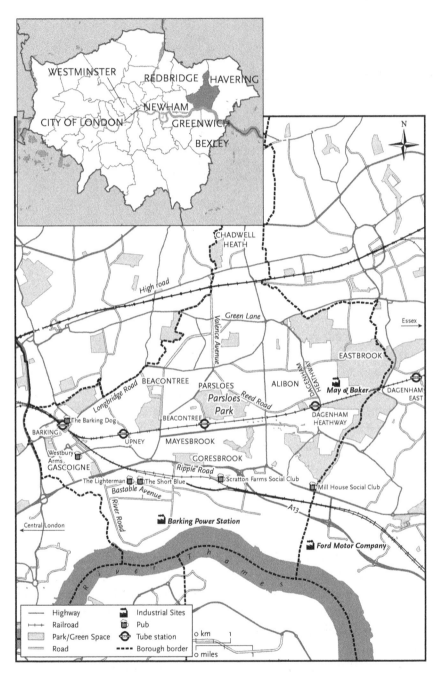

Map 3 Map of the London Borough of Barking and Dagenham.

Historians chronicle the extraordinary emergence of Barking and Dagenham as a feat of urban planning during London's modernist expansion to the east, and as a landmark of Prime Minister David Lloyd George's creation of Britain's contemporary welfare state. The core of the borough is the Becontree Estate—the largest single residential estate ever constructed. In 1920, the London County Council's architect said that "the proposal to convert a tract of land, three thousand acres in extent, at present covered chiefly with market gardens, into a township with a population of 120,000 is something altogether unparalleled in the history of housing" (Tames 2002). The public housing complex symbolized George's promise to reward servicemen returning from World War I with "homes fit for heroes." At the time, Walter Long, president of the Local Government Board, regarded this pledge as the redemption of a moral obligation to those who had endured the horrors of the Western Front: "To let them come home from the horrible, water-logged trenches to something little better than a pigsty here would, indeed, be criminal . . . and a negation of all we have said during the war, that we can never repay those men for what they have done for us." Others, more cynically, saw government-subsidized housing as "the antidote to Bolshevism" (ibid.).

From 1921 to 1932, 27,000 cottages were constructed on the farmland east of Barking town center. Inspired by the American "Garden City" concept, the development was the product of precise central planning. Main arteries were split by tree-lined center medians. Concentric side streets curled and joined a greater suburban labyrinth, featuring dedicated spaces for petite shopping parades, verdant parks, plazas, and cul-de-sacs, which residents would call "banjos." Initially, a special tramway was envisioned to bifurcate the sprawling suburb, but instead, London's County Council merely extended the Underground's District Line five stops east of Barking Station to reach Upminster—its current terminus. Designed to surpass working class accommodation of the day, houses were structured based on a few templates with little variation. The attached cottages each featured luxuries such as indoor lavatories, fitted baths, electric furnishings, telephone lines, and front and back gardens. To emphasize the self-sufficiency of the new living standards, developers even planted privet hedges in residential front yards.

New opportunities for work accompanied the government's infrastructural investments, and together attracted thousands of transplants. Initially, the first tenants were so poor, the estate came to be known as Corned Beef City, after the only meat they could afford. However, May & Baker's chemical plant relocated to Dagenham from Wandsworth in 1922, the Barking Power House electric station was established in Creekmouth in 1925, and in 1931, the Ford Motor Company built a factory on several square miles of Dagenham's riverfront that Edsel Ford (Henry's son) had purchased for £167,700 in 1924 (Hudson 2009). These employers, especially Ford, provided dependable jobs for the residents of the new estate. Through the 1930s, a series of new cars were introduced at Ford Dagenham including the 8-horsepower Model Y in 1932, the 10-horsepower CX De Luxe model in 1933, the first Prefect model in 1938, and the 8-horsepower Anglia in 1939 (Ford News 2011). By 1940, the factory was converted to war production and over the next five years produced 360,000 fighting and transport vehicles (e.g., light vans, army trucks), 262,000 V8 engines, 34,000 Merlin aero engines, as well as a significant proportion of Britain's tractors (Neville 2009). At the time, employee numbers had reached 34,000 (Ford News 2011). The plant continued its expansion after World War II with the Pilot, Consul, Zephyr, and Zodiac ranges, with employment peaking in 1953 at 40,000 workers onsite producing more than 3,000 cars every day on four million square feet of land (Hudson 2009). Further housing developments followed labor demand after World War II, when the construction of the Thamesview Estate brought another several thousand public housing facilities onto the expanses of reclaimed marshland to the south of Barking and Becontree in 1954. The census population of Dagenham soared from 9,000 to 90,000 between 1921 and 1931, and the combined populations of Barking and Dagenham increased another 50% before 1951.

However, people did not relocate to Barking and Dagenham in this era solely for economic opportunity. For the working class men and women who migrated mostly from London's congested, tumultuous East End, the original move was also about personal reformation—greater independence, greater dignity, greater simplicity. Leafy Dagenham was pleasantly separate from the distractions and competition of central London, the population of which was rapidly growing and diversifying with Britain's imperial and industrial transformations. At that time, the East End was populated and commercialized by upwardly mobile Eastern European Jewish immigrants and, as early as the 1960s, by South Asians fleeing the contentious politics and poverty of the Indian subcontinent. The neighborhood's docklands were closing, and a way of life was altering (see Dench et al. 2009).

A homogenous refuge for London's white working class where nearly all were employed by a few key industries, the London Borough of Barking and Dagenham resembled a present-day university campus for incoming East Enders. Employers encouraged residents to develop associations around billiard clubs, bowling leagues, and competitions for chess, cricket, football, tennis, and shooting. The Power House supported a horticultural society, a staff magazine, and a superannuation fund (Tames 2002). The local council institutionalized the New Jerusalem "cradle to grave" vision of the Labour government elected in 1945. Tames notes that the headings of the 1960s "Official Guide" exhibit these paternalistic ideals and objectives. The importance attached to children, health, welfare, and the disadvantaged is attested by an impressively lengthy list of departments, agencies, and programs: Adolescents, Adoption, Blind and

Partially-Sighted Persons, Chess Clinics, Child Care Officers, Child Guidance Clinic, Childminders, Children's Homes, Chiropody, Day Nurseries, Deaf and Hard of Hearing, Dental Clinics, Disabled Persons, et cetera (ibid.). Barking and Dagenham's Council estates were a white working class haven.

However, Barking and Dagenham could not insulate itself from more profound trends in global economics and demographics portended by the East End's earlier transformations. After the mid-1970s, East London's economy went the way of the Ford factory, which endured successive downsizings coinciding with increasing competition in the European car market and Ford's gradual loss of market share. Facing growing financial and overcapacity issues, Ford restructured the company's European operations and, in turn, stopped car production in Dagenham. The plant's number of employees dropped from over 28,000 in 1975 to 7,300 in 2000 (UK Parliament 2000), and in February 2002, the vehicle assembly line stopped for the last time (Neville 2009). As that market declined, unions weakened, labor laws liberalized, and industrial jobs followed a more global move offshore. Britain's postindustrial economy had little use for Barking and Dagenham's tradesmen, as it shifted to high technology and a broader service sector.

Today, the borough's biggest businesses are in logistics and transport, along with some crafts. Manufacturing in the borough is light (fuel nozzles, beds, staircases, flooring), cheap, and in decline. There have been proposals to establish a recycling industry and more housing along the dilapidated river region south of the Thamesview Estate. The river is a makeshift industrial park, a junkyard of multipurpose warehouses, import clearinghouses, parking lots, piles of rubbish, and empty plots of land. The semicircular River Road is a decrepit promenade of rusted metal and garages behind chain-linked fences in front of bare, marshy landscapes littered with plastic wrappers and discarded auto parts. To the east sits what remains of the Ford factory and the electrical power station that still produces nearly a third of London's power.

Alongside the economic changes, the borough's demographics have also altered. Since the Thatcher government's shift to privatization in the 1980s, many of Barking and Dagenham's pensioners and buyout beneficiaries chose to purchase their council flats and sell them off at sizeable profits. When jobs were eliminated, any remaining members of the working class who owned their homes also sold and left the borough. A new generation of residents entered the closed campus that Barking and Dagenham's estates once composed, to take advantage of mortgages and rentals that were a fraction of those in inner London. While some purchased the homes, many new immigrants were assigned to council-owned row houses and tower blocks. Some were highly skilled members of Britain's increasingly diverse middle class, seeking to settle their families in a quieter environment. Others were unskilled laborers seeking work in London's construction or service sector, or joining family members from abroad. Still others were refugees simply seeking a fundamental upgrade to their quality of life. By 2000, East London was diversifying, modernizing, and joining London's globalizing city.

History Retold

Behind these structural trends reflected in demographic statistics, production numbers, and economic charts, a fundamental and wholly unexpected lifestyle transformation was taking place. East London was suddenly subject to the very cultural changes from which it had sheltered earlier generations of EastEnders. It was not that people of immigrant origin supplemented members of the white working class; the newcomers were actually in the spaces once occupied by— and forever associated with—working class white people's former neighbors, friends, colleagues, unionists, and drinking partners. The smells of exotic foods pervaded hallways, unfamiliar music was amplified through nearby windows, and foreign languages were spoken on buses. Corresponding to different demands, import grocers opened on local high streets, neighborhood pubs closed, and empty commercial spaces were renovated to create makeshift mosques and other houses of worship. Though Barking and Dagenham's remaining working class white people have been witnessing these changes for 30 years, they are still revising their narratives of them, reinterpreting their meaning and, in so doing, reimagining their past.

"Everything's gone straight to hell," said Nancy Pemberton, as she reached to stroke her dog, Molly. At 59 years old, the Pembertons had lived in the Thamesview Estate almost since its initial construction. Nancy is a busybody retiree, who is an avid gardener and political activist. Her husband is a retired fireman, and while they own their home, they chose not to sell as a matter of principle. She brought us both steaming hot tea, and sat alertly in her living room listening to the music of the Beatles and Credence Clearwater Revival on the ambient radio. Fixed to the gas fireplace chimney was an award of recognition Ron had won from the fire brigade years ago; above it hung an analog clock that had stopped at just past 12 o'clock. The living room's glass cabinets contained hundreds of hand-painted figurines.

"It was a community back then. It was predominantly English. There was an Asian girl. And there was one black boy whose mother was a big, fat lesbian who didn't live the quietest of lives. But we always got on, and the English were the majority. It has always been diverse what with us living so near the river. But I remember when we went around the houses for a Christmas charity about 10 years ago, and I noticed all the black faces. Now it's a million times worse."

She continued, "The immigrants who came in the fifties all worked, they learned the language, crunched in a small house until each of them could afford their own. They were English, or as English as could be. These people in the 1950s didn't expect something for nothing. They integrated. They didn't try to change us into Africa."

We moved to Nancy's front yard, which featured five Union Jack flags. An enormous one fluttered from the top of a 12-foot pole, while another was fixed to the cottage's façade, draped over a window box of primroses. Three more small flags were pinned to a vine-covered terrace to the left of the front door, emerging from the leaves like they had blossomed from flower buds. There were also two planter boxes which—planted with strategically placed red, white, and blue flowers—would bloom in the design of two more union flags.

"The schools used to be 90% English, and now they're 90% African. The Asians live more like we do, but the Africans are different."

Pemberton went on, "The EU is actually promoting migration to England. It's the best place for benefits. And we've already got enough of our own who are too lazy to get off their asses. I got off the train in Barking one night and there were dozens of Romanian women with children, and it's clear they had been on the nick [thievery]. Vile people, Romanians. Then you walk outside, and it's so loud with all the halal shops and rubbish in the streets. We look like a suburb of Nairobi."

"What can you do about it?" I asked.

She shook her head disappointedly, and reached down to pick a few weeds from the moist planter boxes. Straightening her posture, she stared pensively across the street and yearned with a hand on her hip.

"If I could just bring back Maggie Thatcher. She would never have let all this happen."

Further north in Dagenham, Lou and Maggie Griffiths live in a rented home in the middle of the old Becontree Estate. They invited me into their cramped living room, a cup of tea waiting on the coffee table. Every other flat surface in the room was covered with ceramic statuettes of dogs, cats, and other large felines. The air was heavy and thick with cigarette smoke, and the sofa was covered in a layer of white dog hair. Lou and Maggie are retired. He is a darts aficionado with a raspy, bass voice and appeared tough as old boots.

"This borough was full of East Enders," Lou proclaimed loudly. "People were very friendly. It was easy to settle in. People had come in after wartime, and the neighbors were good. There was a sense of community, more so than there is now. Since about 2004 or 2005, there was change in the borough that came with the influx of other cultures. Goresbrook Ward was previously 5% foreign; now 50% or 60% of the ward is foreign. It was a massive change that happened too fast for people to cope with. There's a heavy Muslim population. Africans have flooded in. They don't seem to mix with the existing community. There's no infrastructure to deal with it, so everything got fragmented."

He went on, "We live in a multicultural society and I think that's good. But when it happened so quickly, the existing community feels threatened. In the 1960s when the West Indians came in, no one area was taken over and they mixed in. But the way we've been flooded, it inspires the animosity of right-wing groups. It's a matter of adapting, but some of these people don't speak English or make any attempt to fit in."

Lou paused to light the cigarette he had been rolling. His voice was raw from a pack-a-day smoking habit, but he maintained a booming laugh that seemed to shake the wall behind me and jitter the Persian cats on the shelf nearby. Maggie looked on with a visible sense of enchantment. They were a warm couple, who remained active in their local Tenants and Residents Association—Barking and Dagenham's most local form of authority and civil society.

"Years ago, you used to look out for one another. People used to go around with a collection if someone died," Lou says. "A lot of the new communities don't want to mix in. I think we can learn a lot from each other, but they don't want to learn. Look at Dagenham Heathway! Sixty percent of it are those African shops, and they don't sell nothing to anyone else. Immigration should have been stopped years ago, and now people are thinking the worst: 'They're taking our jobs' and things like that. We don't go out hardly, and I can't get settled [financially]. This house is a rental, and we've been on the Council's [public housing] list for three years. We just had so much debt that we had to sell our old house before it got repossessed or fell apart around our ears!" he roared with some sorrow.

In interviews with a variety of the borough's residents, there was very little variation in their depictions. As I moved from venue to venue, ward to ward, each new narrator seemed to pick up where the previous storyteller had left off.

"In 1971, Barking and Dagenham had full employment," said Fred Toulson, a seasoned schoolteacher. "You could move from one job to another—from the print to the factory to the dig to the drill. There were close-knit families."

He continued, "In the first class I taught in 1971, every single kid's parents worked at Ford's. Nobody left Barking and Dagenham. Ten years ago, there were no black kids in my school."

"It was a friendly place," said Harriet Johnson, a resident of Thamesview for 42 years. "Everyone knew each other, until all the bigots came. We got overrun by Indians, blacks, Lithuanians and Polish people and all that. Before that, it was a beautiful estate. It was reclaimed land. We used to have cows and horses walking down the roads."

"Back then, you could go out at night and parents didn't worry," said Norma Davies, a pensioner and activist. "Ford's was down the road."

Davies went on, "The kids used to play in the streets and used to respect their elders. The people have changed. You don't feel safe. Everyone used to look after one another, knocking on each other's doors. Since Ford's moved and May Baker's tablet factory shut, it's gone down. There are no jobs and that's why the children are hanging about in the streets. They've got nothing else to do."

"People don't talk no more," said Pam Reed, a bartender at the Mill House Social Club, one of the borough's few standing working men's clubs. "Kids don't come to your house and have a sleepover. You used to always have friends around, kids' parties, you know? All the people who were brought up here have moved out. I've worked all my bloody life and I'm going into banks and seeing Africans come in with thousands of pounds in their hands, sending it back to Kenya or wherever they come from. And you wonder why we have a recession? Bleeding hard to work out! None of their money that they earn here is going back into our country."

Each rendition offers alternative perspectives of the same narrative, and occasionally apocryphal details about livestock, employment, and demographics. The 2011 census calculates that 50% of the borough is white British, 22% is of African or Afro-Caribbean origins, 16% is of South Asian origins, and 8% is of Eastern European origins (Office for National Statistics 2012). The more the borough changes, the rosier the memories become.

Social Displacement

Over time, the working class whites of Barking and Dagenham have developed an increasingly refined—even if not necessarily accurate—collective memory. To a large degree, this unified narrative is indeed a product of an ever-shrinking population—a population selected for their lower material well-being (vis-à-vis departed homeowners), now with fewer stories to go around and a more easily amalgamated perspective.[1] However, perhaps more importantly, this smaller population is increasingly funneled to interact in the borough's few remaining venues of cultural life—none more prominent than the public houses.

Public Houses

Pubs are endangered in Barking and Dagenham today. Their primary consumers, white working class men and women, have less and less disposable income. With the loss of basic warehouse and manufacturing work, they can no longer afford to spend precious pence on pints at the pub, let alone tickets to local football matches. Meanwhile, the cost of pints has steadily risen thanks to a wave of government taxes on alcohol, and many regulars have been further deterred by the United Kingdom's 2007 national smoking ban. Given the adverse circumstances, at least 20 Barking and Dagenham pubs have closed since 1999 (Closed

Pubs 2012). Some were demolished and replaced, like the Church Elm on Dagenham Heathway; now, a public library with new public housing upstairs sits on the site. Others sit dilapidated and condemned on unsold land. The Short Blue on Bastable Road still has signs touting "Disco Friday Night" hanging from the second floor, taunting regulars who pass by en route to the nearby shopping parade. The Westbury Arms sat dormant on Ripple Road for 10 years, until rioters torched the abandoned building during the London uprising in August 2011.

The arson was not random. The Westbury Arms had been a Barking fixture since 1899, and was built on the site of an alehouse called the Hand-In-Bowl, which dated to 1736. Its closing in 2001 removed the Gascoigne ward's primary social outlet. "Men, mainly men, would stand around in their cloth caps and sup a pint with friends," wrote one local about the pub (Vickers 2012). "Old folks who could sit quietly and enjoy the ambiance and be accepted as part of the furniture; they were alone, but they were never lonely." During Barking and Dagenham's recent transformation, pubs serve as the last bastion for working class whites to convene in a relatively homogenous environment to meet, crack inside jokes, make obscure references, and retell stories to each other—and in doing so, to preserve a situated sense of solidarity. For East Londoners frequently complaining about people "not talking anymore" and "being a community," pubs are precious.

While in Barking and Dagenham, I frequented the Lighterman, the Thamesview Estate's only remaining pub. It was named for the tugboat operators who pulled barges on the River Thames. Inside the single-story, 20-seat lodge, light banter is typically exchanged between the loquacious barmaids and charismatic regulars at the bar, while gruff, older gentlemen slouch in a booth against the side wall. There is a single slot machine, where people frequently invest the change they receive after purchasing a few £2.80 pints of Carlsberg. The washroom is bare, with a dysfunctional faucet and a seatless commode connected to a pullchain. House music reverberates at moderate volumes, except in the back of the pub, where it echoes off a cinderblock wall painted with an eight-foot-long, eight-foot-high union flag. Before I visited, I was advised to bring a local escort. Even then, when I first entered, the banter quickly dissipated and the house beats felt louder amidst the scrutiny. "We don't really get strangers in here," Jessi Bowen, the barmaid, later explained. "It's a community, and don't get me wrong, we serve anyone. But all these guys are on the estate. It's like a family." As the last pub in Thamesview, the Lighterman is subtly treasured. Fifteen years ago, the pub's local owner drove an acquired Rolls Royce sedan onto the pavement in front of the pub, where it has been left untouched ever since. "That the hood ornament is still attached tells you what people think of this place," Kieran Turner said to me, while he smoked outside in an early May drizzle.

As with extended family, not all who frequent the pub are well known or particularly well liked. Regulars greet each other, some more hardily than others, with a nod or a jab at their preferred football team. Either salutation is more acknowledgement than they typically attract on the streets of Barking and Dagenham, where the wrong look or attire can lead to a mugging by hoodlums. "People come to the pub to have a rest from the outside," said Terry Hammonds, an 18-year-old from Becontree whom I met at the Barking Dog, one of the borough's largest pubs, which is run by the national chain J. D. Wetherspoon. "This is where they have their time together. They're just looking for a beverage and a chat with other Englishmen. They can't get that outside. Here, you can play darts, watch sport, and talk." As more pubs have closed, regulars have had to shift loyalties to new institutions, leading to social mixing that previously did not take place. While this has brought different people into new interaction, it has also enfeebled the sense of cohesion in consolidated clienteles.

Outside the Barking Dog, a dozen people leaned against metal barriers, smoking cigarettes and occasionally commenting on passersby along Barking's station parade. Hayden Thomas, an unemployed 28-year-old, admired the scenery: "I know who she's talking to," he said, tilting his head toward a young blonde woman shouting into her mobile phone. "She's a shithead. I can't stand her." He drew in smoke from his cigarette and surveyed pedestrians coming and going. "Who's that? I don't know that cunt. There's no unity because there's not enough of us anymore. There's more of them [foreigners], and I think you just get used to it."

Thomas continued, "You say 'alright' to them [fellas at the pub], but you're not going to say much more. If anything happens, you know they'll be there. You see them around." In this way, with sometimes the weakest of ties, the pub recreates the norms of reciprocity and implicit solidarity that the regulars like to think once existed in their borough. And when each pub closes, a particular sociocultural milieu—once recovered everyday—is lost forever.

Private Houses

As public houses have declined, the cookie-cutter cottages and uniform tower blocks of Barking and Dagenham's estates have become not only the venues for the preservation of working class British culture, but also the site of many social problems. As many East Londoners have children at an early age, homes tend to bring together three and sometimes four generations of a family on a regular basis. While two- and three-bedroom accommodations only hold a limited number of people, families tend to be tightly knit and congregate regularly if for no other reason than childcare. In old age, grandmothers are often looked after by their children. However, as many nans are only in their forties and fifties, they frequently help their daughters with their children and household chores. For this reason, young working class women are reluctant to leave their Barking and

Dagenham neighborhoods. A move to another ward mere blocks away is viewed as significant, let alone a move to another borough in London. When I asked Jessi, the Lighterman's barmaid, whether she still lived in Thamesview, she replies, "Oh God no. I've moved away." I ask her where. "I'm over in Goresbrook now"—a five-minute bus ride, or 20-minute walk, from the pub.

Ironically, the early pregnancies that bring mothers and daughters so close are often the consequence of an initial desire for greater separation. Like other British municipal authorities, Barking and Dagenham's Council housing administration prioritizes claims made by expecting or recent mothers over almost any other resident. As a result, many teenaged men and women have children in order to gain greater privacy from their parents and family members. Since they cannot afford their own rental, pregnancy appears as an easy shortcut for young lovers. Alas, only a few of these relationships last and lead to long-standing marriages. The result is an epidemic of single mothers and absentee fathers. Tellingly, the conception rate per 1,000 women under the age of 18 years in 2010 was 19.6 percentage points more for Barking and Dagenham than the mean conception rate for all of England and Wales (UK Office for National Statistics 2012). Once settled in a council flat of their own, young women have little choice but to return frequently to their parents' homes if they want to pursue work, further education, or maintain any sort of a social life.

This close interaction between generations facilitates the inheritance of oral histories and identity constructions by younger generations who remain in close contact with grandparents and great grandparents. "My nan is like me world," says 24-year-old Harry Carlisle. "I don't know me dad, I don't talk to my mum. She's never really been there, after having me at 17. My nan is a proper, old-fashioned, East End lady. It's people like that who put this country together. She looks around and can't believe the sorry state we're in. My granddad would be turning in his grave. There were bombs all around, and my nan was getting up at 5 am to get this country working. It's true what she says: 'This country can't support itself this way. We have enough bums here already without flying more over.'" With Harry's immediate connection to his grandmother, less is lost in translation across the generations. This preserves communal self-understandings about white working class people's role in British society, their collective ideals, and their understandings of propriety.

Indeed, in households, traditional norms endure in the contemporary era. There is strong value placed on neighborliness in Barking and Dagenham's white British households. If I called ahead, every resident of each home I visited invited me in for tea. Many offered biscuits. Several people asked me over after meeting in the pub or shopping parade. In interviews, residents frequently faulted others for not greeting each other on the street, making small talk on the bus, and contributing to local charitable campaigns. That is not to suggest that such actions are conventional today, if they ever were. But that they are not conventional provides substantial fodder for conversations and gossipy condemnations over propriety. Families remain almost invariably matriarchal. While this is indubitably connected to fathers' absenteeism and high levels of imprisonment, it is also true in two-parent households. Gloriously fulfilling stereotypes about their East End ancestors, Barking and Dagenham women tend to be loud, brazen, garrulous and nosy, but with a keen interest in family life and social affairs. They are strong, petulant, but inevitably long-suffering characters quick to recapitulate the most personal of tragedies.

In light of the departure of so many key members of Barking and Dagenham's white British community over the past 30 years, old bonds of communal interdependence have also been re-centered at the level of nuclear families. Surviving small businesses tend to be family-run, with employees who are exclusively kin. Jessi, the Lighterman's barmaid, is married to the owner's son. The other bartending shift is held by her sister-in-law. Elsewhere, Fiona Harrison is the 23-year-old owner of a flower shop. She works six days a week, relieved only on weekends and during her doctor's appointments by her sister and boyfriend, respectively. The shop was previously owned by her father's boss's wife, whom she always referred to as "Nan." "I wouldn't call a random person 'Nan' anymore," she explains. "But that's what she was. Today, people have just moved in from different areas, and people just keep to themselves more. You used to know everyone from somewhere or from someone's family. The older people still know a lot of the other older people, [... but] a lot of young people hang around, smoking, mucking about, stealing things from the shops. So, oh God, people trust each other less." Less than half of Barking and Dagenham residents responding to a 2011 police Public Attitude Survey felt that their local authorities were adequately dealing with crime and displays of antisocial behavior effectively (London Borough of Barking and Dagenham 2010b). Reduced social trust more generally has led middle-aged adults to be ever more insular and nepotistic.

A reliance on family members to run businesses and care for children is also a reflection of the fewer professional opportunities for Barking and Dagenham's working class. In the absence of the Ford factory "family" and the favoritism of white British business owners, today's economy places a higher premium on objective educational achievement—a value not typically passed down from generation to generation in white working class households. In many ways, the children of such households find themselves outside of an increasingly globalized education system—a system preparing individuals for a future of stringent competition for viable jobs (Standing 2011: 68). In the past, the children of Barking and Dagenham typically finished school at 14, took a job at the Ford factory, got pregnant, and lived off their housing benefit, salary, and pension. According to Council administrators, the borough has the worst levels of literacy in London and the second worst numeracy. The 2011 Joint Strategic Needs Assessment for the borough indicates that white pupils continue to perform at levels significantly lower than the national average (London Borough of Barking and Dagenham 2011a). There are fewer people with advanced qualifications, and more with low qualifications, than in other London boroughs. The educational level is said to resemble that of the East End in the 1970s, when Bangladeshis began to move in. Achievement is thought not to be "for the likes of us." "Adults did not have the benefits of a strong education system," said Fred Toulson, the school headmaster. "In schools, there are bulletin boards dedicated to kids who graduated and went to uni. There was no history of higher education. Parents tore up one of my student's coursework and told him he was a 'boffin.' You're ridiculed for being 'too clever by a half,' or for being 'a bit bookish'" (see also Willis 1977: 2). Many of the young men industrious enough to be admitted to universities do not take up their positions—distracted by family difficulties, hesitant to take on further debts, and unexposed to role models who may establish new norms of professional success.

While achievement among white working class women is not much different, they are also subject to social exclusion for their achievement. Gender roles remain rigid in households, and Barking and Dagenham has the highest rate of domestic violence per 1,000 residents in all of London (London Borough of Barking and Dagenham 2011b). "Mum always goes to school, if there's any problem," explained Toulson, describing gender roles. "If it's major, then dad goes too and he sits there quiet-like." Fiona at the flower shop said, "In my family, my dad was never the easiest man to talk to. But my mum was, and she would always speak with Dad for me. My friends would often not speak to either of their parents much. Dads often don't have much time for their kids. Some parents are very forceful with their ideas on their kids, and don't give them a chance to form their own opinion." Compounded, these trends render a white working class community heavily subject to self-understandings and behavior initially practiced by an ever-present generation of elders, who have retained young people inside their own distortions of time.

Turning Back the Clock

In 2007, Barking and Dagenham's borough Council administered a survey to several hundred residents. It asked, "What can we do to make Barking and Dagenham better?" According to Council administrators, the most common answer was: "Make it like it used to be 50 years ago." The average white resident could not conceive of progress coming from the future. While this response connects closely to the prominent images of an idyllic past, it also represents people's discomfort with and confusion about the social and economic processes that have led to the borough's current state. Amid the extraordinary amalgamation of narratives that constitute Barking and Dagenham's past, there is little consensus about how it transformed so substantially, so quickly. Today's politics is therefore a fight to characterize this transformation, which enables power brokers to assign blame and set agendas accordingly.

At a town hall meeting at a church in Dagenham's Alibon ward, Member of Parliament Margaret Hodge and her staff went from table to table to hear complaints and requests from constituents. A Labour politician, Hodge had held the seat since 1994. Volunteers dispensed pizza, tea, and shortbread to mostly elderly locals who gathered around six tables for what is called a "surgery"—aptly named, as community members typically alert the representative to social and economic ills needing resolution. Hodge approached Eleanor Hodgkins and Poppy Moore first.

ELEANOR: But where are [these foreigners] coming from, Margaret?

HODGE: Many are second- and third-generation immigrants. A lot of people have sold their houses and left Barking and Dagenham. Listen, you're never going to change it back again. All you can do is make it better for your children.

POPPY: But Margaret, they're in and they're out. Why do we let them do it?

HODGE: With the buy-to-let people, no one is buying who has a commitment to the community. But you can't control it. It's no one's fault: the government, the Council, no one's. But you can recreate the community spirit.

POPPY: The smells from the houses will make you heave! And on the Heathway, there's too many strange stores selling odd meats and vegetables.

HODGE: Well, some people like it.

POPPY: Margaret, would you please live here for two or three weeks and see what it's like?

HODGE: I'm here pretty often. . . . Listen, times have changed and we have to move on with them.

ELEANOR: I feel sorry for my grandkids.

HODGE: Look, we want good schools and jobs for them. What worries me is the 18-year-olds coming out of school or college with no work. That's the fault of the Tories and this government with all their cuts.

POPPY: You would have made the same cuts.

HODGE: Not like this. Every young person would be employed, apprenticed, or in training. Now come on, don't mope. You don't have it that bad.

POPPY: [Brief pause] We're getting things taken away. I can't even get my eyes tested.

HODGE: Yes, you can.

POPPY: No, I can't.
HODGE: Yes, you can.
POPPY: No, I can't.
HODGE: Yes, you can.
POPPY: No, I can't.
HODGE: Yes, you can. Don't feel so cross.
POPPY: It makes me feel cross just to walk up the bleeding Heathway.

Hodge excused herself to take a phone call on her iPhone. She had been trying to get a supportive local councilor tickets to the weekend's big West Ham football match at Wembley Stadium. Poppy looked at me and asked, "How can she tell us to make a change? How can we? We're pensioners. If [English] shops are shutting, how can [immigrants'] shops afford to open up? We could really do with a decent clothes shop. The politicians all go up there and say what they're going to do. But they never do it."

Labour politicians have struggled to walk the line between maintaining the loyalty of white working class unionists without estranging Britain's many ethno-religious minority groups, who represent the party's future growth. The twin pulls of populism and pluralism have restricted Hodge and others from point-ing fingers at foreign immigrant groups or entitled welfare kings and queens—making for a murky message in Barking and Dagenham. Local minority groups have appreciated Hodge's restraint, but the white working class has condemned her betrayal and, in 2005, elected 12 politicians affiliated with the British National Party (BNP) to the 51-seat municipal Council. The BNP emerged as a splinter group from the far right National Front party in 1982, and has since championed the same platform, largely unsuccessfully. Their agenda seeks the expeditious return of immigrants to their home countries and preferential treat-ment for indigenous British citizens. After an initial burst in pre-election polls, the party's leader, Nick Griffin, lost a challenge for Margaret Hodge's seat in 2010 (London Borough of Barking and Dagenham 2010a). Barking and Dagenham still features many of his supporters. "I voted BNP," says Poppy with a mix of pride and guilt. "I can't help it. They call them Nazis. But they're not. They're Britain for Britain. Labour sent [immigrants] all down here and [Hodge] won't tell me where they come from. I think they fiddled the votes, so that the BNP did not get one candidate in." She continued, "Barking and Dagenham has always been white working class, but the Council was always for us. What did my grand-parents work for? An Asian women told me that I'm a racist. So I said, 'Well you made me one.' Why can't Margaret Hodge see the change in this place?"

Since New Labour revolutionarily embraced neoliberal market economics in 1994, the party has steadily frustrated unionists and working class whites—their staunchest supporters since Clement Attlee was Prime Minister in the mid-twentieth century. Labour found that they could get away with this philosophical shift and their recruitment of visible minorities' backing because their base had far more profound disagreements with Conservatives over the welfare state and with Liberal Democrats' support for the EU's supranational governance. Subsequently, Labour politicians chose to cautiously avoid charged debates over British identity and social change—suggesting an aloof disposition to Barking and Dagenham's white working class frustrations. "When you're sick, you need to be able to describe your symptoms to the doctor," said Alec Edwards, a Council bureaucrat. "But these people cannot describe what's happening to them. And like body parts, there are some ills that people don't want to talk about. The BNP feeds into this. They also don't want to talk about these symptoms. They'd rather blame others, totally representative of the people who vote for them." He also noted, "The equivalent to private parts is immigrants. We are an island nation, so there is a natural aversion to people who wash up on our shores. They all get absorbed, but we have an inability to talk about it."

The BNP addresses immigration head-on. In fact, BNP politicians address little else. A 2008 London election flyer that was distributed across Barking and Dagenham features two photos. The first, a black-and-white exposure, captures a neighborhood block party in the late 1950s. With a table of food in the foreground, there is a line of exclusively white women in housedresses posing behind it. A mother holds her daughter in her arms nearby. A crowd of people chitchats in the background under banners of flags stretching across a street of uniform brick homes. Underneath this image, the second photo features three Muslim women, each wearing a hijab (Islamic headscarf) and a niqab (Islamic veil). The first brandishes two fingers toward the camera (a nonverbal expletive), the second menacingly tightens her fists, while the third shields her eyes with her hand. In large font, the flyer laments, "The Changing Face of London: From this . . . to this . . . Is This What You Really Want?" Smaller text elaborates: "Consider this, this is the way London used to be. At ease with itself, friendly, happy, secure. A capital city with a sense of community values and social inclusiveness. If you would like London to be like this again, then support the British National Party, the party that puts local people first."

Although the BNP won over 20% of the Barking and Dagenham Council chamber in 2006, thanks to about 16,000 votes, they subsequently lost all 12 seats in the 2010 general election (London Borough of Barking and Dagenham 2006). It is not that they lost any support. The party garnered 30,949 votes in the borough, but a mobilized Labour opposition challenged BNP incumbents in every ward and won hotly contested victories to go along with Hodge's dismissal of Nick Griffin for the Parliamentary seat (London Borough of Barking and Dagenham 2010c). Today, these voters are without a representative sharing their views. "The majority of white English people here have given up," says Harry Carlisle, a BNP supporter. "They have punched us into the sink so much that there's going to be a civil war. There's only so far you can go before there are riots and uproar. It's on a wobbly edge right now. There's no one else to talk to, to listen to us, to hear our story and take action." He continued, "It'll take one big thing to spark it all off. And when it starts, it ain't going to stop. You can feel the tension. It will be released, and in such a way that the whole country's going to have to do something about it. How long are people going to put up with it?"

Observably, Barking and Dagenham's working class white population has expressed with their frustration in variable ways. While some have continued to support the Labour Party, others join issue-specific movements through their tenant and residents associations. Others have appealed to the exclusive politics of the BNP and similar, more openly violent organizations like the English Defence League (EDL) or the English National Alliance. Still others have withdrawn from the spheres of political expression completely. This raises this book's primary research question: why do similar people under similar socio-civic circumstances take different forms of political action? The remainder of this examination of Barking and Dagenham addresses this question, and explores perhaps a more basic, but equally important enigma: why are people who for decades have been politically unified by their working class status unable to look past ethnocultural difference and unite with new—albeit foreign—members of the working class?

The External State

White working class people in Barking and Dagenham speak frequently about the government—or, as it is more commonly called, "They." *They didn't fix my radiator. They keep letting the foreigners in. They don't listen to us lot.* In speech and frequently inscrutable allusions, residents hinted to the separation they feel from the state. On the one hand, the state is the essential purveyor of housing, welfare benefits, healthcare, and a variety of other public services, not to mention its representative functions. On the other hand, despite its intimate relationship to citizens' quotidian needs, it remains intensely distrusted and external. To the vast majority of people I encountered in Barking and Dagenham, the state is the all-powerful, unapproachable, unpredictable provider. It is sometimes generous, frequently adversarial, but always uncontrollable.

While such a Kafkaesque portrayal is reactive to the perceived unresponsiveness of today's local government, it also has deep historical roots. To Barking and Dagenham's early residents, the local government was a proactive, if not overbearing presence. As part of the "cradle to grave" paternalism enforced by the Council's honeycomb of departments, agencies, and programs, the government also micromanaged residents' behavior. Ordinances were enacted to enforce the uniform grooming of privet hedges in front yards. If any tenant departed their cottage or flat, the state would remove any embellishments they had made to the house and replace them with standard-issue fittings. One-upmanship was frowned upon by a utopian nanny state that provided everything an East End transplant could dream of, in exchange for strict obedience to the rules of a well-regulated environment. This veneer of egalitarianism contributed to the greater sense of solidarity, and would sensitize the citizens of Barking and Dagenham to the exhibition of material differences later in its history. It also created an instrumentalist—rather than activist—relationship with the state.

As expressed by the borough's working class white citizens, externality frequently comes from political representatives' material well-being. "All the prime ministers have come out of Eton," says 30-year-old Ollie Marks, referring to the school traditionally associated with the upper class and aristocracy. "Democracy is an illusion. [. . .] The immigrants get all of the attention because it's part of a divide and conquer strategy." "The government means nothing to me," said Theo Garrigan. "If the Queen died tomorrow, the only thing that would change in my life is the head printed on my bank notes. It's everyone out for themselves. As soon as we start getting involved, we get arrested." "Politicians look out for themselves, and create services for rich people," said Oscar Bradley. "If they lived out there with us, they'd experience what we go through. The rich and poor are separated. [. . .] David Cameron concentrates on his type of people, the people who can afford decent homes. And the working classes are left to do their own bit."

However, others suggest that the state's externality has only emerged after breaches of confidence. "The politicians listen, but there's no action," said Norma Davies, the pensioner and activist. "We've been saying that we need to have more police, but they've been cut back. Years ago, you could go to the Council and they would help." She continued, "But people think that no matter who gets in [to office], nothing will get done. People are just treated as numbers, without compassion." "The Council promised me a fence," said Lexie Browning of Thamesview, "because all these people keep looking through my bedroom window and are seeing me sleeping. But they took so long, we just had to do it ourselves. I've given up. I don't feel safe here." Over pints at the Lighterman, Kieran Turner said, "It's very strange. With the Olympics, they were pumping money into Stratford, but there are still poor people. What are they going to do? Money gets spent on things other than us." Turner went on, "I don't mind going half and half with the Council. I used to propose things to the Council, but they found it unacceptable, so I've lost interest. A lot of people don't vote, because it doesn't matter who gets in." Several interviewees said that they also do not rely on the government to resolve civil or criminal disputes anymore. They cite experiences with social service representatives removing a child from their custody, encounters with judgmental council employees, and unfair court verdicts. The government is no longer welcome in white working class lives—unless it is delivering a check.

Tenants and Residents

Because of both this dissatisfaction and the conception of the government as the aforementioned aloof provider, there is a general norm of yielding to the state and its elites—no matter how passionate a citizen may feel about an issue. Since the 2010 election that saw Labour remove the BNP from any electoral representation in the borough, Barking and Dagenham has featured very little political activism. Shortly after the election, when the Conservative–Liberal coalition government made across-the-board spending cuts, there were protests and rallies at town halls across London. Barking, however, was quiet. Council bureaucrats say that they did their best to mitigate the bite of the cuts, but there was still a significant effect—but little reaction. After peaking toward the middle of the twentieth century, today's unions are much smaller, less organized, and not very vocal. Since 2003, the Ford Factory has focused on diesel engine production and employs a mere 4,000people in engine, transport, and stamping operations (Hudson 2009). The civic culture and block parties of earlier days have also dissipated. At Scratton Farms Social Club, they organized a party in the neighborhood fields for the royal wedding in April 2011. Residents said it was the first time they had experienced that kind of event in 15 years. A year later, the Council set aside ten small grants to fund community parties for St. George's Day, the English national holiday. Administrators received 11 applications, three of which were from people who were not of English descent.

The most significant hubs of political activity in Barking and Dagenham are the tenants and residents associations (TRAs). Each of the borough's 17 wards has a TRA that meets monthly to discuss community affairs. Topics tend to be exceptionally localized—like a noisy neighbor or a repeated burglary. The Council provides a modest budget for tea and neighborhood events, but offers limited oversight of technically independent organizations. TRAs tend to be the breeding ground for Council political representatives, and are occasionally the venue for proxy wars about wedge issues like diversity and housing. Associations are typically composed of retirees, and led by presidents who can be quite autocratic and intolerant of difference.

Nancy Pemberton, the Thamesview resident with an affinity for Union Jack flags, has served in her TRA for 20 years. "I write to the local paper, and have a go if I have a bee in my bonnet," she says. "I think that I have some power locally, and I now I have some friends on the Council. People come up to me and tell me things that are going wrong," she says, with a sense of duty. Nancy felt agitated and empowered enough recently to write to David Cameron, then the Prime Minister:

> David Cameron
> 10 Downing Street
> London
> SW1A 2AA
>
> 10th February 2012
>
> Dear Mr Cameron,
>
> I am writing to ask if you would stop any more house building in the LB Barking & Dagenham but particularly in Barking.
>
> We used to be a very close community but over the last 15 + years this has changed so much and certainly not for the better.
>
> It would seem that immigrants from all over the world are encouraged to come to our borough to live, thus driving out the indigenous community one by one until now we have the situation where we are in the minority in a place we have lived for most of our lives.
>
> Before you start to think of this letter as a racist rant, it is anything but. We have always been a hugely diverse area but the immigrants who came over with their families in the 1950's were completely different and they hate what is happening here even more than we do. When they came they had nothing given to them; they had to work hard, learn to speak English and they integrated; they have our values.
>
> Unfortunately, because of the overgenerous benefits offered to the rest of the world, the people swarming into our borough (into council housing ahead of local residents in need) feel they have a right to everything for nothing and they have absolutely no respect for us or where they live.
>
> Despite thousands of pounds being thrown into promoting 'community cohesion', this is never going to happen because the recent arrivals are only interested in their own cultures and, to a large degree, this is being encouraged by all the services created especially for them at great financial cost, while we sit on the sidelines and watch all this; we watch our elderly being frightened to go out because if they get on a bus they are likely to be the only

person speaking English; they are pushed and shoved at the bus stops while these people (mainly Nigerian) walk to the front every time.

The only thing they are interested in is shouting loudly on their mobile phones and making a lot of noise in the many industrial units they have taken over in our area for their happy clapper events, where because they go under the guise of a church, they do not pay business rates. They are ruining job opportunities and the chance of new businesses coming to our area.

I work hard in a voluntary capacity for our Tenants & Residents Association. Despite advertising everywhere, being part of a very active group who try to include all elements of society and different organisations working in our area to improve where we live, these immigrants never ever join us and are really not interested in what we are trying to achieve in our area.

Our house prices have fallen alarmingly over the last couple of years because so many immigrants are buying to let here and mainly social tenants are moving in who care not a jot for the area; have no interest in where they live and if they don't want something they tip it over their back garden or into the street. This is costing thousands for our Council to keep cleaning up after them. When it comes the time for us to move, as it surely will come, we probably won't be able to move into anything more than a caravan because of the value on our homes dropping and the pitiful amount we get in state pension, that we have worked our whole lives to earn the right to, unlike recent arrivals who gain access to pensions, health care, free travel and countless benefits without contributing a penny.

It is time that people who make decisions about how we should have to live our lives came and actually saw these areas they are sending all the immigrants to; came and saw the devastating effect this is having on communities, on public services. Of course this won't happen because you are all cocooned in your cosy little exclusive areas where the problem of immigrants never touches, it's just words on a paper.

Our forebears fought two world wars to keep our country free; not to have us treated as second class citizens in our own country and subservient to the most corrupt organisation that ever existed, the EU. They died so we would not be invaded by Germany but it is slowly happening by all our laws being made from within the EU dictated to by Germany.

I dread to think what our country will be like as our grandchildren grow up. Will English still be the main language spoken here; will Christianity still be the predominant religion; who knows?

Please come to our borough Mr Cameron, without any advance warning. Get out at Barking Station and see how the third world looks, despite all the money being spent to 'improve the area'; then walk around and see if you can identify any English people or hear English being spoken. It's very difficult these days.

I am proud to be English and I love England but I hate seeing it disappear and our language being lost among all these other tongues. I hate seeing our way of life eroding and all our values being ignored. I hate all our little bits of green being built on to house even more immigrants, who are a drain on our society, certainly of no benefit to us.

People coming to live here, to live off us in the main, should be required to take a driving test before they are allowed on the roads and for this they should *have* to speak and read English fluently; should be checked for infectious diseases (as we were once TB free); and should have sufficient money to live on and be able to support their families. Whatever is this nonsense about them taking driving tests with interpreters (for which we taxpayers pay highly). It's no wonder there are so many bad drivers around and accidents that we are left paying the cost of; not to mention the horrific cost of car insurance, even to drivers who have been claim free for over 40 years. Are you going to do anything about this?

We have always had more than enough of our own wasters, spongers, trouble makers, villains; we really don't need them being imported in from the rest of the world to luxuriate here under our benefits system that pays them far more than someone working extremely hard to support themselves and their family. That is the most terrible state of affairs for any self-respecting person to have to put up with . . .

Come to Barking; come and see how a town with tons of history attached to it looks in today's society; it's a crying shame and we, the people who have lived here all our lives, deserve better. Stop building new homes for immigrants, our schools can't cope already. In a class of 24 you have maybe one or two English children these days; how terrible is that. 67 languages spoken at our local primary school! One language should be spoken—English—this is still, just about, England.

If someone wants to come here to live then they should be prepared to live like us and speak like us, not expect to transport their culture here, it's not working.

I hope I will not get an automatic response to this letter. I would like to think you would have the courtesy to read it—really read it—and wonder why someone would feel so bad they would have to write such a letter.

Go out and ask the people; they all feel the same; we are getting a raw deal and no-one cares unless you are an "asylum seeker" or just an immigrant, then nothing is too much to ask!

Yours in hope that you will actually read this; will realise that things have gone way too far now and have to change.

Stop immigration immediately; give priority to British people for jobs; ensure our manufacturing industry gets contracts they deserve and they don't go to Germany, who would never give such contracts to us.

Ignore rulings from the EU; what can they do? They need us, we don't need them.

Please, start to put our country and people first for the first time in years.

Yours,
Nancy Pemberton

Nancy clearly felt like her words had a chance of being read and absorbed by 10 Downing Street. This sense of competence was rare among people I met in Barking and Dagenham. For many, voting is the only civic activity undertaken, and this tends to be done out of a sense of duty and habit—not because of expected impact. Nancy has an extraordinary sense of internal efficacy. But like many of Barking and Dagenham's TRA leaders, she had been in power for over a decade. This marginalizes not only dissenters, but also younger participants and ethnic minorities.

Nicki Josephs is a 22-year-old single mother, who was placed in a new council flat after the birth of her daughter two years ago. She grew up in a four-bedroom, one-bathroom Dagenham cottage that housed 11 people. A heavyset blonde with visible hair extensions, she sat on her sofa stroking two cats, Missy and Cookie, who were perched on her black leggings. She recently joined her local TRA.

"I don't think anyone knows where to turn," she said, releasing a plume of cigarette smoke. "I got involved with the TRA when I got burgled. I don't think they have an impact though. It's more about the police. They said they'd circle more but we were let down. I think you need to get more young police officers so that youths don't feel threatened by them. My voice ain't big enough." She went on, "I think the government is interested, but they've got a lot on and not much money. They're paying a hell of a lot of money to house people in flats. It costs £800.00 per month for my flat, and I pay £7.00 a week."

"Do you vote?" I ask.

"I don't vote," she said, in a way that suggested she had thought hard about the decision. "I know that's how you get your voice heard, and it could make a difference, but I'm not interested. I'm a single mum, I'm not working in order to support my two-year-old. So instead of doing nothing, I joined the TRA to contribute something to the community. I know that there are some things we don't get told. There are some things that are hidden. I think the government is at the center [of everything] though. I'm certainly not, or things would change. Instead, they're getting worse. There's no respect anymore. Young people are on the outside. They can't speak out for what they want."

Lou Griffiths, the retired darts aficionado who had been a member of the Becontree TRA for many years, noticed that activism had declined. "Years ago, if you didn't like something, you'd go protest and march," he says. "But now, we have fragmented communities, so people don't pull together. You're lucky to see the odd letter in the newspaper. No one turns up for meetings. After years of no communication from the government, people just assume that politicians are there to feather their own nest.

"It's going to break soon," Lou said ominously. "Something's going to give way, but will it be in a good way or will it lead to anarchy and more riots? I think you'll see more of them riots. It just takes a small spark. The younger generation just feels like they don't have a future. There's nothing there for them. There's no job security, benefits, and there's a lot of abuse. We don't have much contact with young people, because they don't have much interest in politics"—at least not on the surface.

The BNP

With older citizens' monopolization of tenants and residents associations, there are few venues for political expression by people under 50 years old. And beyond TRAs, there are few role models or solicitations of their views. However, the BNP fixed that by telling perennial Labour supporters that it was acceptable to be angry. BNP leaders recognized that dissenters among Labour's base possessed a great deal of political capital, and that the general veneer of political passivity was actually suppressed aggression. One of the more fascinating trends in white working class politics is just how little separates the social and political attitudes of BNP and Labour voters. In dozens of interviews, nearly all working class whites griped about European Union oversight "and all their human rights laws." Nearly all believed that immigration was out of hand, that the government "shut the barn door after the horse had bolted." Nearly all were frustrated with the "politically correct brigade" favoring the rights of immigrants over the entitlements of citizens. And nearly all had a low opinion of the government. But in nearly all of my interviews, I was genuinely unsure about individuals' partisan leanings based on their policy preferences.

While a legal political party in the United Kingdom, the BNP straddles the line between democratic and undemocratic. Through their electoral ventures, the party works within democratic channels to gain power. However, to win elections and influence opinion, party members employ exclusivist and occasionally violent tactics. Until a 2009 court order, the BNP did not admit nonwhite individuals. Interestingly, their first "ethnic" member was Rajinder Singh, a septuagenarian Sikh who came to Britain in 1967 and authored a regular Islamophobic column for the party's *Freedom* newspaper. In Barking and Dagenham, BNP leaders used to walk around with burly bodyguards dressed in black. Members have been accused of using intimidation tactics. Their posting of British Union flags was so ubiquitous that it has become a widely interpreted symbol for xenophobia, much to the chagrin of ex-law enforcement and military personnel. At their public rallies, leaders condemn people of diverse ethno-religious backgrounds and urge their mass deportation. Many of these gatherings have deteriorated into violence, as rival minority groups confronted BNP personnel. In a series of investigative reports, the *Guardian* newspaper accused the party of using "front organizations" and other "techniques of secrecy and deception . . . to conceal its activities and intentions from the public" (Cobain 2006). The BNP reportedly operated using a "network of false identities" and clandestine meetings, at which party members were instructed to curb public hate speech. BNP supporters' acceptance of these tactics is the primary characteristic that distinguishes them from many white working class Labour voters who otherwise wish to see the same policy changes.

Among BNP voters in Barking and Dagenham, many depict their vote as one of desperation. "The BNP was the only way to have a voice," said Lucy Iverson in the Gascoigne ward. "It had nothing to do with being racist. We were just bursting at the seams. They ruffled a few feathers. And we did get a change of [national] government in the end. But you know, Labour will always be here." In Thamesview, Harriet Johnson noted, "I think that the National Front should come in for a bit. And I don't even like the National Front, but they'll level the estate out. In the council block over there, there's not one family of whites and there are English people who could use that home. In that section, it's all blacks. Then they open up all their [African] happy clappy churches. It's not a nice place to live. You want someone to look after their own, the English people first." Several young men suggested that the BNP treats support for their agenda as a litmus test for patriotism. Their current slogan is "Love Britain."

Toby McEwing is the 22-year-old manager of a betting shop, one of many that appear in nearly every ward's shopping parade. He completed two years at

London's City University, but dropped out before completing his final year due to the accumulation of debt from short-term "payday" loans and the need to support his mother, nan, and two young siblings. "I never used to get involved in the politics," he says, "but when I went and voted for the first time, I met [BNP leader] Nick Griffin who was arguing for British jobs for British people, and I agreed with that. I also went to a demonstration against Muslims Against Crusades. I just thought the army is fighting to keep our country safe, and some people fail to appreciate that. It was what young people my age were talking about. I agreed with the philosophy of British jobs for British people. I knew a lot of people out of work and wanted them to have a job. The way it came together, there were a lot of people who got their votes counted because a BNP candidate got elected. For them to do that, it made me feel like what I voted for made a difference."

The BNP not only depended on the externality of the state; it also depended on the vision of the state as ultimate provider. Per Dancygier (2010: 35), such great government-procured resources produced not only white peoples' grievances, but also their perception that their protest might address the perceived inequity—that it might, essentially, restore the provider's earlier favor.

Political Displacement

Since their loss in 2010, a significant number of BNP supporters have backed the ascendant United Kingdom Independence Party (UKIP). However, Toby and many other BNP backers have felt voiceless. After the euphoria of its revolutionary 2005 victories in Barking and Dagenham, the BNP went on to win its first three county Council seats in Hertfordshire, Lancashire, and Leicestershire in 2009, along with two seats in the European Parliament—a body it had repeatedly denounced. One Labour councilor from Dagenham noted that the BNP would have won a majority of the Council seats had they fielded more candidates that year. The party was raising more money and starting a youth brigade. However, elected representatives in Barking and Dagenham proved to be absenteeist and incompetent while in office. They were unresponsive to citizens' claims and often did not attend meetings to vote or meet constituents. With their removal from office in 2010, the party imploded in a tempest of personal betrayals and infighting. Sidelined supporters ceased to have a single presence in government, and there was increasing scrutiny from the press and equality advocates monitoring their speech. Thousands of Barking and Dagenham's working class whites felt silenced and out of bounds.

Vincent Dogan was born and raised in Hackney. He joined the BNP at 17 years old after suffering a brutal mugging by a gang of black teenagers. Now

38, he has been involved ever since. "I had an utter revulsion and hatred toward blacks," he told me over lunch at a Dagenham diner. "At the time, I wanted something Nazi, and through the whispers, I knew the BNP was that party. The party was like a second parent to me, a moral guide. The militarism, the racism, the hatred appealed to my anger. It channeled my emotions into something positive. Kids are very impressionable."

He moved to Dagenham in 2004 to mobilize support for the party. His father was a Turkish Cypriot Muslim who married an English woman and naturalized as a British citizen, before dying a few years ago.

"I didn't give a toss about the ideology. It was the hunger for power. It's the most overriding aspect of politics. Not money. Without power, you can't do anything, whether for good or bad. I gave my heart and soul to the BNP, but now it's full of pricks, misfits, and degenerate people. Good people left because of what Nick Griffin did to people who once looked up to him. He betrayed all of us. He's guilty of treason to the people and the nation. All that hope has been flushed down the toilet so that he can secure his position as leader and money-grabber."

"When I arrived here in 2004, [Dagenham] was a sight for sore eyes. There just weren't as many ethnics living here as in Hackney then. The first thing I noticed when I came out of Dagenham Heathway Station was how white it was. And I told people here, 'You've got a nasty surprise coming your way.' I saw it as a political opportunity. The white demographics were vastly in favor of the BNP. If you're not part of the [Liberal Democrat, Labour or Conservative Parties'] trick, you're not mainstream. They all agree on everything, except for the minutiae of tax. They all want to stay in Europe, allow migration, and destroy British industry. We've lost our identity."

"When you've got whites walking around with trousers beneath their arseholes, listening to gangster rap and mimicking their physical mannerisms—I was in Tesco [supermarket] the other day, and I wanted to shake the cashier and tell him he's not one of them. These days, you've got the Black Police Association and ethnic organizations like that. But when the native population wants to organize, it's construed as racist. That is a hypocritical double standard. People like David Duke; I'd like to speak to him someday."

Dogan continued, "Sometimes totalitarianism can do some good. We can take a little something from each of the different governing ideologies. I like the appeal of not being afraid to stand up for yourself. I find the militarism appealing. I don't want to invade Poland, but when I see the black and white images of 'Triumph of the Will' [Nazi propaganda film], I think it's proud, forthright, unashamed, strident. The events that occurred after 1939, some might consider them aggressive nationalism. That's not what I would favor, because European nations shouldn't attack each other. That kind of fascism would not work here. To quote Mussolini, 'Each fascism finds its own iden-tity.' To a young mind, it can be inspirational, but you have to change with the times. The idea was a vision of what could be better than what we have. That's a triumph of the will.

"The way the BNP went about it was unprofessional, the electioneering. You don't win by sitting at a table and passing out pamphlets like we did here at the Heathway. You win by door-knocking, talking to people." Dogan went on, "I would never have pulled a Brevik [the xenophobic Norwegian convicted of terrorism] though, because I don't like prison food. It might sound weird, but I understand his ideology. I don't agree with what he's done because he killed some people that were completely innocent. Somebody must have channeled his political thoughts in a negative way. Do it through the ballot box. But there are some things I would do that would make Stalin blush. Politicians should be executed to leave an echo-ey Halls of Parliament."

Dogan is now trying to create a new political party to capitalize on other estranged BNP supporters and their militarism. "People join it to recreate the 1930s, but that's misguided. The BNP was not about that. Its goal was to re-store Britain to greatness. Since the British Nationality Act in 1946, this coun-try has known nothing but problems. When the white birth rate is lower than the ethnics, you know things are heading down. The Luftwaffe's actions were small compared to our current demographic annihilation. The immigration since 1945 was deliberately designed to change this country. People said that we needed them for postwar labor shortages, but that is a lot of shit. They just didn't want to pay proper wages."

"But your father's family is Turkish Muslim," I interjected.

"If the BNP had a problem with me, then that's their problem. I know what I wanted, and I wasn't going to let some fuckhead stop me. Sorry to put it in abusive terms, but sometimes an emotional response is useful." He contin-ued, "Muslims are setting out to build masjids [mosques] everywhere. If push comes to shove, they would want this country to be Islamic."

"But what about your Muslim family members?" I asked.

"I'm not sure."

"Would you be in favor of comprehensive repatriation," I probed, "knowing that you would be on the boat, too?"

"Possibly," he responded, pensively. "I might go, because that would mean that my work here is done. I don't think the Titanic was big enough. There is a void to fill today. [. . .] Ex-BNP members just need a little electoral success to get started again."

The opening of the Becontree Heath Islamic Centre on Green Lanes in August 2010 injected new life into dormant tensions. Barking and Dagenham's Council granted permission to build the mosque despite the Development

Control Board's decision not to recommend construction due to concerns about parking, loss of rental units, and crowding around prayer times. Local residents sent hate mail to the Council, and subsequently contacted the nascent, militant, openly racist English Defence League to get involved. A local branch was opened, and EDL leaders immediately organized marches that quickly turned into confrontations between white British and South Asian Muslim men from groups like Muslims Against Crusades. Harmony House—a shelter for refugees in the Goresbrook ward—has since endured bricks erratically thrown through its windows. EDL members have also frequently interrupted meetings by opposition groups such as United Against Fascism. After the failure of electoral tactics, radicals are now using alternative measures to communicate their welled frustration.

The London Riots

It is difficult to explain confidently why riots take place. It is usually possible, however, to identify an impetus. In August 2011, London Metropolitan Police officers shot Mark Duggan, a 29-year-old black man who was suspected of planning a handgun attack, and riots erupted in his Tottenham neighborhood to protest police misconduct. In response, satellite violence took place across parts of England and much of London, including Barking. Indeed, Barking was the site of the riot's most iconic video imagery—when a group of young men pretended to assist a blood-covered bystander whose jaw was broken in the violence, only to rummage through his backpack and steal his wallet and mobile phone, leaving him to stagger away in a daze. The perpetrators were later identified to be from outside of the borough, but for days, Barking market's electronics and sports apparel shops were assaulted by a mix of locals and people from other parts of London. News media underscored the multicultural character of the rioters and portrayed the revolts as a unified expression of frustration by poor, unemployed youths in the depths of a recession. However, interviews in Barking and Dagenham suggest that rioters participated in the looting and violence with much less coordination and agreement than suggested. While some depicted the riots as opportunistic thievery, others construed meaning in the violence, but few acknowledged unity.

"I went out [to the riots] for the fun," explained Finn Peterson of Barking. "All my mates were out there, and I thought I'd join them. They were just bored. There's nothing to do but commit crimes. All the things that go on in Barking, Dagenham, Newham, and Stratford. That wasn't doing something about the problems we face; that was making things worse than they already are. There was no point. It was just fun. Around Barking and Dagenham, all you need to know is that people are going to do what they want to do. Nothing is going to stop them." Peterson clearly felt little camaraderie in the revolt. Other respondents suggested that every rioter had a different reason for their participation—whether protest, thrill, political expression, or poverty.

Some young men interviewed acknowledged the riots' political significance. "The Government is squeezing everyone," asserted Kyle Downey, an unemployed 21-year-old from Marks Gate. "Everyone's broke. And rioters wanted to do something about it. They were sending a message to the government saying, 'You can't control us'. If everyone rose up, we'd outnumber them 10 to 1. I don't like how they'll say they'll do something when they come into power, and then do nothing. For the little man, there is no other way to put your message across than to hurt them or to hurt their profits." "The riots are a way young people fight against their oppression by the ruling class," said Joseph Fallon, a 19-year-old McDonalds employee who will attend Kingston University next year. "We feel like we don't have control. We're being ignored and stereotyped by the government as being in gangs. Rioting is a more direct way of releasing tension. If they do it in a civil way, then they're more likely to be ignored." However, for working class whites making a political statement in Barking and Dagenham, any politics of class unity was contradicted by the socially divisive changes they sought.

Displacement and Anomie

The sense of shifting social boundaries has undermined white working class interviewees' solidarity, as they yearn for another life and higher status. This has meant that the younger generation has aspirations to move up and break free from their parents' community and its sinking place in the social order. In their avoidance of relegation to society's periphery, many Barking and Dagenham residents viewed neighbors as a threat. Social ascendance is increasingly perceived to be an individual, rather than collective, endeavor. As such, interviewees observed an increasing number of fellow working class whites violating earlier norms of reciprocity and breaching the social bonds established by their grandparents. "[Other white] people look at you and judge you," noted Callum Everett at the Spotted Dog pub. "But if you're wearing a brand new tracksuit, they'll think you got money. If you're different, that's when you get picked on. So people are joining groups just to defend themselves. [. . .] Everyone is against each other. Gangs are all about postcodes: IG11, RM9, E3."

Paul Bibby is a 20-year-old plumber who is currently contracted by the Barking and Dagenham Council to repair housing estates. "You don't really know everyone the way you once did," he says. "Even the English people lack respect now. Because all the foreigners created more anonymity, you can now get away with a lot. [. . .] If you were here in the 1960s, everyone was the same. Culture, religion, country, goal. Now you've got so much variety, people can't cope. Can you imagine 20 different wild animals in the same room? Those people in the 1960s had it harder. I work in council flats, and the standard of living there is not nice. They're struggling. In the sixties, there was no underclass because everyone had to work. Many of those people are members of today's underclass. I don't see how things are going to get any better."

"Does that stop people from trying?" I asked.

"One of my mates from work got sacked for getting caught looting, and he was on the same wage I'm on," he replied. "People think they have no chance of moving up except through the lottery. That guy had gotten the job through the 'Youth Offenders' program. It's not worth it. I'm against crime. But there are a lot of people living a nice life from lives of crime." The quick (and ephemeral) wealth of criminals only incentivizes this moral collapse in Barking and Dagenham, as envy sweetens the temptation of deviance.

A major issue is that it is not clear to many of the working class white people whom I interviewed that hard work and educational achievement pay off— that the economy's meritocracy actually functions fairly. "People that work all their lives from the bottom of the ladder, they should get more from life," said Terry Hammonds. "The people who never give up, the underdog. Some people make it there, but so many people give up halfway. They're lazy. They can't be asked. I've signed up for jobs and jobs and jobs, without response. But I keep going. You have to believe in yourself. I don't believe in the system. I believe in myself." Self-reliance and individualism is threaded through the statements of many of the under-30 interviewees. It is reflective of their interpretations of a new economy—one premised on greater risk for greater reward; one premised on greater flexibility for the employer and the employee; one that sees work not so much as a relationship or an extension of one's community, but as an instrumental exchange, or at worst, as a civil form of exploitation. However, it is also reflective of their interpretations of a new society—one that does not feature the collectivism and normative agreement associated with Barking and Dagenham's past.

Many young men are torn between lives of hard, thankless work with little prospect of social ascendance and the shortcuts of criminal pursuits. Theo Garrigan said, "I'm fully trained in cleaning science. I have no problem with the job market. I know people are saying that the economy is fucked, but they're looking at the wrong jobs. They only look at the jobs that they want to do. Look for the jobs that no one wants to do, but that pay you the same wage." He insisted, "I think if you're willing to work hard, you'll reap the benefits. If you're not honest, you don't get nowhere in life."

"Does that make it difficult to see last year's rioters get away with stealing?" I asked.

"If I were out [of prison] during the riots, I would have done it. I'm not sure I would have thrown missiles at Old Bill [the police]. But I would have looted. If the Job Centre pays me GBP 53 per week and expects me to get by without committing a crime, it's just not possible. People wanted money. But the government imprisoned people for 14 months for stealing a pair of shorts. The amount it costs to put them away would have paid their benefits for twice that amount of time. You get three meals a day, showers, toothpaste, toothbrush, deodorant, free training, and a bed to sleep in."

Young men and women in the borough have no real models of upward mobility. "I just want a good life," said Callum. "Nice job, family, nice cars, a beautiful wife. But that's just a dream. I don't know anyone that has that though. Those who come close get it by robbing. I see the queen and the royals on telly with all the flashy stuff, and then I look at my pockets and think 'I want that.'" Rhys Williams said, "It might help if I had a model to follow. There are some people who I admire, but just because I think they're cool people, like [musician] Frankie Ocean. None professionally. I've seen people in TV adverts, like [musician] Billy Bragg grew up in Barking. But I don't know anyone who's climbed up the ladder. There's John Terry." Terry ascended quickly through the Barking youth ranks to captain the English National Team and the famous Chelsea Football Club. However, throughout his meteoric rise, he has been revealed to be a heartless, racist, philanderer who had an affair with his teammate's girlfriend. Barking and Dagenham's crisis is economic, but more importantly, it is normative.

Remarkably, one of the most prominent attempts to reinvigorate white working class solidarity and reestablish a sense of moral structure comes from the bellicose English Defence League. They organize around some of working class white citizens' most basic senses of injustice: fundamentalist Islam, criticism of the British armed forces, unpatriotic behavior, and the fate of Britain's contingency of British people. Ashton Roberts is a 24-year-old artist, who was enamored for some time with the EDL's campaign. "I saw the EDL as a group that stood up for us, and didn't call us racist when we said what we believed," he explained. "People of the same culture and class as me were standing up to terrorism and to groups trying to take our freedom away—like the people burning [Memorial Day] poppies and insulting the history of our country's victories over Fascism. I read about the EDL and saw that they're not exclusively for white people. One of the scouts, this black guy, asked me to stand up for my people. [. . . But they and] the BNP exploited us. They know we don't have a voice. They know the government doesn't give a shit about us. For 20 years, we haven't had a voice. But to get that voice, we have had to agree to be torn apart." Many Barking and Dagenham residents have consented to such an exchange. Said one Labour councilor, "No one realized the extent of the anger, the dissatisfaction and the loneliness."

Mute Button

Unimpressed with Labour's priorities, profoundly distrustful of government, and unwilling to join forces with working class immigrants, Barking and Dagenham's working class whites are now engaged in a largely unstructured, alternative form of minority politics. They tend to be focused on local affairs, fighting for scarce public resources and wary of institutionalized discrimination against them. The difficulty has been having their claims heard, and taken seriously.

In interviews, working class white people tended to preface many fervent statements by first clarifying that they are not racist or prejudiced. This was not a trend among a few individuals; rather, it occurred 32 times across the 40 interviews with nonelite sources. Some examples follow:

NICKI: I'm not racist, but the solution is to get rid of [the immigrants].

GEORGE: I'm not racist, but this used to be a nice community of English people, before all the Albanians and Africans came over.

JESSI: I'm not racist, but this country's covered by blacks and Bosnians.

BLAKE: I'm not racist at all. I've got black cousins and nieces. But the Polish have been taking all of the work and running prostitution and drug rings.

JOEL: The West Indians make me goat curry all the time. I'm not a racist. I fucking love goat's curry, pardon my language. But the principle of English families not coming first is just not right.

PAM: When they get off the bus, they don't say "thank you" or "excuse me." But I'm not racist. I've got a grandson who's half-Sikh. My niece is seeing a black boy.

FIONA: The shops around here used to sell more homemade things. Now they're—and I don't want to be racist, but—they're not English, and they all sell the same things.

HARRY: I was supposed to go door-to-door [for the BNP], but I just don't think I'll say the right things or do the job. I think I come across a bit ignorant, and I don't have all the right information to put out there. I might sound racist.

While such disclaimers suggest awareness about intolerance, these individuals had not endured hours of sensitivity training. Instead, they were concerned that their ideas would be disqualified, when they are in fact genuine expressions about how their lives are being transformed. Accusations of racism are interpreted as yet another means of controlling working class white people's expressions, and declaring them invalid. So the preface serves as a caveat that at first appeals to the impressions of outsiders, before appealing to what the individual perceives to be the their true sentiments. "Kids have always picked on difference," noted Nancy Pemberton. "Spotty. Fatty. Honky. Blacky. But I think the anti-racists have made it worse. They look for trouble. They construe everything as racist—like my Union flag. But it's not racist; it's our country's flag and it's up for the Queen's Jubilee anyway. They'd say the same about the cross in the undertaker's window. These people are ruining our country. And we're the only ones who can be racist." Indeed, participants were not concerned so much with being labeled a racist, as they were about the effect of such a label on the perceived veracity of their grievances. Racism is, in this sense, not a branding. It is a "mute button" pressed on someone while they are still crying out about a sense of loss—from a position of historic privilege, frequently in terms they have difficulty articulating. Therefore, the preface "I'm not racist" is not a disclaimer, but rather an exhortation to listen and not dismiss the claims of a purportedly new minority.

This perceived minoritization informs the sense of social, economic, and political displacement among East Londoners. As will be discussed in the next chapter, Youngstown has experienced a similar collapse in its way of life, but its politics are informed as much by the desire to reinstate the past as a desperate search for more stability. British respondents benefit from greater state support and a functional local government, but struggle to coexist with the immigrants who filled the void left by a previous generation. Like much of the United States, Youngstown's citizens can trace their roots to immigrants. Instead, they struggle with the insecurity that pervades their social, economic, and political lives.

4

After the Fall

THE POLITICS OF INSECURITY IN YOUNGSTOWN, OHIO

Where had it all gone? The things that had made it a community—stores,
schools, churches, playgrounds, fruit trees—were gone, along with half the
houses and two-thirds of the people, and if you didn't know the history, you
wouldn't know what was missing.
—George Packer

This chapter examines white working class political behavior and its context
in Youngstown, Ohio. Based on interviews with 75 people—20 of whom are
elites—and ethnographic observation during three months of full immersion, it
offers an analysis of subjects' attitudes and actions. I begin with a discussion of
Youngstown's history and its narratives of memory. I then explore the multiple
forms of economic, social, and political insecurity that condition observed political behavior. In the end, I outline the nature of white working class subjects'
marginality.

Collective Memory

There is a post-apocalyptic feel to Youngstown, Ohio.

It is a city with two symphony halls, a world-class art museum, and a large
historical gallery and archive. It has a 450-acre wooded green space designed by
Frederick Law Olmstead (of New York Central Park fame). Its center features
dozens of monumental architectural specimens, a 15,000-student university, a
20,000-seat stadium, five towers of over 12 stories each, and a downtown skyline
largely untouched by modernism.

However, its core is decimated. Boarded-up windows are ubiquitous, the city
has thousands of empty lots, and relics of old factories and deserted railroad
tracks litter the banks of the Mahoning River. There are few pedestrians at any

Map 4 Map of Youngstown, Ohio.

time of day, and very few cars passing under the traffic lights that dangle from telephone wires above intersections. People drive through slowly, like submarines exploring an oxidized Atlantis of brick, mortar, and corroded metal.

There was a time—any local will tell you—when the city was the steel capital of the world, when the city's center was a bustling commercial hub, when you could step off the train on Monday and find a job on Tuesday.

"This place was a boomtown," said John Avery, commencing the common narrative.

"We had a good steel business," said Debbie O'Malley. "If you couldn't find work on one block, you'd find it on the next. [. . .] We put out good products [. . .], good stuff. Those chairs I have from the company are still as good as the day we first bought them."

"When the steel mills were going full blast, working three turns, seven days a week, you'd have to blow the soot off your porch glider but people had good jobs," said Gil McMahon. "You knew everyone on your street."

For years, the foundries and furnaces of about a half dozen companies provided not only jobs, but also housing, loans, supporting industries, philanthropy, and the sites for political organization and social life. "How're things?" one neighbor would ask. "Sweeping the steps," the other used to reply—a nod to the productivity and prosperity symbolized by porches covered in a layer of black dust, often called "paydirt." Indeed, on hot summer days, the ambient air was said to be so laced with graphite particles that it shined in the sunlight.

The beginnings of Youngstown's steel industry date back to 1844, when a vein of black coal was discovered on David Tod's Brier Hill estate (Linkon and Russo 2002: 18). The region had already seen the development of pig-iron blast furnaces, the first of which was developed by the Heaton brothers near Yellow Creek (present-day Struthers) in 1803 (Allgren 2009: 35). A stretch of mills thirty miles long along the Mahoning River developed throughout the late 1800s and early 1900s, including three main plants: the Youngstown Sheet & Tube Company of Campbell and Brier Hill; the Ohio Works of the United States Steel Corporation, just west of Youngstown; and the Republic Steel Corporation, located downtown (ibid.). Rapid population growth fueled the city's meteoric industrialization, thanks to the arrival of immigrants from the Levant and every corner of Europe. By 1930, nearly half the city owned their homes, and by the 1940s, Youngstown's population reached 170,000 (Linkon and Russo 2002: 38; Buss and Redburn 1983: 2).

For over a century, Youngstown was home to an oligarchy of powerful families who structured labor and leisure. The habits of daily life always rotated in turn with the cycles of steel production (Allgren 2009: 38). The cadences of steelwork, the rhythm of labor, set the tempo for the average worker's pace through life. Labor, alongside attendant political and social concerns, was a pervasive oral tradition passed on from generation to generation (Allgren 2009: 39; Bruno 1999: 104; Peyko 2009: 12). Steelmaking and the steelworker—symbols of goodness, productivity, and power—defined the spirit of the city (Linkon and Russo 2002: 67–68). And in turn, from bowling tournaments to amusement parks, steel companies largely defined opportunities for social life (Allgren 2009: 38). Most Youngstown natives spent entire lifetimes gazing up at the silhouettes of hulking mills, man-made creations capable of altering the natural horizon (Bruno 1999: 25). It was an industry town.

To compete, workers unified in some of the earliest agitations to protest labor practices, wages, and working conditions. The Mahoning Valley's first attempt at organized labor traces back to a meeting held by the Mechanics of Youngstown in 1843 (Linkon and Russo 2002: 21). The town's first strikes occurred in 1865 and 1869, when 1,500 coal miners dropped their pickaxes for four months. A third strike occurred in 1873 (ibid.). In January 1916, strikes at the Youngstown Sheet and Tube and Republic Iron and Steel Mill sites turned violent. Four blocks of

East Youngstown were razed to the ground by fire, eight strikers were killed, 12 wounded, and more than 100 were injured (Linkon and Russo 2002: 28–29). Later in Youngstown history, workers would communicate their resistance by instigating unofficial or "wildcat" strikes, creating subtle delays in production, or taking back "what the company owed them" by stealing materials from the job (Bruno 1999: 123–125).

Enduring ethnic segregation and discrimination, however, belied the unity of protest movements. Factories allocated housing and jobs to correlate employee desirability with a social hierarchy that placed white Protestants at the top, followed by the mix of Central and Eastern Europeans, Jews, the Irish, Italians, and finally African Americans at the bottom. Conventional representations of work as the exclusive domain of white laborers and the trumpeting of Protestant values over those of newcomers fed the early rise of the Ku Klux Klan in Youngstown during the 1920s (Linkon and Russo 2002: 28–31). The group gained prominence in local politics by voicing opposition to the perceived growing influence of Youngstown's immigrant population (ibid.). Early nativist sentiments were evidenced by local newspapers' account of how protesting foreigners were spurred on to riot by Bolsheviks (ibid.).

Under circumstances where transparent governance was effectively nonexistent, the growth of the Ku Klux Klan provided the backdrop for a reactionary expansion of organized crime syndicates. Aside from their involvement in illegal activities like bootlegging and gambling throughout the 1910s and 1920s, mafias protected the interests of Italians and other immigrant communities against incursions by others. They also provided for immigrant families during periods of economic decline and defended immigrant access to jobs outside of the mills (ibid.). In this way, the mob was institutionalized as an alternative police force "providing a measure of fairness" in a seemingly unjust, prejudiced, and conflictive environment (ibid.). Sicilian and Neapolitan crime families benefited from flourishing black markets for prohibited substances and gambling, which led many to seek supporters in official public positions (Schneider and Schneider 2005: 34).

"The Golden Days"

By the 1960s, organized crime in Youngstown reached new heights, as rival factions associated with mob families in Cleveland and Pittsburgh converged (Linkon and Russo 2002: 213). Conflict over control of illegal activities provided the impetus for a rash of gruesome bombings that painted a picture of Youngstown as "Crime Town, USA," according to a 1963 cover story in the *Saturday Evening Post* (Kobler: 76). As construction and urban expansion boomed, organized crime infiltrated both the legitimate business sector and local politics (Schneider and Schneider 2005: 41). Following the dissolution of a truce between the two mob factions in 1977, the Pittsburgh-aligned mob ensured that a newly elected mayor would install a preferred candidate as police chief (ibid.). Such practices continued well into the 1980s; for example, a reform candidate for the 1980 Democratic mayoral primary was intimidated and forced to withdraw from the race (ibid.).

"You couldn't separate the mob from politics," says Bill D'Antoni, a former public official. "Government was like, holy. [...] The mafia had a lot of money in grassroots politics. [...] The whole Democratic Party was controlled by the mafia. It's money. You need to pay precinct committeemen on election day, you need TV, and generally the mayoral candidate raises money and that's done by cutting deals with people who have money. Everybody respected the mob. [...] I don't care if you were a billionaire. You didn't fuck with the mob."

"I don't know why they didn't shoot me. I guess because they still wanted business in the county. They moved their gambling outside the city, like at the Liberty Ramada Inn. We're talking about gambling and maybe drugs. They also controlled the construction companies and the inspectors, so if we paid $10 million for two inches of asphalt on a street, they laid one inch and kept the other five mil. It rained hard a year later and the street looked like Hell. They might as well have just painted the street. If they didn't control you, they could intimidate you. I don't know why but I wasn't intimidated. I was scared, but I didn't take any money. Maybe because I'm a mental case. But I'm like a cat in a fight. I've been threatened. The FBI told me that I shouldn't go out with my friends on Friday nights anymore."

"If you need a project, it takes wealth. It isn't done with just government money here. If you want a job, or to get off the hook with law enforcement, you might be able to do something like that. The higher you go, the more money has influence. And that'll be true in a hundred years. [...] Money, not even dirty money, it corrupts you. People expect something back. If you know someone, you can get something. If you have a traffic problem, you get the right lawyer. Anything here can be influenced by money. [...]

"When white working class people say that the mafia days were "The Golden Days," they're full of shit. [...] We were bystanders to the mobs' competition. The layperson was not affected. They were careful not to have collateral damage. If you're outside of it, then you don't see it. [...] They didn't know half of what was going on, and the reason they were happy was because you had a paycheck every week. The mafia was doing their thing, and you didn't care because you had a nice house, a nice car, and 50,000 jobs. Hell yeah they were the good old days, but not because of the mob. It's plain as my nose."

With City Hall sidelined, the public sphere was dominated by three nongovernmental entities: the mafia, the unions, and the steel companies. With conflict concentrated at the top, average citizens were taught early that if they did not get too close, they would not get burned. Many Youngstowners reminisce about running errands for mafia bookkeepers and bootleggers in their youth; they tout the importance of their union membership and comrades; they recall clutch favors called in to government agencies by friends of friends during times of need. However, they generally stayed on the fringes of a war over the city's resources, and remained content with the stability of their jobs, homes, and sense of community shared in Youngstown's churches, clubs, and bars. All the while, politics was managed in backrooms.

The Collapse

The bliss of this arrangement was abruptly interrupted with the swift collapse of Youngstown's steel industry in the late 1970s and early 1980s. "Black Monday," or September 19, 1977, was the day when Youngstown Sheet and Tube announced the closing of its Campbell Works. The closure of the Brier Hill Works would follow five years later. Following suit, US Steel would shut down its Ohio and McDonald Works and Republic Steel would close its Youngstown Works shortly thereafter (Linkon and Russo 2002: 47–48). In a matter of six years, Ohio State Employment Services estimates that 50,000 jobs were lost in basic steel and related industries, costing Youngstown's working class $1.3 billion in annual manufacturing wages. Unemployment climbed to a staggering 24.9% in 1983 and a wave of personal bankruptcies and foreclosures resulted (ibid.). The primary mental health center, Parkview Counseling Center, witnessed a threefold increase in its caseload during the 1980s, with increases in rates of child and spouse abuse, drug and alcohol abuse, divorce, and suicide (Linkon and Russo 2002: 53). Youngstown's per capita murder rate between 1980 and 2000 was often the highest in the country, and stood at eight times the national average during the 1990s (Linkon and Russo 2002: 64–65, 193). Youngstown was up against a transforming economy that valued high technology, the lower overhead of developing countries, and access to sea lanes to fulfill global demand.

Many members of the Youngstown community did resist the prospect of deindustrialization after the mill closure announcements were made. Almost immediately after Black Monday, workers organized a petition asking the federal government to provide better protection for the steel industry (Linkon and Russo 2002: 167–168). Four days later, five buses packed with 250 Youngstowners drove to Washington to protest (ibid.). The city's religious organizations, advocates for the working class community, organized the Ecumenical Coalition of the Mahoning Valley (Bruno 1999: 46; Buss and Redburn 1983: 23). Legal activists Alice Lynd and Staughton Lynd and the National Center for Economic Alternatives fostered national research networks, recommended legislative agendas, and led the occupation of steel company administrative buildings (Linkon and Russo 2002: 50; Lynd and Lynd 2000). The most highly publicized coalition endeavor involved the proposal for community-worker ownership of the mills. To raise the needed funds, the coalition began the "Save Our Valley" fundraising campaign in conjunction with local banking institutions. However, these efforts were futile. Local union officials inadequately bargained with corporate representatives after the steel companies announced their decision to shut down the mills. Due to infighting and a disorganized approach, local officials had little influence on the deindustrialization process (Bruno 1999: 147; Buss and Redburn 1983: 29). Up against harsh economic realities and without an infrastructure of public leadership or crosscutting social capital, Youngstown struggled to break bad habits and recover.

Without the steel industry providing the resources for side businesses and black markets, attention shifted to government coffers that looked increasingly bigger as the private sector deteriorated. Since 1990, Mahoning County has witnessed the indictment of its sheriff, its prosecutor, a judge, and twice its congressman, Jim Traficant, on corruption charges. In 1998, the city made national news when mafia hitmen botched the assassination of its prosecutor, Paul Gains. More recently, a county grand jury led by Gains indicted the county auditor, the treasurer, a county commissioner (who would become mayor), and the Jobs and Family Services director for accepting bribes from a local business mogul in 2007. The case was eventually transferred from the Federal Bureau of Investigation (FBI) to the State of Ohio for prosecution. Even though Youngstown's economy is decimated, its oligarchy has continued to preside over a broken city.

Youngstown's residents remain perplexed by their struggle. "We have a city that—I just don't understand why—has not been able to redefine itself since the steel industry wound down in the seventies," said Philip Massey, a salesman who moved to Youngstown in 1979. "I see a nearby city like Pittsburgh thrive, when its industry left in a big way. And now it has a vibrant downtown area, with supported sports teams, and major well-respected universities linked to its progress. They have found ways to become a center for education and research and business—60 miles away. There's a little bit of that in Cleveland, and in Akron, where they have responded with resilience after the loss of the rubber industry. Now you can't swing a dead cat in these places without hitting a new restaurant or development. We're surrounded by success stories. But a reputation as a mob town doesn't help. [. . .] There is a perception that to do business here you need to do it with more than your customers. Sunshine laws don't exist when Vinny

Nono's representatives are talking with city officials. [. . .] I'm just not sure what it is that makes our officials behave the way they do."

People in politics are less perplexed. "It started because for so long a time, it didn't really make a difference who was mayor," explained Marty Nash, a Democratic Party operative. "Before the steel industry left, you had a powerful congressman and a strong economy that would succeed no matter what you did, and a corrupt local administration who ensured the mob could run their operations, and people were satisfied with that. The Democratic Party was handing out hundreds of jobs at a time. Your cousin Tilly who couldn't count to ten could find work. It's patronage, so there was a lot of interest in maintaining the status quo. Then after it collapsed, because there had not been a talented infrastructure of public service, you didn't have anybody sitting on the bench who could check in and take on the tough issues. Then you had a brain drain, and anyone with an IQ above 80 got the hell out of here. That convergence made it impossible to elect good people. Now, more than ever before, there are fewer and fewer public sector jobs. So it's harder and harder to stick incompetent people in these positions."

The result has been an exodus—of business, of social life, of people. After peaking with a population of 170,000 from 1930 to 1960, Youngstown is down to 67,000 residents, according to the 2010 census. Amid this general population decline, African Americans stayed in Youngstown at higher rates than the white population and have consequently ascended from their status as an institutionalized out-group to a near majority demographic. As Table 4.1 shows, over the last 50 years, Youngstown's white population has declined from over 80% of the city to a mere 47% share today. For residents, this shift has been dramatic and fast.

Table 4.1 **White Population of Youngstown, OH Over Time**

Year	Percent White	White Population	Total Population
1960	80.9	134,784	166,689
1970	74.2	103,765	139,788
1980	64.8	74,825	115,435
1990	59.3	56,777	95,732
2000	50.9	41,737	82,026
2010	47.0	31,508	66,982

Note: For 2000 and 2010, respondents were given multiracial options. These statistics include only those respondents that identified as single-race white.

Source: US Census Bureau 1963, 1973, 1983, 1990, 2000, 2010.

Many departing families have fled to the city's suburbs or left the region altogether to pursue work elsewhere, creating a "doughnut" phenomenon whereby the core of Mahoning County continues to be hollowed out. Across the counties of Northeast Ohio, the amount of developed land per person rose 23% between 1979 and 2006, even while the population of the same region dropped by 7% in the concurrent time period (NEOSCC 2013). Today's Youngstown occupies the same amount of land as it did when its population was tripled. Bird's-eye views of the city are peppered with condemned homes and empty lots where houses once stood but were burned down. Abandoned buildings, some of which were the Northside mansions of foremen and steel barons, have become havens for criminal activity. They are used as street hotels by prostitutes, as drug rings by dealers and addicts, and as warehouses to store property hoarded from home robberies.

A key anti-crime measure employed by City Hall is to demolish these homes, leaving open pastures where homes once stood in formerly middle-class neighborhoods. Over 3,000 vacant houses have been demolished in Youngstown since 2006. Residents frequently marvel at how many houses remain on their childhood block. "If you drove around ten years ago, it was like night and day," said Jimmy Plummer, a 26-year-old handyman who also hauls scrap on the side. "It's just a vast emptiness of houses now. People moved, the houses get stripped by scrappers, they get vandalized, they become an eyesore, and then they get demolished. My aunt's street used to have seven houses on her block. It now has two houses, and my family owns both of them."

There is very little external investment into Youngstown—particularly for commercial purposes. The only major retail chains that have branches in the city are Rite-Aid and CVS pharmacies, fast food restaurants, and downscale grocery stores like Family Dollar and Save-A-Lot. Neighborhoods are filled with shuttered businesses: muffler garages, bars, tire centers, roofing and construction offices, maintenance services, and travel agencies. There are few barber shops, gyms, home furnishing outlets, hardware stores, or salons. There are few hobby stores for sports, art, photography, or crafts. There are few copy shops, stationers, clothing boutiques, cinemas, coffeehouses, candy shops, or bakeries. These are not mere luxuries, but staples of the nonessential but nevertheless conventional leisure and service industries inherent to contemporary American markets.

As a result, white working class residents flock to the few, treasured bars and clubs that remain. Nearly all of these institutions—Molly's on the Westside, the Boulevard Tavern on the Southside, the Royal Oaks on the Eastside, and the Golden Dawn and Army-Navy Garrison on the Northside—are narrow, brick structures without windows. Dark and solemn, often without music but always with a TV, they each feature a curved bar near the entrance with intimate booths that stay empty except during meal hours. The owners typically bartend and employ family members. They know their regulars by first name, often after decades of service during which they have observed the collapse of their community from the inside, wondering when their luck will turn.

"Until you tear down the mills, you won't be able to move on. People will always think, there's always that hope they'll open back up," said Father Candiotti, a local priest. "Just like if you lose a loved one, you grieve for a long time. And when they finally imploded the oldest of the blast furnaces, there was a group of steelworkers who stood watching on a nearby hill, crying. Those were the brutish-looking steelworkers who went to work everyday and finished it at the bar with a double—sitting there, weeping."

Contested Memory

Like a mother who assiduously keeps her adult son's room in the condition of his childhood departure until he returns, Youngstowners are reluctant to alter the structure of their city, desperately preserving what's left of a bygone era in anticipation of its resurrection. The narrative of Youngstown's past is therefore omnipresent. Amid this civic formaldehyde, the community tightly monitors anything new. The white-working class population is a victim of its earlier success, its accompanying dependencies, and a residual conservatism. Everybody in Ohio appears to think that Youngstown has hit rock bottom and has nothing left to lose—except for the people living here.

"We were better off under organized crime," said Ralph Mickelson, a retired steelworker. "All the streets were plowed, there was no nonsense. Now cops have their hands tied behind their backs and a patch over one eye. At least back then, the trouble they created was among themselves. Now we're all suffering."

"[Former Congressman] Jimmy Traficant cared," reminisced Hank Thompson, an industrial painter. "He was always right. Jimmy had his fingers in bad things, but he was the man. He got caught, but they all do it. So you take him out and put in another guy who's stealing instead. When the mobs were running things—the Strollos, the Predos, the Carabbias—you didn't see all these drug houses, car jackings, shootings, and murders. If you crossed them, yeah, they'd knock you off. But you probably deserved it. And they always paid in cash. It was better back then."

"Everybody wants the big stroke," said Bryant Daniels, who formerly held public office. "There have been scrambles for a Lufthansa air cargo hub here, the world's first indoor NASCAR race track, an Avanti car body factory. That drives things. Somebody from the outside is going to rescue us and make it like the steel mills again."

Most now envision the city's comeback hinging on hydraulic fracturing. "Fracking," as it is called, entails the use of pressurized water, sand, and chemicals to displace natural gas embedded in underground shale foundations so that it rises to the surface, where it may be harvested. The prospect of a fracking boom nearby on city and county land has some residents seeing dollar signs, but others are wary of severe environmental repercussions and corporate irresponsibility. Still others have noted that fracking hubs in Western Pennsylvania and West Virginia have not seen the benefits for which Youngstown hopes. While oil and gas has created thousands of jobs, nearly all of them are being filled by people from outside the region with technical experience or specialized training. Three-star hotels, where workers from around North America stay, are booked solid for months in advance. Fracking's local economic trickle-down effect remains indeterminate. A movement of skeptical residents placed a municipal charter amendment on the 2013 ballot that would ensure citizens greater control over land use decisions. With this question, Youngstown was confronted—vividly so—with a referendum on the narrative of its past.

The results were not close. The amendment lost against the hope that fracking was the key to Youngstown's future. To replace the dilapidation of an enormous local industry, many Youngstowners can only fathom the majestic arrival of another industrial behemoth. There is little sense of organic growth, incremental investment, or structural change to reinvigorate the region. There is a way things are done in Mahoning County, and it is with a signature product and the singular identity that accompanies it—no matter what dependencies or what externalities it creates. The narrative of Youngstown's past constrains its future.

Distrust

For a city so anxious to place so much faith in a single industry with a questionable track record, Youngstowners are caustically distrustful. "There's a lot of anger in the area, stemming from the late 70s and the closing of the steel mills," explained Max Greenfield, who has worked for different public officials. "They just don't believe in promises, in the future of the community, leaders, they're very skeptical about everything. We do focus groups with white working class families and they're highly antagonistic and have almost a fervor to get into an argument. They have a feeling that they've been battered. There have been so many promises made since the fall of the steel mills, and that's the root of it. This was once a wealthy community, and it ain't so wealthy anymore. People know it, and there's a tremendous amount of resentment between the haves and the have-nots."

Nash, the Democratic staffer, said, "[White working class people are] socially conservative, slightly racist, with a huge chip on their shoulder, distrustful of most public and private institutions, extremely cynical, and extremely susceptible to demagoguery. They have a chip on their shoulder particularly as it relates to private institutions like the steel industry. This is an immigrant community that had difficulty with work and discrimination. This was such a tough town that it's in our culture. In the mills, it was one ethnic group against another and everyone against African Americans. So it remained balkanized for a long, long time."

"Having a chip on your shoulder is a prerequisite for living here. Black Friday saw people lose all of their livelihood in the space of a day, and our inability to recover created a pervasive sense of hopelessness that is also part of the culture. The distrust of private institutions goes back to the way industry treated workers until the union movement formed, and even thereafter. Banks and powerful institutions were always run by white Anglo-Saxon Protestants. We have a reputation as a tough union town, but that's only necessary when you have tough management. They were basically killing workers, and the workers rebelled. It all goes back to what you had to do to earn a living. Distrust of public institutions was after a demonstrated inability to cope with the destruction of the steel industry, the incompetence of political figures, and the fact that most people accepted their corruption. That didn't matter when things were good, but it became a sore spot when things got tight and crime exploded, services weren't being provided, streets weren't getting paved, and everyone was on the take. This city was wide open."

Nash continued, "It's natural to distrust your officials when they can't get the job done. [Ex-Congressman] Jim Traficant couldn't get elected in almost any other congressional district, and this situation set him up to be the king. People feel like they've been failed, and he had a message of 'us against them.' He made people feel like they were fighting back, despite the fact that he was one of the least effective congressmen in the history of the chamber. The guy was corrupt as the day is long, but Jimbo could get away with almost anything because no one here would say the emperor had no clothes."

A key hindrance is that while Youngstown is a city large enough to sustain (and large enough to need to sustain) a veneer of accountability, it is a city that is small enough to operate on a cronyist system of favors. Indeed, despite its culture of intense distrust, would-be whistle-blowers are conspicuously few. Youngstown is tightly knit like a small village. Social networks are very dense, thanks to a society that has added few newcomers and seen many young people leave since the 1990s, concentrating coteries and rendering them relatively static. So even when problems are uncovered, there is a general reluctance to speak out about them, for fear of a backlash or due to established relationships. Dense networks, long memories, and a great deal of arbitrary power keep tongues tied.

"I've had to arrest friends when it's necessary, but I'm not going to pull over a kid I went to school with," said Officer Kilburn, a police patrolman. "I had the chance to break up one of those betting rings with the SWAT team, but I stayed in the station because I knew all the guys we were busting. You can be more aggressive if you don't have family here. The problem is that if you call out everyone every time something corrupt happens, everyone's going to hate you. Sometimes you have to let things go, or tiptoe around it. [. . .] You need to pick and choose your battles. Just keep names in your black book. It sounds like a movie, but if someone starts spouting off, people here will come after you. Throw a monkey wrench in someone's business? Get ready. The 'Youngstown Tune-Up' is real."

As a result, it is frequently difficult to distinguish rebellious behavior from democratic behavior, particularly under a dysfunctional local regime. Indeed, much like unique species of fish are able to survive around sulfuric vents in the deepest crevices of the sea, Youngstowners have adapted to extraordinarily difficult conditions. Amid severe economic, social, and political insecurity, they identify alternative ways to subsist and create proxies for civil society and governance.

Economic Insecurity

Lost steel industry jobs were always more replaceable than the unique normative structure that welfare capitalism provided. For over half a century, the steel industry was invested in social safety nets, company housing, and community programs that were as much a legacy of unionization as an acknowledgement by steel companies of their dependence on Youngstown's future generations. Welfare provisions were a means of economic reproduction. With the precipitous decline and collapse of the city's mills, municipal government was thrust into the role of "provider," after years of passivity.

However, government did not have the resources to mimic Big Steel. Municipal programs were earmarked for only the very poorest, and City Hall was ill equipped to protect workers from the realities of the neoliberal capitalist forces that were let loose. Today's workers are disenchanted by what they perceive to be a culture of exploitative greed in the local market, and implicitly (and sometimes explicitly) remorseful about how good they had it.

"Nobody cares about the quality of work anymore, what things look like behind the scenes, safety," said Will Macmillan, a union electrician. "The cheapest bid gets the job." Ralph Mickelson added, "There is no work ethic or loyalty—to your employer, or from your employer. It's at the bare minimum. In some instances, hard work pays off, but in others, it gets you scorn from other workers."

A former mill hand, Lou O'Malley, said, "These days, the big boys, the people with the big money don't want to pay the gazeetas. They want something for nothing. We're sending too much of our business overseas and getting terrible quality back. But I guess you've got to go with the flow. The losers are the white working class people."

Such sentiments are reinforced when government agrees to deal with companies that offer their workers few benefits and little stability. Desperate to bring any jobs and tax dollars into the region, and therefore reluctant to impose any conditions on prospective investors, local government bows to companies' whims.

"We will give away the farm," said Katherine Kemp. A middle-aged woman with business acumen and a refreshing directness, she has worked in city planning for over a decade. We met in a dark, wood-paneled bar in the southern suburb of Boardman.

"We got V & M [the city's only remaining steel producer] in the ballpark of 30 million dollars to locate to a place that they were probably already going anyway. We scrambled and pieced together tons of incentives during the federal stimulus."

"How do you compete otherwise?" I asked.

"We don't. Nobody has any reason to relocate to Youngstown or the region. There may be a small reason for logistics companies because of our low overhead and placement between Cleveland, Pittsburgh, and Chicago. But until the shale gas companies came along, there's no reason. Our workforce is not distinguished. Our university is lackluster. We do have an aging population, so we can attract some health care companies. When companies do come in, you Google their name and realize that they've been indicted in one state and barred by the Chamber of Commerce in another. We're a magnet for shady types."

"How much does that have to do with politicians' propensity to expect bribes?" I asked.

"Most companies that are decent won't do stuff like that. So it's a detriment. Word gets out about stuff like that. Cheap whores don't get classy johns." She sipped a glass of wine.

"So how can Youngstown attract a decent company?"

"If there's an existing company run by people who grew up in the [Mahoning Valley] region, they'll stay here because they are deeply loyal. The networks are so strong. My dream is that one of them goes Fortune 500, and just doesn't turn into an asshole."

Kemp reclined, and continued, "There's a genuineness about the place. But don't expect to get a good workforce if you're going to pay them nine bucks an hour. You gotta treat people well, or you're not going to do well. Youngstown has a real history of being exploited by employers. Originally, yeah, by the steel industry and the legacy is still here. There is still a strong mistrust of authority and in particular government. Ohio has weak governance structures generally. We sort of cater to companies' economic demands and this area is pretty much the same. City Hall is located on a side street and you can't even see its sign. The government doesn't exploit working class people; we just go along with employers' every demand."

Remarkably, local government is just as obsequious with the fracking industry in discussions about a resource over which Mahoning County holds a monopoly: the land underneath them.

"Everyone is scared shitless to say anything," said Nash, the Democratic staffer. "The Chamber of Commerce, elected officials won't. But they're being short-sighted. We're sitting on $1 trillion. Where else are they going to go? They can't frack in China. We're sitting on the stuff and they got to go through us to get to it. We are so used to rolling over for anyone who wants to come in here; you don't have to do that with energy. Somebody has to take a leadership position on labor and environmental issues to make sure we get some benefit. [. . .] It's a question of leadership, in a region where there hasn't been any."

Crony Capitalism

A key hindrance is that government offices positioned to represent the public interest have a propensity to maximize personal interests first. Most visibly, personal relationships have tainted the redevelopment of downtown Youngstown, where success has been contingent on things other than business. Downtown's purported renaissance features a tattoo parlor, a few restaurants and bars, and a vintage shop. The tattoo parlor was co-founded by a former city police officer. Shortly after its opening, several other parlors in the city were reportedly closed down by inspectors for health code violations, and a competing store was not permitted to open on the same street.

Among the bars and restaurants, Dooney's was owned by the then-mayor's son, Chris Sammarone. After investments from city politicians, the owner of the Lemon Grove bar was accused of falsifying earnings reports in order to raise further capital and resist closure. "He owes so many favors," mused one regular, "they've got him by the balls. He can't rock the boat." The owners of Avalon Pizza have reportedly received special treatment from the former mayor, Charles Sammarone, who forbade city building inspectors from citing blatant violations of safety standards.

The vintage shop, Greyland, is the only clothing or furniture store to open in decades. However, City Councilman Mike Ray has repeatedly threatened to close it as part of a campaign against "thrift stores." Shortly thereafter, a promotional event at the store was interrupted by plain-clothes police officers who antagonized attendees and intimidated the proprietors. The owner was so concerned that he began suspecting any passing police car for weeks thereafter.

"I tried to start a bar downtown, but the mob owns all the liquor licenses," said Freddy Kristeva, a 59-year-old Westsider. "There is a finite number of licenses given by the city, and they bought them all up and control who they go to.

They don't want me competing with their joints, and if I do, they want me to pay 30 grand and agree to buy the pool tables, dartboards, and video games that they rent. They insist on your cooperation or they burn down your building. I mean, it's not that it's a bad deal; it's just control."

The most well maintained buildings outside the university—the city's largest employer—are banks and churches. The highly touted "business incubator," which was cited in President Barack Obama's 2013 State of the Union address, is promising for its facilitation of high-tech start-ups. However, it is next to meaningless for the working class people who are unqualified for jobs as computer programmers or scientists.

In interviews with three business officials in City Hall, Mahoning County, and the Chamber of Commerce, I inquired about Youngstown's sources of economic growth and received three completely different projections. One underscored call centers, food processing, distribution logistics, and metal mining. The second emphasized the arts, higher education, and high-tech start-ups. The third attributed all growth to oil and gas. "Mahoning County doesn't have a five-year plan," conceded Karen Amalfitano, a county official. "It doesn't even have a one-year plan. None of our departments know where we're going to be. We're shooting off the seat of our pants."

"We were always known for our labor unrest," said George Ellis, a member of the Chamber of Commerce. "But our private sector labor force is only 9% union. We've transitioned away from that. I think the culture is changing."

"How is the culture changing?" I probed.

"I heard from a young person that my generation worked to live, while the new generation lives to work."

Under the circumstances, they have little choice.

Instability

"You're constantly reminded that you're replaceable with someone else who demands less money," said Didi Schumer, a hospital clerk. "It's worse as you get older. [. . .] Companies are giving people more work and finding ways to cut people's jobs. Hard work doesn't pay off. They know you'll get the work done, because you're replaceable."

The instability and insufficiency of conventional jobs in Youngstown alters individuals' approach to the rest of their lives. Working under the consistent threat of dismissal, many are reluctant to plan for the future. Companies' unwillingness to pay living wages or provide benefits has many employees keeping one eye on their qualification for government provisions like Medicaid and food stamps, as they ponder career decisions.

"These days, if people get jobs, they hang on to them for dear life," said Hank Thompson, the industrial painter, as he looks up from a welded frame. "You hear about some getting tired of working somewhere and threatening to leave, but who are you going to bump out at the next shop over? A lot of companies will lay you off as soon as business slows. I got a wife and four kids."

He patted his brow, and raised his airbrush. "I'm going to get lung cancer like this. If they would open that racetrack casino [proposed for Mahoning County], I'd take a job there, so I can be in the air conditioning all day with broads walking around me."

Others eschew formal work altogether and partake in an enormous underground economy that is equally unstable. Youngstown is a hub for secondhand sales, garage work, and under-the-table commerce. Without paying taxes on earned income, many individuals feel less of a stake in governance.

"People learned how to get by on the side," said Maddux Miller, a shopkeeper. "And if it wasn't you who was doing it, it was your neighbor or your family member. While organized crime has broken down, the economy has declined and the blue-collar desperation has gone unchanged. The DNA is the same. The history has not left us. People overlook the same activities that made organized crime powerful. Drugs, betting, they just look the other way. It's like Mayberry [Andy Griffith's fictional television town with friendly but incompetent police]."

Youngstown is a locus for the drug trade. Heroin, crack, and marijuana are sold in significant quantities, typically out of vacant or rented properties. "The cash is coming from the [wealthier] suburbs and townships," Maddux explained. "And Youngstown's businesses are subsidized by the dealers who rent out empty rooms in their stores and restaurants—the same rooms that were once used by racketeers, bootleggers, and money launderers. Today's drug dealers are much more localized than before. It's still the Wild West, just lower level. Guys are now block-by-block. There are over 40 gangs that have replaced a small handful of rings. Over the years, we've just gone from a few big hustlers to hundreds of little hustlers. They're on every street."

Citizens also supplement their income by fixing cars in their backyards, mowing lawns for other residents, hauling materials in their trucks, and offering friends handyman services and light construction. Mahoning Valley residents are also prolific scrappers. Many collect, trade, and sell the widest imaginable variety of household wares, memorabilia, and furniture, convening at the twice-weekly Four Seasons Flea Market, estate sales, and pawn shops.

Ralph Mickelson's porch is littered with items he found on the street. "I scrap," he said, hoisting a discarded carburetor. In the corner was a pile of paint buckets stuffed with magazines and newspapers, a bag of charcoal, a jug of antifreeze, a recycling bin, and toddler's furniture. We sat in two recovered office chairs set facing the front yard. Ralph keeps his eyeglasses and a cordless phone on the rail, with his shotgun just inside the door. "I did a lot of things to make sure my kids ate."

Many young, white working class adults who have yet to leave Youngstown have embraced insecurity as a way of life. Available jobs are increasingly flexible positions that have replaced benefit-earning, longer-term roles and can be easily shed during declines in sales or in response to unexpected rises in overhead costs. Rather than invest in younger employees, many companies work on truncated time horizons and value short-term agility over long-term increases in human capital productivity.

In so doing, the market is imposing a similar myopia on its workers, who are unable to invest in their skill sets, relationships, and subsequent communities. They have internalized the feeling of being replaceable. They are unsure how long they will remain employed and therefore choose not to own homes and continue to weigh the advantages of welfare benefits. In this way, market flexibility has also translated to a social flexibility.

"Considering all our debt, we have basically communicated to our young people that there will be no safety net in the future," said Maddux. "The economy is going to hell and there is nothing you can do about it. So the response has been to stop trying to do anything at all. There's no reason to strive. Nothing is guaranteed."

Though they work in the same contingent jobs as earlier generations, young people often espouse anticapitalist perspectives and have low expectations of the government. They frequently engage in episodic personal relationships and semipermanent domestic arrangements—always ready for the next adaptation, convinced that such independence is what is required to survive Youngstown's next apocalypse.

"You just get used to living from one disaster to the next," a young man mused to me at a flea market. "We can't afford to prepare for the future. So you ride the broken car til the wheels fall off."

Leah Perry confronts the countervailing forces. The 29-year-old clerk at a window manufacturer recently purchased a dilapidated house on the Northside, thanks to a loan she received from a friend—not a bank.

"Banks will not give mortgages on houses that they consider uninhabitable. You need a 'purchase and rehabilitate' loan from HUD [Housing and Urban Development]. They assess the property and estimate its value post-rehab. But there's not a single house in this neighborhood worth much more than $15,000. It's modern-day redlining. They're refusing to lend."

After purchasing the house for $4,000, she personally performed the drywalling, mudding, interior painting, demolition work, floor refinishing, and bathroom retiling with the assistance of neighbors. However, she faces the expenses for more technical work like exterior painting ($12,000), plumbing and heating

($16,000), electric wiring ($2,500), and roofing ($11,000)—amounting to triple the ultimate value of her home.

Within weeks of her purchase, the city had already fined Leah for not painting the house's exterior, a code violation. They would cite her several times at costs exceeding the price of paint.

"If I want a certain quality of life, the only way to do it is to do it myself," she said. "The government just makes it hard to work in their framework, so you either have to do it yourself or give up. [. . .] I don't qualify for welfare or health insurance. I had a better quality of life when I was working part-time at $9.00 an hour. I'm making enough money to exist, but that's too much for the government, because the city doesn't have a program for me. [. . .] [The office of] Jobs and Family Services doesn't take any action. I guess I could do what other people do and not report parts of my income. But I want to live honestly. [. . .] We're all one step from welfare. You are one bad car accident, one unexpected lay-off, one medical bill away from losing your house."

One Step Away

Many of Youngstown's citizens occupy the space between poverty and middle-class stability—a precarious place that incentivizes families to balance their pursuit of a living wage with their maintenance of government assistance. The city's per capita income is $14,996, while the average household earns $24,800 per year. Youngstown leads the country in concentrated poverty, with 33.8% of its households living beneath the poverty line (United States Census 2010).

Eddie and Gillian Phee, both 42, run a stall at the Four Seasons Flea Market where they sell clothing and watches. Both were laid off in 2010 within a couple months of each other. Eddie was working for an aluminum factory that produced siding and window frames, while Gillian worked in logistics for a plastics company. Their home was foreclosed and they have not been able to find work since. They earn about $2,500 per month for a family of four.

"We're stuck between a rock and a hard place," Gillian said. "You can't get a job or you'll lose your medical [Medicaid]. But if I don't get a job, we're not really making enough. Each month, we want our numbers [income] to come in right—high enough to pay the bills, low enough to keep the medical coverage and food stamps. The American Dream works for some people. Other people just live day-to-day. If you do have a dream, this town will find a way to shoot it down."

Will and Caroline Macmillan, 48, are in a different position. She is an art teacher, and he is an electrician who vacillates between jobs assigned by the union hall. "Eight years ago, I ran my unemployment out and the government refused to grant an extension, even though the whole state of Ohio was struggling," recalled Will. "I didn't know what to do, and I called down to the welfare office. It was tough to go that route. We got a Medicaid card and it was better than my usual union coverage. I realized at that time that the welfare money at $225 per week was half of my unemployment payments and a quarter of my salary when I was working. Why would somebody want to work a minimum wage job if they can qualify for welfare and not have to get up every morning? I mean, I didn't want to work at Dunkin Donuts and lose my Medicaid either."

Caroline, who only works part-time because the couple cannot afford childcare, said, "In 2010, there was absolutely no work to be found. Thank God for the government's extension of unemployment benefits, because we could have lost our house. We otherwise would have had to drain our retirement accounts to make all our payments. [. . .] It was a little humiliating but I always appreciated that [Will] didn't make me come down to the welfare office with him."

"Things have just been so bad for us that the union's stances have weakened," said Will. "This summer was the first time I have ever been told that it was mandatory to work six 10-hour days a week, unless you have a doctor's excuse. Otherwise, the client could fire you. Then they recently added a mandatory eight-hour Sunday on top of that. The general attitude is that, because things have been so bad, that people seem happy just to have a job."

Tess Delacort has owned a secondhand children's store for 18 years. Despite the relative stability, "I feel this sense of internal panic everyday," she said. "Everyone is struggling right now. I have never been more worried, not since maybe I got pregnant as a teenager. My husband was in Iraq and is now suffering from severe post-traumatic stress. He needs to be hospitalized, so he will soon lose his job, which means the family loses his medical coverage. I take ten different meds a day. So right now, I feel like my family is one month away from homelessness. When he got hospitalized, we were on the verge of a divorce. But I just could not tell my kids that I'm leaving their father and letting him commit suicide. We're all hovering just above poverty. Every month is a struggle."

On the periphery of Youngstown, trailer parks are populated by people who once lived on the edge of poverty. None willingly capitulated to the pressures of their circumstances; they encountered unexpected events or made poor decisions. Violet is a recovering addict, who turned to crack after the unexpected death of her stepchild and her ex-husband's departure. Her neighbor, Sam, spent nearly his entire childhood in and out of foster homes after his father killed his mother and committed suicide when Sam was four years old. After a career in factory work, he was diagnosed with lung cancer and, according to his doctors, has six months to live. Down the block, Fran Sulz recently finished a five-year prison sentence for killing her husband, after enduring 20 years of brutal domestic abuse. She recently enrolled in night classes at the university to "start over." Like Violet and Sam, Fran confronted life's challenges without much familial or community support. Given the short distance separating Youngstown's white working class from the Hillcrest Trailer Park, attitudes toward poverty are unforgiving.

Symbolic Boundaries

In Youngstown, welfare chauvinism is most intense among those closest to qualifying for it. Proximity does not foster a greater concern or empathy, but rather foments greater resentment. In most interviews, white working class people expressed an ability to directly relate to the choices made by people receiving government benefits. Indeed, because they believe that they could just as easily "give up" or "use the system" as welfare recipients are thought to, they are among the least tolerant of such a choice. Concurring with earlier research by Lamont (2000), many respondents place this choice in moralistic terms that reflect their work ethic and integrity. Their resentment is fueled by the way they believe government "rewards" their counterparts.

Stories about people driving into welfare office parking lots in brand new Cadillacs are repeated from neighbor to neighbor to neighbor until it is unclear who exactly witnessed the incongruous scene. Variants of this story describe welfare recipients wearing leather coats and ostentatious jewelry, buying steaks and lobster from supermarkets, and selling their food stamps at a discount and spending the profits on nonessentials. Less acquainted with the choices of wealthy professionals, they are more forgiving or at least less bothered by their behavior. There are no stories whispered about an executive's decision to purchase downscale safety equipment, a stakeholder's drive to close a company, a vice president's gratuitous pursuit to reduce payroll and earn a meager bonus. "Working class white people don't feel like they can control Wall Street or big corporations," explained D'Antoni, the former public official. "They can control their neighborhoods; that's an easier target for their anger."

Such moralistic and logistical distinctions are not always clear. When lamenting the decline of their neighborhoods, many respondents cited the unaccountability of landlords who rent or sell their properties to unsavory individuals with histories of criminal behavior or negligence. However, the same respondents also speak of their own desire to one day move out to the suburbs and sell their own homes to the highest bidder. Others actually rent from the very landlords they discredit. It is also complicated to point fingers at the employment and business practices of companies that white working class people patronize. It is precisely the denial of health benefits that helps keep Walmart's prices low. It is the inclusion of goods imported from developing countries that make groceries and household essentials affordable.

A more arbitrary distinction concerns the framing of welfare itself. Many respondents did not consider registration for unemployment benefits, disability payments, Medicaid, or food stamps to constitute "welfare." Rather, for them, welfare was exclusively cash assistance—state and federally funded programs that provide money to people with little or no assets or income. In yet another construction of moral superiority, cash assistance is thought to be categorically different from food stamps and Medicaid in that payments are effectively liquid, and categorically different from disability and unemployment payments in that eligibility is not a matter of demonstrable misfortune, only demonstrable need. In this spirit, cash assistance is interpreted to be not a matter of assistance, but a reflection of capitulation and system exploitation.

"There are a lot of people who abuse [welfare]," said John Avery, who handles odd jobs for a small factory. "I'm running around busting my hump, while another guy sits on his porch. That's not right. I get food assistance and medical from the government because of my daughter. But I go to work every day, even after I broke my leg. You have to earn it. [. . . People on welfare] are driving around in new cars and I can't even afford a vehicle. The government pays their rent and utilities, and so they spend the cash on gold chains and a Cadillac, when I can barely afford a Cavalier. [. . .] People will take advantage of things any way they can."

Threaded through such statements is an implicit association between cash assistance—though not other forms of welfare—and African Americans. On the surface, respondents frequently made use of coded language by referring to Cadillacs and gold chains, which are predominantly associated with African Americans in Youngstown. However, other respondents referred to predominantly African American neighborhoods, families with multiple children out of wedlock, and other associations based on derogatory stereotypes. Rather than rely on such cues, I asked respondents to identify these people who exploited welfare. "While I do think that there is a disproportionate amount of black people on welfare," said Caleb Jones, a parking attendant, "it is more determined by a lack of education or income."

"Which black people are more subject to?" I asked.

"Yes."

"Did you ever accept welfare or other government benefits?" I asked.

"Unemployment, yeah," he said, sheepishly. "It was a humbling, disheartening experience for three months. I had philosophical problems with it, but I eventually found work digging ditches for a construction company. You know, it became comfortable to get money in the mail. You can really stagnate. I asked myself whether I was not working because I can't find a job or because I don't like the jobs I find. Now, I'm poor, but at least I have a job. I don't get what I want, but I got what I need."

Caleb, Will Macmillan, and other subjects who acknowledged their consumption of welfare were each quick to note the allure of indefinite government assistance, and celebrate their progression back to full-time employment. However, their interpretation of welfare was subsequently less in terms of work ethic. Indeed, none of these subjects admitted to indolence. Rather, welfare is here interpreted as a matter of discipline and integrity. As more working class whites or their peers require government assistance, conventional socioeconomic dichotomies and their normative underpinnings are becoming hazier—altering social boundaries more generally.

"Many working class white people are down today," said Father Candiotti, "because they realize that they are becoming the very people they used to criticize."

Social Insecurity

A city that has always structurally divided rich from poor, the managerial class from labor, Youngstown appears in many ways built to unite the proverbial proletariat against the interests of capitalists. While class-based segregation is less apparent today, the Central YMCA serves as an enduring artifact. A labyrinth of hallways and stairwells, it is a conurbation of three buildings that once made up the largest YMCA branch in the United States. Located mere blocks from Youngstown's key government buildings and business offices, the gym attracts a mix of clerks, custodians, construction workers, police officers, politicians, business owners, and teenagers. However, contrary to the Christian egalitarianism that inspired its initial founding, Youngstown's Central YMCA provides little refuge from surrounding hierarchies.

There is literally an upstairs and a downstairs. For an extra fee per month, members are admitted to the Health and Fitness Division, an exclusive, all-male changing facility on the building's fourth floor with a steam room, reserved lockers, towel service, and private exercise space. There is no female counterpart. Other male members use the men's standard locker room in the building's humid basement next to the heavy weightlifting rooms—popularly known as "the dungeon." The Health and Fitness Division's steam room is known to be a de facto roundtable for the city's (male) power brokers, attended by the mayor and others. While the gym offers progressive pricing to low-income members, the extra cost of access to the Health and Fitness Division is not so pro-rated. So the Division—and the division—is largely kept in tact.

More subtly, Youngstown is also developing a linguistic divide, relatively unique in contemporary American society. Situated along a linguistic fault line separating the Northern dialect of the Great Lakes region from the Southern and Inland South dialects of Appalachia, differences in speech are substantially correlated to socioeconomic status.[1] While professionals and middle-class white people generally participate in what linguists refer to as "network standard" American English—largely consistent with Northern dialects—Youngstown's poor white population is more likely to speak with a full Southern shift that features what is colloquially known as a "twang."[2] The high dialect is therefore thought to be learned as a result of social (or educational) pressure, and associated with "overt prestige" (see Labov 2006). While nonstandard dialects are usually considered low prestige, certain dialects stigmatized by the education system—such as Youngstowners' Appalachian twang—still enjoy a covert prestige among working class men for the very reason that they are considered incorrect (Leith 1997: 96).

With such audible and structured divisions between the managerial and labor classes, the nature of steelworking required close coordination among steelworkers, further facilitating ethnocultural bonding. The workplace functioned as a crucible of social bonds where camaraderie and mutual understanding were forged (Bruno 1999: 54, 137). Accumulated grievances led to the evolution of a once-powerful union movement and collective bargaining arrangements. Steelworkers also took note of and ostracized fellow workers who appeared to be "company men" (Bruno 1999: 69). They recognized differences in living conditions, work schedules, earnings, and attitudes between themselves and those they perceived to be of the privileged class (Bruno 1999: 17, 89). However, they also noted such differences within their own ranks.

Balkanization

Youngstown's working class balkanization was largely driven by steel mills' tendency to assign jobs on the basis of race and ethnicity rather than merit (see Allgren 2009: 36; Linkon and Russo 2002: 31–32; Nelson 2001: 155–164). Whereas white workers largely dominated the skilled jobs in steel-shaping units, African Americans were relegated to jobs in the coke plants and blast furnaces. The Irish were typically found in transportation, Italians in masonry, Slovaks and Hungarians before the open hearth, and native-born Americans and English in supervision (Bruno 1999: 73; Linkon and Russo 2002: 32). Vinny Cosenza worked in a plant for 20 years. "In the mills," he said, "the Irish were the first ones to run the open hearth. When the Dagos came in, the Irish wouldn't show them how to do it. When the blacks came in, the Dagos wouldn't show the blacks. But today, the black man is just as much the little man as the white man." Despite Vinny's realization, interracial working class unity remains rare.

Youngstown Sheet and Tube's worker housing initiative was designed to help the company gain control over its workers (Linkon and Russo 2002: 33–34). The spatial segregation of workers encouraged the perception that they were residents of particular neighborhoods, rather than citizens of the larger Youngstown area (Bruno 1999: 29). Housing was divided into four different sections: Loveland for skilled workmen, foremen, and superintendents; Overlook for American-born employees; Highview for promising foreign-born workers; and Blackburn for African-American and recent immigrant workers (Linkon and Russo 2002: 36). These segregating practices continued well into the 1960s, when banks' lending policies excluded black workers from moving to the suburbs and Youngstown's largely white Westside (ibid.).

Despite the Obama Administration's successful attempt to unify ethnocultural minorities with working class whites in the Upper Midwest, this coalition proved ephemeral. "[Whites and blacks] don't treat each other as if their problems are different; they treat each other as if they are different," Marty Nash explained. "'At least I'm not a dago, a hungey, and at least we're better than the niggers and always will be.' To a large extent, it goes back to the Reagan days' stories about the welfare queen. It takes attention away from who the real enemies are and the Democrats can't bridge the gap in reality. And it doesn't help when the trades and labor have been racist for so long. They've denied opportunities to blacks too. People are more concentrated on maintaining their piece of a constantly shrinking pie, rather than working to try and make the pie bigger."

Bryant Daniels added, "It is such a racially divided place. They know enough that it's not okay to call someone a 'nigger' or be openly racist. [. . .] They know to be outraged if their child says something prejudiced at school. But they could have put that anger into changing something politically instead of directing it towards other members of their subclass. It has caused a disassociation from politics for white working class people, because the Democrats and Republicans are both afraid to turn them out. [. . .] Fundamentally, blacks and whites are in the same predicament, but they have absolutely no sense of that."

However, it is precisely that shared predicament which appears to yield racial sensitivities among the white working class. They believe that there is an honorable response to poverty—their own—and judge African Americans for their perceived tendency to stray from that constructed and frequently betrayed ideal. Many white respondents are quick to recognize exceptions to their generalizations, but their views go largely unchanged.

"Now there are some damn decent black people, and I'd welcome them into my house," said Ralph Mickelson. "But there's black trash, just like there's white trash. A nigger is just a person who doesn't hold themselves accountable. And I know as many white niggers as I know black niggers. There's a lot of white people I just as soon wouldn't be around."

"There are black people and there are niggers," said Paul Podolsky, a 29-year-old chef form the Southside. "Blacks are educated. They respect each other. They don't think they're better than anyone. Niggers think everything should be given to them. They do whatever they want, without regard for others."

Remarkably, similar views were suggested by a Southside priest, Father Kelly. "There is a gangster culture of drugs and out-of-wedlock kids here in the African American community," he said. "It's not a racial thing; it's a cultural thing. So white people left the city."

"How many black congregants do you have in the church?" I asked.

"Two."

"So most of the African Americans here are Protestant?" I asked.

"If they go to church," he quipped.

Since the 1970s, Youngstown landlords have been forbidden to use phrases like "good neighborhood" or "good schools" in rental advertisements. Touting such attributes was understood to be coded means of saying that the neighborhood was predominantly white. One landlord on the Westside told me that she had been instructed by neighbors to rent her property exclusively to white tenants. "I had neighbors approach us and tell us that they would burn down our property if we rented to blacks," said Evelyn Burke, a 64-year-old landowner. "They'd say, 'I'm not saying that I'll burn it down, but someone may.'"

Katherine Kemp, the city planner, says that white and black Youngstowners have long memories that preclude greater unity. "In the 1920s and 30s, the first housing development in the nation was established in Youngstown to attract blacks from the South in order to work in mills and bust the unions. What did those people know about the situation they were entering? Nothing. They just wanted a job and out of Jim Crow. But they were hated by the Italian and Irish steelworkers, who never forgot. In the seventies, when the blacks were getting radicalized, the whites got scared and Youngstown was like something out of 'Dirty Harry.' Belligerent minorities, block busting, real estate people trying to get white people out of the city by telling them that black people are buying their neighbors' houses. The educated African American population from the 1970s was part of that, and their kids became the professional class in Youngstown. So you have the residual carryover of resentments."

"But isn't that ancient history?" I asked.

"The problem is that City Hall is generating more resentment by exploiting racial politics. They use big-time code. Black politicians will say 'It's our turn,' or it's just tone. [. . .] If you're black from the Southside, you're going to be elected by blacks from the Southside. You need a handy enemy and handy friends. Race is convenient for that. [. . .] People think that they need to speak with someone inside their group to eliminate the possibility that rejection of their request is due to racism. [. . .] It's part of a legacy of mistrust that goes back 100 years, abused by steel mils and now politicians."

At a meeting of the Westside Citizens Coalition, a white resident complained to a local police officer that, "There is an attitude in this town that you can sell people dope anytime, anywhere, anyway you want. Throwing bags from car-to-car. In broad daylight. It is an epidemic," he says.

When a black attendee noted that, "it's happening in more than just the Westside," the white resident said, "Yeah, but we don't want our side of town to become like the others."

In the Family

Racial tensions have merely replaced the equally strong ethnic affinities that characterized Youngstown over the last century. At its economic peak, immigrants from Ireland, Italy, Germany, Greece, Hungary, Poland, Czechoslovakia, Belarus, Ukraine, Serbia, Slovenia, Croatia, Russia, and Lebanon all migrated to work in Youngstown's booming factories. After two generations of intermarriage and integration, connections to countries of origin have dissipated, though nearly all respondents still express acute awareness of their ethnic heritages, even when mixed. Rhetoric aside, the most prominent contemporary expressions of this ethnic diversity are from community churches, which frequently align with one group or another, like St. Stephen's for Hungarians, St. Anthony's for Italians, St. Maron's for the Lebanese, and the Holy Trinity Serbian Orthodox Church. The church communities frequently dedicate summer weekends to cultural celebrations like the Simply Slavic Festival, the Greek Summerfest, and the Youngstown Italian Fest.

Although few respondents strongly identified with original immigrant cliques, Youngstown's propensity for clan-based relations has endured. There is a pervasive distrust of outsiders—and not necessarily people from distant countries, but people from nearby counties. "There are times when I don't feel welcome," said Philip Massey, the salesman. "Even though I'm not from Planet Neptune, I did grow up 35 miles away. So I didn't go to one of the local high schools, and people here put a lot of stock into that. But I've been here since 1979, and 30 of the last 34 years. But I can't shake that feeling that people are going to look at me a little differently because I wasn't part of the East High School class of 1972."

With the loss of integral forums for dialogue provided by factory locker rooms, union halls, and so many restaurants and clubs that went out of business, centers of belonging have become fewer and more heterogenous (see DiTomaso 2012). One bastion is the Army–Navy Garrison on the Northside. Offering veteran and "social" memberships to the community, the facility features a horseshoe bar, a dining area with a pool table, and a full-size bocce court in the back. Referring to his fellow members, 38-year-old construction worker Tank Schumaker said, "People around here will do anything for you. They're true Youngstowners, all these guys around here. If they don't have it, they'll try to get it for you—if they're one of the good guys. It's very tight-knit circles. It's just the way it works. If you're short on your bills, can you spot me a fifty? If you need help with your yard—Manny took me to Vegas twice for all the work I've done for the place. That's Youngstown."

He leaned in toward me, closely.

"But, don't ever fuck 'em. You fuck 'em, and you're out."

There was clearly a time when most Youngstown residents had such an association, which overlapped with others into a greater network of social capital. And from interviews, it is also clear that many wish they still did. However, with the closure of such hubs of communal activity, a sense of isolation has settled into Youngstown's white working class. There is a sense that they must defend whatever relationships, monuments, and cultural resources they have left.

Paradoxically, Youngstowners treasure extraordinarily dense social networks and yet report extraordinarily low trust. "White working class people don't know who to be frustrated with," said Gil McMahon, a Westside retiree. "The city, the state, the feds. It's just awfully hard to find a job. Nobody cares about the white working class. We just try to hang on and do what you can for yourself. It's just that, before the mills [shut], we were working and the guys there would walk home together and felt cohesive as a group. The only remnant left of that is the bars, and most of them have closed down. That's where the neighborhoods came together. They'd start with a stiff one at 7:00 am and tell everyone what they were going to do that day."

Mo Kerrigan, an unemployed 65-year-old, said, "There's the NAACP, the Muslim Brotherhood—the white guy? All he has is his little church. White people don't have the strength or support to accomplish anything. All the wealthy [white] people haven't done me any favors; I would have had to do something for them first. And all the black folks look at me and literally say, 'What do you want, honkey?' I was born here, and they say, 'Get out. This is our hood.' I'm the cannon fodder."

Youngstowners are so cautious about who they let through their gates, that it is little wonder that they feel so isolated. Even Tank feels a sense of estrangement beyond the doors of his club.

"Nobody looks out for us," he said. "We look out for each other."

Once someone is in the family, the family never really lets go.

Political Insecurity

Youngstown's government is just another family, albeit one that many people have tried to join since the fall of the steel mills. Its character can be traced back to an earlier era, when the moguls of industry tolerated the political maneuverings of organized crime as an alternative to the growing labor movement (Schneider and Schneider 2005: 34). The groundwork supporting corrupt political dealings in this era would later immunize government officials following the decline in regional industry (ibid.). The modern-day patriarch of the system was Don Hanni, Jr., chairman of the Mahoning County Democratic Party from 1977 to 1994. Known for his populist rhetoric, "Bullmoose," as he was nicknamed, was the county's "entrenched political boss" (Welsh 2009: 82).

"Hanni created Youngstown's version of the Chicago Machine, and we are still living in it," said Katherine Kemp, the city planner. "He created the coalition-building by giving people jobs, following the old steel mill model, and just imported it into the political system. This perpetuated the mistrust between the different groups. He kept them separate, and talked about the Irish to the blacks, the Greeks with the Jews, et cetera. If I got a job, it was because I was 'the WASP they needed,' and he would tell you so. The black community still repeats what he used to tell them: 'Now is our time. If we don't get the goodies now, we never will.' It was always about getting the goodies."

"Hanni was the master of bartering," said Bryant Daniels, the former public official. "He was a network of bankshot favors. If you were in that network, someone would automatically do it. You never had to fix a case or tell anyone what to do. If a certain lawyer appeared before a judge, he knew how to rule. The local civil engineering firm got every contract available. Other firms would try to come in here, receive a great deal of courtesy, but no contracts. County offices were placed in Cafaro family real estate. It was an incredible network of favors. There was so much investment in the status quo, there was no coin in getting something done. All that could do is introduce risk into your well of favordom."

He continued, "What people call the mob today is a more innocuous favor-sharing network. There was always a looming threat of violence, but that was unlikely because the heart and soul was commerce. It was an economic device. And it was actually fairly democratic. There were low barriers to entry. You do your part and you get your part. So there's no incentive to do things differently. We're not exactly spawning entrepreneurs here."

Hanni's tactics were not innovative. They merely reflected the way Youngstowners otherwise managed their own lives: through close, personal relationships. The failure of local government and civil society to take ownership of closed mills or preserve them as historical sites reinforced the community's distrust of institutions and encouraged individuals to seek out "extra help from friends with [the] right connections" (Linkon and Russo 2002: 237). On the city's largely white Westside, Vinny Cosenza has owned a small business for decades.

"People refer to me as 'the Godfather,'" he said nonchalantly over a cup of coffee. "I'm the oldest guy north of Meridian Road. So people ask me if I can do something, and after 31 years, I can get a lot of things done. I'm not going to owe nobody for nothing. I just ask for favors. It's bartering."

"So what are the kinds of favors you barter?" I asked.

"You might call it politics, but if you get into trouble, you'd get out of it here if you knew somebody. If you know somebody, you'll get what you want. A speeding ticket, a DUI charge. I knew people; I still know people. If you want something done, your street paved, I can get it paved."

"Does anyone ever say 'no'?"

"I never get turned down," he replied. "It don't matter what you want. People do things for me, because they may need something later. Quarters, a case of beer, they come see Vinny. That's how this valley works. Everyone knows everyone."

He stands up and changes the coffee filter, before greeting a customer and returning.

"What do you study?" he asked.

"Politics," I said.

"Jim Traficant did a lot for this Valley. It's just bartering. He went to jail for it, but he cared a lot about the working man—the little man, the small businessman, that's what built this valley."

As Mahoning County Sheriff, Traficant accepted a $163,000 payoff from Mahoning County's Cleveland mob faction and a $60,000 payoff from their Pittsburgh rival in 1982. Even after a federal tax court found him guilty of income tax invasion for the bribes and for owing another $180,000 in back taxes and penalties, Traficant was elected to the US Congress in 1984. The subject of a 20-year investigation by the FBI, he evaded corruption charges in 1999 when the federal government convicted several of his aides, the county sheriff, the county prosecutor, and the county engineer on corruption charges. However, Traficant was later convicted on ten counts involving racketeering and corruption in 2002.

In many white working class circles, he is a championed martyr who had the audacity to stand up for the working man. He gained notoriety for his garish 1970s suits and bell-bottoms, his unruly gray pompadour, and his arm-waving, occasionally profane, conspiratorial tirades on the House floor that typically ended with, 'Beam me up, Mr. Speaker.'" Just before his 2002 conviction and after years of bucking the Democratic Party and perplexing Republicans in Washington, he became only the second member of Congress to be expelled by the chamber since the American Civil War. His photos are nonetheless plastered on the walls of Youngstown pubs, and some residents still display his bumper stickers. The Royal Oaks pub has a framed illustration of Traficant being crucified with a crown of thorns. Getting one's hands dirty—in the Machiavellian sense—for the public good is considered a rather high calling. And having been in situations when they needed assistance themselves, many of his former constituents frame political favoritism as a "public service" (Linkon and Russo 2002: 222).

With the increasing scrutiny, however, Youngstown's expansive bartering matrix shrank along with the Mahoning Valley's available resources. Since Traficant's departure, the network is humbler and smaller, but according to respondents, it is an institution that still works the same way.

The Inner Circle

Youngstown is effectively a single-party city in a single-party region. Given the size of its white working class population, Mahoning County has been one of the most surprisingly reliable districts for the Democratic Party in the United States over the past century. With a few exceptions, Democratic Party nominees have won nearly every significant election in the region for decades. In 109 city, county, and statewide elections between 2000 and 2012, Democrats won all but five contests. One such exception was when former Mayor Jay Williams won as an independent in 2005, only to accept the Democratic Party's nomination in 2009 (Mahoning County Board of Elections 2013). "Twenty-five percent of the people here look at the system and they think it's working for them," said Gil McMahon, who runs his local neighborhood association. "The rest don't give a shit if it's working as long as it's a Democrat in office. You could run Mickey Mouse on the ballot and if he's got a 'D' next to his name, you bet your ass he'll get elected."

Given the predictability of election outcomes, the Mahoning County Democratic Party has been able to tightly control access to the ballot, without fear of public repudiation for poor choices.

"The County Democrats just want people to fall in line," said Val Coronado, a former Democratic public official. "The candidates fall in line. The precinct officers fall in line. And that all continues because everyone here just punches a hole next to the 'D' on the ballot. [. . .] People in this town are easy to control. The committees are older, so they've been involved for so long that they're just rubberstamps. The names in the race stay the same, so boom, boom, boom, it's automatic. Positions shift from husband to wife, and when people take power, it's all favoritism in hiring practices. [. . .] The Mahoning Country Democratic Party chairman controls people like puppets on strings. Politics here, people in this area vote with name recognition even when the representatives haven't done nothing for us since the mills shut down in the 1970s. They just keep flipping jobs."

Like the constituents they represent, Democratic officials are disinclined to open their family up to unproven outsiders or people they deem to be untrustworthy. I asked Karen Amalfitano, the county official, if there would be space for a grassroots candidate who earned citizens' trust but had not put in time with the Party.

"I don't believe in that bullshit," she said. "If you want to run for political office, you go to the Democratic Party and ask for their support. I worked those precinct committeemen. They should too. I told the chairman, I'm not just gonna beat my opponent, I'm gonna murder him. You do whatever it takes to bring the Party people to you. The new people trying to go around the party are missing the boat. They feel like they're independent Democrats. Well you can't be an independent away from the Party. You gotta do it from inside. Strength is structured by an environment where people believe the same thing. That's the loyalty. That's your people. And you're not going to win another office if you turn your back on those people. I will help my committeemen until the day I die. [Another politician] backed me in my run, I know his family, I knew him when he was in school. His family can eat at my table any day. He was loyal to me. I says to him, 'Whatever you intend to do, I will help you.' [. . .] In the game of politics, everything is loyalty, respect, and integrity. And if you can't have that, than maybe you should look for another career. The game's the same. The suits just change."

I asked Rick Hanley, a Party official, the same question: "Could a grassroots candidate gain his nomination?"

"He's got no chance," he said. "But that's not Mahoning County. You can't be a fart in the wind and expect to be successful anywhere. Buy a fuckin' helmet. Get skin in the game. If you don't want to get in the game, then fuck off. You can't win a boxing match without taking a hit. Try it out and see how it goes."

"But when outsider candidates are excluded like that," I later asked, "are insiders liable to be corrupt because they can bank on Party support?"

"[People who take bribes] are shitting on the very people they're there to represent. It so wrong on so many levels, I don't know what to say. And it should not occur. There are people who go to work everyday and they don't have the time or attention to know about this stuff. These [representatives] should be taken out and shot. It's a cancer. It leads to a public distrust of the very institutions there to serve you."

"Do you think the Mayor is clean?" I asked.

"Do I think [Charles] Sammarone is clean?"

He looked away momentarily.

"Do you want the honest answer, or the really honest answer?" he asked.

"Really honest."

"Yes," he deadpanned.

"Okay," I said. "Give me the honest answer."

"No." He grinned sheepishly.

"But the Party is endorsing him in for Council President?"

"In a perfect world, I don't support him," Hanley said, straightening his posture. "But I don't have that choice."

"He has an opponent," I offered.

"He's not a member of the Party."

Elected officials guard their inner circle carefully because they depend on each other to get their way.

"I think I know every elected official at the county level and almost every one at the city and township level," said John McNally, a County Commissioner who was running for mayor at the time. "I have to. I want to know who I'm calling when I make decisions. Some people think that's bad, but that's how things get done here. You can't always have a great debate on the Senate floor."

Youngstown's City Council representatives reportedly adhere to a norm under which, in matters exclusively concerning a particular ward, the Council votes for whatever that ward's councilperson desires. This holds true even when the city's various impartial recommending bodies advise the Council otherwise.

Pat O'Neal sits on one of those recommending bodies. "If the committee defies the councilman's interests, they expect the councilman to rally the rest of the council to veto the proposal with a supermajority," he said. "They're supposed to be independent thinkers, but they want to preserve their ability to whip others into line when a vote is pertinent to their ward. Looking out for their particular ward hinders any plan that is in the best interests of the city."

He went on, "If we keep doing things the way we have been doing them—without any sense of benefit beyond political benefits—there won't be much left to argue over. Everyone wants a piece of the pie, but the pie is getting rotten. [. . .] The money is no longer in private hands. The government is the biggest fish left in the pond."

"We have had a pay-to-play mentality and some people just walk away. [. . .] It's even more toxic today because the city isn't as healthy economically, and as a result it's not as healthy politically. It gets at the leadership vacuum taking place. It used to be honorable to serve the city as a councilperson, now they're drawing a healthy salary and benefits. It's a livelihood, not a service."

When it is nearly impossible to lose re-election, there is little concern for transparency and ethics.

Corruption

Today, the name "Cafaro" still opens doors in Youngstown. The Cafaro Company is one of the largest commercial real estate developers in the United States. Founded by former steelworker William M. Cafaro with his brother on Youngstown's Eastside in the 1940s, the company pioneered strip mall and commercial center development, amassing a fortune worth $800 million at the time of its founder's death in 1998. His son, Anthony "Tony" Cafaro, Sr., has since continued to oversee the company's holdings and projects.

In the midst of the steel industry's pull out beginning in the 1970s, the Cafaro family's influence on regional development expanded with the help of back-door meetings and questionable lobbying practices. In particular, the "Cafaro Roundtable" was established "as a weekly opportunity for friends and business associates to socialize" (Schneider and Schneider 2005: 43–44). Tony Cafaro later expanded the Roundtable to include prominent judges, mayors, legislators, and county commissioners resulting in what some have claimed functions as a "shadow government" for all intents and purposes (ibid.). After the federal corruption probes and increased newspaper coverage of these meetings (even after they were moved to a new restaurant venue), the Cafaros conducted their business more privately.

"The Democratic Party was Bill Cafaro's hobby," said Jim LoDuca, a public official. "Christ almighty, Bill had Kennedy at his house when he was running in 1960. He was reputed to be influential in the appointment of federal judges. They invited county prosecutors and judges on private plane trips to see a swearing-in ceremony, baseball games, hockey games. The old neighborhood stuck together."

The Cafaros are equally well known among working class people. Mo Kerrigan said, "My uncle ran [a restaurant] on the Westside. [. . .] He got into some trouble from the city, because they created some zoning laws that would revoke his license. So he went to a guy who was connected to the Cafaro family to ask for help. Sure enough, the problem got fixed. But every Saturday, when most places' backroom banquet facilities were hosting weddings, his backroom was reserved with a table full of food and drinks for meetings. But he needed a favor."

Gil McMahon said, "When I first got laid off from [Wean] United, I worked for the county's disaster services office. My director's brother-in-law was a Cafaro. At the time, the City Commissioner was going to cut two of our staff members as part of a budget deal, so the director jumped into his car to go to the hill [Cafaro headquarters in Brier Hill]. Within 20 minutes, we got a call from the City Commissioner's office saying that our jobs were safe. That boss, he'd disappear in the afternoons all the time, and leave a phone number where we could reach him in case of an emergency. One time, we got curious and we called the number. It was [Mafioso] Joey Naples' music store."

More recently, John J. Cafaro, the brother of Anthony Cafaro, Sr. and former Vice President of Cafaro Corporation, was implicated in the Traficant corruption scandal (Schneider and Schneider 2005: 43–44). In 2010, he was also charged by federal prosecutors for concealing a $10,000 loan contribution to his daughter Capri Cafaro's unsuccessful 2004 campaign for Congress (Krouse 2010). She currently serves as an Ohio state senator representing Trumbull County.

"The Cafaros hate when people tell them 'no,' and once you do, they hate you forever," said Marty Nash. "They hate me to this day. On the political end, they ran things around here for so long, they just can't believe when anyone says no to them."

Perhaps most prominently, Anthony Cafaro, Sr. was charged by Mahoning County with organizing a conspiracy to prevent the county's relocation of its Department of Job and Family Services office from the Cafaro-owned Garland Plaza to the county-owned Oakhill Renaissance Place in 2006 (Milliken and Skolnick 2012). The County had been renting the Cafaro property for $400,000 per year for 19 years, when they chose to purchase the Oakhill property in bankruptcy court and move the office there. The County was also paying for maintenance costs associated with the plaza, and in its final year of tenancy, the total taxpayer bill was approximately $1,150,000 (Milliken and Skolnick 2012).

In an attempt to keep the property out of the county's hands, Cafaro allegedly guaranteed a $100,000 line of credit to Andrew W. Suhar, the Oakhill bankruptcy trustee. He also allegedly went to the residence of Boardman businessman Sam Moffie in an unsuccessful exhortation to file a civil lawsuit to block the county's purchase of Oakhill. Moffie would later reveal to Cafaro that he was wearing a wire for the FBI. Recognizing that Cafaro was a "very powerful guy," he believed that it would do him more good to have Cafaro as a "friend [rather] than an enemy." He said that while the FBI could not do "pigeon squat" for him, the Cafaros could "destroy" him (ibid.).

The state alleged that County Commissioner John McNally, IV, County Auditor Michael Sciortino, and Treasurer John B. Reardon were accepting bribes by receiving the Cafaro Company attorneys' assistance, which was reflected in legal bills totaling $876,139. They were also charged with counts of perjury for denying discussions with Cafaro and his attorneys. Lisa Antonini, the former county treasurer and Democratic Party chairwoman, was also implicated on money-laundering charges (Vindicator 2012).

On July 11, 2011, the Oakhill criminal case was dismissed by the Lorain County Prosecutor's Office and Ohio Ethics Commission special prosecutors on the grounds that they were unable to retrieve tapes from the FBI for the required period of evidence discovery (Milliken and Skolnick 2012). In an interview with US Attorney Steven Dettelbach about his office's scrutiny of corruption in Youngstown, he did not recognize the name of John McNally.

"Who's that? I don't think I know him," Dettelbach said.

"He won the mayoral primary and is likely to be the next mayor of Youngstown," I explained.

He pondered.

"He was also the subject of an indictment by the county on corruption charges," I added.

"If there is a pending case, I personally don't want to comment on it."

"Are you not familiar with the Oakhill case?" I asked.

"No."

I turned to his communications officer, Mike Tobin, who oversaw the interview.

"Mike, you guys haven't heard of the Oakhill case in Youngstown? It's just been in headlines for awhile."

Mike smirks, "Well I—"

"I'm the one being interviewed here," Dettelbach interjected. "You can direct the questions to me."

"I'm just surprised the US Attorney overseeing a region consumed by corruption cases doesn't know about this case," I explained.

"Oh that's the one that might have involved the Cafaro family," Dettelbach suddenly recalled.

"Yes, Cafaro is one of the defendants," I said.

"So I've been recused from any involvement in any cases dealing with the Cafaros. My law firm represented a member of the Cafaro family, so the Deputy Attorney General recused me."

In 2014, the federal government handed the matter to the Ohio Attorney General and Cuyahoga County Prosecutor, who indicted McNally who was then Mayor of Youngstown. In a March 2016 plea bargain, Mayor McNally would later plead guilty to four misdemeanor counts—two counts of falsification, one count of unlawful use of a telecommunications device, and one count of unlawful influence of a public official. It is thought the state is building a broader case against the Cafaro family. "I don't think there's a black mark on the city," he said after the sentencing, which included a short probation period. "I don't think there's a black mark at all."

Before this took place and before he won the 2013 mayoral election, McNally and I met at the Golden Dawn bar and restaurant, an institution on the city's Northside since 1934. Notorious for hosting backroom meetings in the mid-twentieth century, the Dawn has remained a favorite hangout for white Youngstowners and a strong supporter of McNally's campaign. A large green endorsement sign was draped across its roof.

Around the polished bar tended by 93-year-old co-owner Ralph Naples, the interior walls dripped in memorabilia from nearby Ursuline High School, Youngstown State University, and Ohio State University. Upon entering, McNally was greeted by burly regulars yelling "Ey, Johnny!" and "Holy Mackerel. Looky here!"

"How's your son?" McNally asked one gentlemen in a booth.

"He's got a good attitude," he replied, "but he's still only about 140 pounds."

Before our discussion progressed beyond the courteous, McNally was greeted by six more people, including his own father and the sitting mayor, Charles Sammarone. Nicknames for him ranged from "Jack" to "Johnny Mac."

"You're clearly a popular guy," I said.

"It's like family here."

"Some people," I said, "they say that the Oakhill case is personal relationships gone too far."

"I don't think it's personal relationships gone too far," he said. "I think my colleagues made an awful decision [to relocate the county office] without political relationships. The fact is [Oakhill] should have been torn down, an empty building on Market Street. I think the move was a bad decision. I think it's inevitable that people see it as personal relationships gone too far. I think I was banged on because I said the Cafaros are my friends, because I went to school with their kids [at Ursuline High School]."

"Is it a conflict of interest then?" I asked.

"In the Mahoning Valley, I'd have to disqualify from every event if that was necessary when I had a friend that was involved. Where's the threshold? When I've been called for assistance ten times? At what point are they a friend and I need to pass people on to someone else?"

"If you were the judge presiding over the Oakhill case, given your personal relationships, would you recuse yourself?"

McNally is a practicing attorney. He sighed and looked toward the bar.

"I think in that case, you have to recuse yourself because of all the players," he said. "In the judicial scenario, you're damned if you do and damned if you don't. That would be difficult."

"But why is being a judge making verdicts any different than the verdict of a legislator?" I asked. "Doesn't each role require objectivity?"

"Yeah, you can say that. But the judge is not determining the best interests of the community. The elected official does."

"Public Service"

Years of shoulder shrugging have softened the political grounds for tactics and behavior that exist in the shadows of government. Smaller acts of "public service" rarely receive public scrutiny because they are less egregious than the rackets and six-figure bribes of yesteryear, but their near ubiquity in corners of Youngstown's city and county government suggests a wide tolerance or indifference.

"Corruption is—I don't want to say accepted—but people are complacent about it," said Maddux. "When indictments are handed down, people are not okay with it. But there is a cultural acceptance in a broad way. [. . .] Today, it's more nuanced."

Kickbacks make Youngstown run. Modest payments of $2,000 or $3,000 at a time are generally understood to be required to receive certain officials' support and grease the wheels of government facilitation. It is particularly common when business owners are soliciting city funding to improve their façades or relocate.

"A few thousand bucks, that's part of the game," said Katherine Kemp, the city planner. "The Youngstown Initiative is a perfect vehicle for it because you can shave off a few grand in the cash you hand out."

"Why do politicians sell off their integrity so cheap?" I asked.

"Half of those guys have debts up the yin yang. Holding public office, you're expected to buy dinner or a round of drinks wherever you go. Being a politician is a net loss around here. A lot of those guys have had real estate deals go sour. You look into their tax delinquencies, and you see that they have messy financial problems. So they're desperate and that results in dinky $3,000 deals. A lot of them get into the business because they think they can make money off of it. [. . .] Building inspection is a payola business. Landowners pay to not get their businesses inspected. They pay code enforcement officers, and the politicians get a piece of that."

According to multiple respondents, Mayor Charles Sammarone was prolific in these deals and regularly provided special treatment.

"I was gently encouraged to treat certain people differently," said Natasha Jackson, a building official who says she was ordered to approve unsafe structures and rescind stop-work orders. "There is blatant, just blatant nepotism. [. . .] I'm afraid of retribution [for my dissent]. I don't know what kind, but we joked about attaching a mirror to a stick to look underneath my car before starting it. I literally had anxiety attacks before going to work."

"The mayor [Sammarone] once pinned my colleague up against the wall, stuck his finger in his face and yelled, 'I own you, motherfucker. I own you.' [...] We gave [my supervisor] a bottle of anal lubricant because we all knew he took it up the ass so much from the mayor. We'd have meetings where he'd hang his head and preface the mayor's instructions by saying 'I can't believe I have to tell you guys this, but ... ' [...] We had to cancel our department's Friday lunches for fear that the mayor would barge in and accuse us of conspiring or not working."

George Ellis, a member of the Chamber of Commerce, says that Sammarone also interfered with the establishment of new businesses.

"When we have a big business come in here wanting to set up shop for millions of dollars and hundreds of jobs, I've got the mayor calling me to tell me which contractor I should use to put in utilities. [...] I have had to put in burglar alarms, security in my house. My wife makes sure that no one sneaks into my garage when I pull out in the morning. I have absolutely had powerful people threaten me."

Joe Hinski, a city administrator, had to delay five or six projects in order to avoid the mayor's micromanagement.

"The mayor's an old-school political guy. He wants to support people who support him politically. I assume that means campaign contributions. I'm just trying to caretake this, until we get a new mayor in. I don't know that this guy knows how to do projects, and yet he wants to be in control. We're just playing four corners, like in basketball when you slow down the game. Waiting for him to get out, we run marathons here. Not too many sprints."

Hinski also witnessed frequent mismanagement by First Ward councilwoman Annie Gillam.

"[Gillam] wants to get her husband hired on projects, and she's said some ignorant things," he said. "It's not at the point where I need to turn it over to the feds, but it's somewhat disturbing. [...] We just go to four corners with any project that you think she'll be involved in. In most cases—90%—she doesn't have the power to hold up a project. On the others, yeah, we have to put some relative on the payroll, hire the husband's [construction] company, or whatever."

Multiple respondents report that the city's finance director, David Bozanich, facilitates these deals from City Hall.

"Bozanich told me, 'Yeah, I let Annie [Gillam] steal; it promotes world peace,'" said Kemp. "He knows exactly what goes on and makes sure that everyone wins on every deal. Multiple winners and no losers. The tax base is increased, the work force benefits, the employer benefits, the development costs are brought to a minimum, and the politicians are happy because they're pockets get lined. But the real loser is you and me when we pay property taxes, gas taxes, license plate taxes. [...] It's the taxpayer, and we're hemorrhaging them. They're all leaving the city. It's a chain reaction. The lead corrupt politician surrounds himself with useless sacks of shit minions who are loyal. They're not visionaries; they do what they're told. And as the big kahuna stays in power, he accumulates them. And when it's time to repave the roads, there's no money left. Bozanich is just like a mobster. He has a running list of what everybody wants and who is owed what."

"So there are losers," I said. "It's not true."

"You don't understand. He doesn't know the difference between the truth and bullshit. It's semi-true and semi-false and you don't feel any sense of conscience about it. All these years of desperation, it changes you. Look, this is a capitalist system. There isn't a deal that doesn't make me want to take a shower and drink seven glasses of wine. And I'm not even religious. It's just messy. You just do what you can to get by."

"Twenty years ago, would I defend a guy like Bozanich? Probably not. But it makes the city work. Meanwhile, we keep inventing new lows. The world of financing innovates to make this stuff possible. Everyone else is doing it, and disenfranchised communities aren't seeing any money. Meanwhile we use all the tricks available to make the bottom line work. [. . .] There's not a lot of goodness to it. But it gets the job done."

Referring to the tolerance of small-scale corruption, Hinski said, "It is counterproductive in the long run. But if you're using it in the right way, everyone goes along with things and you have the ability to get stuff done. Concentration of power is good if it's being done for good. It's only bad when it's done for bad. Ideology is great if you can afford it. People want the trash picked up, the fireman there in time, and the wastewater purified. The government doesn't need itself involved in theoretical debates better placed in the Supreme Court. Wherever I can be a dictator, I try to be benevolent."

Alone Together

In light of City Hall's benevolent governance, each working class respondent was asked who looks out for his or her interests. Typical answers were "nobody," "you and me," and most commonly, "I look out for myself." Their answers did not suggest a sense of prideful independence, as much a sense of resignation and disappointment. As earlier sections have exhibited, collectivism is envisaged to be a matter of provision rather than cooperation. This is exacerbated by Youngstowners' proclivity for social distrust. Consequently, while many white working class citizens are estranged from conventional forms of organization and institutional assembly, others espouse vigilante forms of activism— renegades for what they believe to be the civic good.

Vigilantism can be constructive or destructive, individualist or collective, but it is always pursued as yet another public service. Constructively, a variety of neighborhood groups assemble to plant gardens in the vacant lots left by demolished homes in Youngstown. Others carry out spontaneous street cleanups.

"Most folks are jaded," said Freddy Kristeva, who belongs to a group of activists.

"So why do they come to your meetings then?" I asked.

"People don't come to our meetings to ask the government to solve things. People come [. . .] to solve things ourselves. The government won't stop river dumping, so we deal with it. We won't call City Hall or the mayor, because we know they won't do anything."

Grocer Billy Morris, age 44, voluntarily cuts lawns and plants trees around his Southside neighborhood. "Several of my neighbors have asked me to get more involved in their local meetings, but my personal motto is to not wait for somebody else to do things for you. Just do it yourself," he said. "Some people say that I should let the government [do it], but I know they're not coming. Every man and every business is out for themselves."

More destructively, Ralph Mickelson and his neighbor prefer to respond to a local gang with further violence. "We had a problem with black boys coming into the neighborhood, two dozen at a time, tearing up the gardens, beating on cars, getting in fights," he said. "My neighbor sat outside her house with a rake, I was cleaning my shotgun on my porch. They said they'll call the police, and I said 'Go ahead!' [. . .] Vigilante justice deters. If I'm sitting up here with a gun, they ain't coming. But that's a Band-Aid. But that's pretty much the only way to get things done. You've got to try to force change that one group doesn't like. The minorities are in control of the ship."

He continued, "I've gotten away from every organization. I left the Army–Navy garrison, coin clubs. It just feels like your beating your head against a brick wall. So you get complacent like everyone else. [. . .] We're on the outskirts all the way around. Shit trickles downhill. If there's anything to get, we've got to get it for ourselves."

Mickelson's sentiments were echoed by Gillian McPhee at the flea market. "A Spanish kid stole a watch from my stand, so I chased his ass outside to his car. [. . .] I said, 'Eat rocks!' and chucked a brick through his back window. You got to take care of things yourself. That's how we do things in Youngstown. [. . .] You can't call the city government or police to complain about drug dealers hanging out and selling outside of my house. You just have to do it yourself. If you want anything done, you need to confront them."

More commonly, citizens have resorted to arson when the government has not moved quickly enough to demolish a vacant or dilapidated building. After the city's population dropped in the 1980s and the real estate market bottomed out, Youngstown witnessed an average of 2.3 fires a day, resulting in an estimated loss somewhere between $1.75 and $9 million annually (Linkon and Russo 2002: 223; Maharidge 1985: 35–36). Fires were often set with accelerants and gasoline-filled garbage bags, which often exploded just after firefighters arrived on the scene, increasing the number of injuries (Linkon and Russo 2002: 223–224; Schneider and Schneider 2005: 44–45). Fires became so frequent that fire-fighters would practice "perching": they would sit in the streets and wait for the first signs of that evening's expected batch of house fires (ibid.).

Arson was yet another Youngstown "public service." While insurance fraud was the likely animus behind the rise in arson activity, private demolition companies also profited handsomely from the situation (Linkon and Russo 2002: 224–225). It costs about $3,000 to demolish an average home in Youngstown, $8,000 if as-bestos abatement is necessary. However, after a house is scorched, the remaining valuable material can be stripped, sold off, and the debris may be discarded (ibid.). Demolition contractors would charge full price for their services after a fire, and make a sizable profit given the reduced removal costs (ibid.). In a perverse way, the regular explosions also provided firemen with job security, such that they were often reluctant to report possible arson cases accurately. Fire department records taken during this period are ambiguous, as little distinction was ever made be-tween arson and accident.

In scope, white working class citizens' propensity to take matters into their own hands mimics the behavior of some elected officials and government ad-ministrators. They make claims in such a way that circumvents institutionalized, democratic processes. And when such circumvention is widely practiced and ac-cepted, a moral hazard emerges for each new claimant. Why follow rules that no one else seems to follow? However, white working class respondents frequently act alone—if at all—rather than in collusion with others. Excluded from the inner circle of governance per usual, they have now also lost their sense of col-lective power, and have witnessed the relative rise of a historically subordinate African American population.

Consequently, they do not yearn for a lost homogeneity, but rather for the social apparatus that historically structured the city's diversity. Long mar-ginal to the American economy and marginalized by their local government, Youngstown's white working class people are grappling to maintain a foothold in the society they once defined. Most were taught early that if they did not get too close, they would not get burned.

5

Institutions

STRUCTURES OF A CRUMBLING POLITY

And was Jerusalem builded here
Among these dark Satanic Mills?
—William Blake, *Jerusalem*

The case studies of Youngstown, Ohio and East London, England set out to better understand the nature of marginality in white working class milieux. Interview and ethnographic data exhibit two communities characterized by drastic economic transformation and demographic change, which has left many people consumed by their collective and individual falls from grace. Unable to cope with the trauma from the twin collapses of commercial and social life, the populations examined are also subject to governments disconnected from their preferences, and their own incapacity to do much about this. To this point, we have closely examined the social, political, and economic circumstances that contextualize important trends: the observed disconnection between citizens and their government, subjects' poignant nostalgia and sometimes aggressive nativism, the rise of anti-system political organizations like the BNP and EDL in London, and the extent of corruption in Youngstown. However, we have not developed a clear understanding of what produces these broader, collective trends, and what explains the individual-level political choices that support them.

In this chapter we return to this book's primary research question: why do similar people under similar pressures and circumstances engage the political system to variable extents and in divergent ways? A prominent explanation concerns the nature of local institutions that structure political activity in the two venues. Are there significant differences between them? How do institutions frame, regulate, or restrict political behavior? I begin this chapter by laying out the observable variations in respondents' political behavior. I then describe three key institutional factors that enable the problematic trends in democratic politics across the cases. The first pertains to the single-party landscape of both political constituencies; the second points to different institutional rules governing local government; and the third addresses the weak infrastructure of social capital left in the wake of Youngstown and East London's union histories.

Observable Variation: Political Behavior

Youngstown and East London exhibit a full typology of political behavior. Per Figure 5.1, I classify these according to whether individual actors are active or passive, and whether the orientation of their activity and passivity is through or in support of democratic channels of self-expression. In Quadrant I, those citizens engaging in conventional and unorthodox forms of political and civic engagement are represented. This list is not necessarily exhaustive, but it is derived from a compilation of common forms of engagement. While they may be actively engaged for normative, instrumentalist, or traditionalist reasons, they are nevertheless observably active (see Held 2006: 251).

Quadrant II contains those citizens who are actively attempting to undermine, disrupt, or destroy the political system. These individuals are actively anti-system. Quadrant III is composed of those citizens who report themselves to be temporarily inactive in the democratic political system. Some of these individuals feel no current motivation to participate. Others are too busy with other matters of priority. Still others might be fully satisfied, or might simply not know the means of participation. As discussed earlier, democratic governance—to some

PRO-SYSTEM		ANTI-SYSTEM	
I. Active:	Activity that engages the institutions and channels of the democratic system:	**II. Active:**	Activity that impairs, disrupts circumvents or overthrows the system:
	Observed in East London and Youngstown		Observed in East London; Only Elites in Youngstown
III. Passive:	State of inactivity within the system:	**IV. Passive:**	Committed inactivity and withdrawal from the system:
	Observed in East London and Youngstown		Observed in East London and Youngstown

Figure 5.1 VARIATION IN POLITICAL BEHAVIOR. The four quadrants model the observable behavior of individuals who are anti-system or engaged, passively or actively, in East London and Youngstown.

extent—depends on the assumption that all citizens are complacent and trust-ful enough to not participate in the deliberation of every political issue, and only participate in those about which they are most invested or passionate. Finally, Quadrant IV encompasses those citizens who report having permanently with-drawn from the sphere of civic life. These individuals are passively anti-system.[1] Importantly, this model understands (in)activity and systematic orientation as individual political-behavioral choices.

The activism of democratic engagers (Quadrant I) and rebels (Quadrant II) is easily distinguishable by the nature of their observable behavior and affilia-tions. However, the difference between the passivity of individuals sitting out (Quadrant III) and the passivity of the withdrawn (Quadrant IV) is not be-haviorally observable. Indeed, both are inactive. Instead, the difference is that the passive anti-system individuals *never* intend to become active democrats, while the passively engaged individuals still *may*, given a change in circum-stances or resources. While the former is effectively divesting from participa-tory opportunities, the latter remains alert in their abstention.[2] Still, all that is observable to the researcher is a signal. So I ensured that I interacted with re-spondents to understand the basis and nature of their choices, as anything else risks speculation. It is important here not to conflate actors' self-conception of their behavior with the objective appraisal and classification of the behavior. This is because actors' behavior may defy their self-understood purpose. As a result, the form of behavior and its effect on the robustness of the demo-cratic system is central. Does it degrade, diminish, atrophy, or circumvent the system? Or does it reinforce, reproduce, maintain, or support the system?[3]

This passive anti-system behavior is widespread in both Youngstown and East London, where there is a disconnection from the state and public sphere. In Youngstown, the perception of the state's weakness or favoritism marginalizes many citizens from making claims. DiTomaso (2012) has referred to them as the "apolitical majority." A sense of self-sufficiency is pervasive. "Don't depend on somebody else," warned Billy Morris, a 44-year-old grocery store employee. "I've seen family members and friends complain to the city, but nothing gets done. You can't even get the councilwoman to return phone calls. Every man and every business is out for themselves. [. . .] You try not to depend on anybody. [. . .] The only time I sit still is if I'm eating, driving, or on the throne [toilet]." Few res-idents redirect their political capital toward forms of protest, even though such actions do not depend on the weak and corrupt government for claim-making. They still know that the government remains ultimately responsible.

In East London, citizens do not believe the state is weak, but rather see it as endowed with limitless capacities. Respondents regard the state as the locus of great, arbitrary power, wielded by an inscrutable, unpredictable bureaucracy that appraises citizens' wishes without any consultation. "Fuck the government," said Kyle Downey, an unemployed 21-year-old. "It's hopeless. People in power are going to stay in power. It's all rigged. They'll stay in power no matter what you say. So your vote is wasted. I've thought about getting involved. But before I figured out how I can make my point, things get already done."

Active anti-system behavior is less widespread, but nevertheless present. In East London, groups like the British National Party and the English Defence League are cultivating frustration with the government. In pursuit of their xenophobic and racist platforms, they employ intimidation, violence, and other coercive tactics to supplement their more peaceful protests and electoral endeavors. Some respondents also report participation in the 2011 London riots, during which many individuals looted and destroyed property, independent of any organized effort. "I don't vote because I don't see what they do," said Oscar Bradley, a 21-year-old forklift apprentice. "You need to blow something up. That's the only way England stopped. The last time was 7 July 2005. Either that or you commit a crime. It's about getting the attention of people at the top. The riots just proved that the underclass is more powerful than the upper class. We just don't work together. I think it was pure frustration and opportunism. Some kids were trying to take advantage of the situation, and showed how frustrated they are." In Barking and Dagenham, this sentiment was expressed by male and female respondents of different ages. Indeed, the BNP's electoral base proved to be quite broad when, despite not winning a single council seat, they attracted over 30,000 votes in the borough in 2010.

In Youngstown, active anti-system behavior is rare. Its most common manifestation is in the form of bribery among elites. Indeed, parts of Youngstown's civic sphere have and continue to run on a matrix of favors and kickbacks. However, among white working class respondents, not one exhibits active anti-system behavior. Some observers might contend that this is due to the absence of an anti-system organization like the British National Party or the English Defence League in Youngstown, which would otherwise capitalize on the sentiments of marginalized actors. However, counterpart organizations like so-called patriot groups, militias, and the sovereign citizen movement reportedly do exist in the counties surrounding Youngstown. None have garnered a foothold in the city or its suburbs, however. After three months in Youngstown, I sought out the members of such organizations in Mahoning County through police records, but the only two reported incidents both involved African American sovereign citizens, one of whom was serving a prison sentence at the time. Any explanation of white working class marginality and political behavior in East London and Youngstown will need to consider this variation.

Institutional Explanations

Despite some variation in individual actors' political behavior across Youngstown and East London, and despite key differences in the methods of governance in the United Kingdom and the United States, the observed nature of white working class people's marginality is remarkably similar. Both cities exist in a post-traumatic environment where the industrial dependencies of an earlier socioeconomic era endure in the absence of that era's primary industry. Both populations are characterized by a nostalgia that inhibits their economic adaptation and sustains rigid social boundaries. And both governments are severely disconnected from the local white working class communities. These parallel trends are enabled by three key institutional attributes: (1) single-party political landscapes; (2) the formal externality of the state; and (3) the weak infrastructure of social capital left by Youngstown and East London's union histories.

Single-Party Landscapes

Single-party systems leave Youngstown and Barking and Dagenham without competition for citizens' votes, and consequently without real accountability for political officials. The lack of competition also impedes the flow of ideas for improving civic life. Citizens' views are not solicited to craft fresh legislation, and as long as they are with the dominant party, prospective representatives are less inclined to put forward innovative platforms that alter a comfortable status quo. In the past, this political stability was a product of both regions' status as factory towns. So much of their livelihood depended on their respective manufacturing industries that politics simply adhered to the community's universal interest in preserving the primary means of commerce and favorable arrangements for local workers. The factories not only employed the majority of the working citizens; they also sustained supporting industries—everything from office supplies to construction work—and factory paychecks were the base of a service, leisure, and household sector. Political choice, like everything else in a factory town, was a matter of falling in line. Today, even though this unique economy has disappeared, its conformist politics has endured.

In East London, although the BNP won over 12 seats in the Barking and Dagenham Council chamber in 2006, they subsequently lost all of them in the 2010 general election, despite galvanizing even more votes (London Borough of Barking and Dagenham 2006; London Borough of Barking and Dagenham 2010c). With Labour representatives now in 47 of 51 council seats, the period between 2006 and 2010 saw the greatest number of non-Labour councilors in the Barking and Dagenham Council chamber since 1968, when the Conservative Party won 13 seats. Today, these former BNP voters are without any representation whatsoever. For most, the 2010 election demonstrated the futility of democratic mobilization. While some have opted for the emerging United Kingdom Independent Party (UKIP), others have joined the ranks of the English Defence

League so that they do not go voiceless. Without stiff competition, the Labour Party has not been pushed to consider white working class perspectives in light of a national platform that is supportive of less restrictive immigration and integration programs. With the ascendance of UKIP, a more competitive partisan landscape may accommodate white working class populism. At the national level, the Liberal Democrat and Conservative coalition has since sought to curb border access for Eastern Europeans and to set tougher conditions for immigrants to access government benefits.

In Youngstown, Mahoning County has been one of the most reliable districts for the Democratic Party in the United States over the past century. With a few exceptions, Democratic Party nominees have won nearly every significant election in the region for decades. In 109 city, county, and statewide elections between 2000 and 2012, Democrats won all but five contests (Mahoning County Board of Elections 2013). While some candidates have opted to run as Independents, few are successful, and many are ultimately absorbed by the Democratic Party anyway. A recent city councilor with Democratic leanings was known to affiliate with the Republican Party only to avoid a competitive primary. With the city's demographic change, the Democratic Party has been challenged to diversify its candidates to accommodate a growing African American population. Even though the Party has not endorsed a single black candidate for a county-level position, few African Americans even ponder affiliation with the Republican Party or partisan separation. So the Party's inaction goes unpunished.

One implication is that corruption and dysfunction continue with impunity in Youngstown. The local newspaper mused how the 2013 mayoral election featured a series of competitors offering the public little choice:

> John A. McNally IV, one of the leading candidates, has a criminal indictment on his political record; DeMaine Kitchen, the other frontrunner, is accused of sexual harassment and is a tax scofflaw. Then there's John Crea, who sits in the Mahoning County Jail charged with three counts of aggravated menacing, to which he has pleaded not guilty by reason of insanity. Crea already has been convicted of aggravated menacing and disorderly conduct. Claudette Moore, the only woman in the Nov. 5 general election contest for mayor, claims that God told her to run and that he is guiding her campaign. Moore has also publicly admitted that between 1989 and 1991 she was a cocaine dealer in Youngstown. And for good measure, she says her father was a hit man for the Mafia. (The *Vindicator* 2013)

The Democratic Party endorsed McNally, who eventually won the election with a looming federal indictment on corruption charges. When he pleaded guilty to a series of misdemeanors and was placed on probation while in office, he defiantly vowed to remain mayor and run for another term. "The dependence on the unions and a single party has destroyed the area," said Caleb, the parking attendant and Democratic Party defector introduced in the last chapter. "If you can't lose, then what do you care about following rules? If there's no accountability or competition, then you lack the incentives to do the right thing."

Single-party landscapes allow the party in power to be less consultative. Labour representatives have adhered to the national party's turn away from the leftist, labor-oriented politics that characterized party ideology until the 1990s. In turn, they have focused progressive platforms on a more expansive understanding of Britain's working class that incorporates minority groups and immigrants, even as many Barking and Dagenham residents choose not to. Without a competitive opposition, Labour has not lost seats despite their patronizing dismissal of white working class views. Youngstown's Democratic Party has not been forced to navigate difficult political actions, because they take very little action at all. For decades, politics has been a means for many politicians to enrich themselves at the expense of their constituencies. While rhetorically supportive of their voters' ideals, elected officials from the county's Democratic Party are at worst, corrupt, and at best, stagnant.

Katznelson (1981: 18) attributes the lack of a strong working class party in the United States to the segregation of workplace politics from community politics. This, he argues leads to the "the isolation of the working class from the dominant classes who resided outside the community," and "the segmentation of the society within the territory, dividing workers from each other along ethnic lines" (1981: 73). Importantly, Katznelson contends that the American political sphere is characterized by debates over limited resources and "symbolic posturing that utilized a language of racial and ethnic competition" (181). Such ethnic divisions can be traced back to the colonial era, Morgan argues (1975: 386). He writes that the white servant class turned to racism to distinguish themselves from the black slaves, whom they considered their subordinates. This racism, as expressed among middle- and upper-class whites has, as Massey and Denton contend, resulted in the "hypersegregation" of American cities that has further perpetuated urban political fragmentation (1993: 10). Today, the distinctions that once protected poor whites from associations with ethnic minorities now weaken working class whites' capacity to make political claims.

This is perhaps where Donald Trump's 2016 presidential candidacy (and to a lesser extent, that of Senator Bernie Sanders) has had the most structural impact on American politics. His candidacy has disrupted the complacency of white working class voters—an enormous constituency—tired of backing a mix of Democratic and Republican candidates with whom they do not identify or trust. And despite being a plutocrat complacent in the inequities and political corruption he laments, Donald Trump's message embodies the sentiments of white working class people. A month before the 2016 Ohio primary election, more than 1,000 Mahoning County Democrats switched parties to vote for him (Skolnick 2016). Ultimately, Trump would win just over 50% of the county's Republican votes, along with 29 of the 32 Ohio counties that the state designates as "geographically isolated and economically depressed" (Suddes 2016). Trump has created a new, independent fraction inside the Republican Party that may also attract defectors from the Democrats. However, it is unclear whether this is a cult of Trump's personality or an enduring fraction that reproduces itself with candidates in local elections in a manner that offers alternatives to otherwise single-party regions.

Formal Externality

If a lack of competition makes the Democrats and Labour unaccountable to white working class voters in Youngstown and East London, respectively, the institutional structures of local government bodies render a formal sense of externality. However, disparate circumstances mean that City Hall operates in different ways across the cases. Embedded in a global city, Barking and Dagenham's Council bureaucracy recruits from a pool of highly qualified civil servants, many of whom commute from middle-class suburbs and other parts of Greater London. They are also therefore unexposed to immediate ramifications of the decisions they make and the rules they enforce. More cognizant of best practices around London and elsewhere, they tend to appeal to centralized standards more than local preferences.

EAST LONDON

In a variety of discussions with Barking and Dagenham Council bureaucrats, some—though far from all—exhibited a condescending view of the borough's elected representatives and the white working class constituency. It is not that they disrespect representatives and their constituents, but as with so many other British bureaucrats, they impose what they believe to be a rational, informed filter on the actions others demand. They also view themselves as permanent and qualified for decision-making, as opposed to the relatively ephemeral, common legislator. "Nobody cares about the people in this borough," said Maisie Drake, a homemaker. "The housing here is going to people moving in from outside the borough, so there's no space. They don't see it from our point of view. They'll dump you in the most horrible place. [. . .] People just go and do what they want anyway. They're fighting amongst themselves." While appraising claims is part of their remit, this arrangement can appear patronizing in a borough where the average Council bureaucrat lives in the middle-class suburbs of London and has anywhere from two to seven years more education than the people he serves. "The government, the Council, they don't live around here," said Pam Reed, the bartender at the Mill House Social Club. "They don't see what's going on in our streets. They've got big houses out in the country." Bureaucrats retort that residents view the Council as a cure-all with little regard for the limitations of government resources and procedures that must be followed.

The rift is wider between politicians and their constituents. Margaret Hodge, the Labour MP for much of Barking, is an heiress to the world's largest privately owned steel-trading corporation and wife of the late Sir Henry Hodge. Her official title is the Right Honourable Lady Hodge MBE MP, by virtue of her husband's knighthood and her appointment to Her Majesty the Queen's Privy Council. As British electoral rules do not require Members of Parliament to reside in the district they represent, Hodge lives in the exclusive Canonbury neighborhood of Islington—an upscale borough in Central London, where she previously served as a councilor. Jon Cruddas, the Labour MP for Dagenham, keeps a home in trendy Notting Hill near London's West End—a one-hour drive from his constituency. He holds a PhD in Philosophy from the University of Warwick. Both Cruddas and Hodge have served in Labour's Cabinet and been tapped for leadership positions.

Despite having substantially more access to his elected representatives than others, Ryan Sampson, a member of one Tenants and Residents Association, is skeptical of both MPs. "The borough has two career politicians, not constituency politicians," he says. "They may not have woken up to it because they're too busy in Westminster, but what Labour needs is activism. People are feeling marginalized because the state is retracting along with the support system they've come to depend on. Benefits are getting cut full scale. This causes new anxiety and pressures, but also resentment. People have the view that people come off the boat and get everything. [. . .] Big business are [sic] the people who run this country. Every cabinet member is a multimillionaire. They haven't eaten egg and chips. They don't know what it's like to be on the housing list for four years, to not have the heating turned on, to not have enough money to support your children. We forgot to listen to the working class."

I raised these concerns in an interview with Hodge personally. Her office is located in a small two-story cottage, tucked away from Barking's bustling market promenade, near a preschool and a Sikh temple. An unassuming building with overgrown weeds along its perimeter, it is nevertheless equipped with a security door and intercom system. While her staff works upstairs, the single downstairs room is a voter mobilization bunker equipped with highlighted canvassing maps of 17 wards and long plastic work tables with stacks of Labour Party flyers, and decorated with campaign posters from the past decade. Hodge is a small, robust 67-year-old woman with an air of sensibility and dignity, marked by a dash of self-pity.

"I don't fit it right, you know," Hodge says, once we sat down together. "They're suspicious of me. They respect me because I do the work. But I don't like the football. I don't go to West Ham matches. I don't go to the pub and get the pints. I'm not vitriolic, and demanding that every pedophile be hanged. My family is Jewish and we're middle class. It's not where you live, but where you spend your time."

"Do you mind if I eat," she asked courteously. I didn't. "Very busy right now, so little time for lunch." She tucked into a sandwich delivered by an aide.

"Barking and Dagenham does not have the world's most capable authority," she continued, still chewing. "It's Tammany Hall. The Labour Party six years ago was old, white, male members of trade unions. Now it is diverse, multicultural people of different ages. A lot of my people are there. We built the 'Margaret Hodge' brand, not the Labour brand, because Labour has been unpopular. The problem is that the old Council is low-spend, low-rent, and the state is perceived to be the only provider, so they have failed to invest in any civil society infrastructure. This lot just doesn't get it. They don't fund the voluntary sector, full stop. There is no understanding of civil society, and public services are crap. I depend on grassroots politics now. It's all about connecting, engagement."

"What do you find effective?" I asked.

"With white working class people, their politics start at their front door. They are very traditional. They are unchallenging of authority. They believe they should be in council housing. [. . .] The ones who are stuck here are the ones who can't move. The people who say to me, 'I can't get over the changes happening,' that's code for immigration. They really are at the bottom of the socioeconomic ladder. Many are out of work. Low educational qualifications. No skills, they're being replaced by migrants. It is sort of cultural in that they are stuck in their dependency on Ford's as the employer, on the government to provide benefits, and on the local Council for housing. There is no ambition or aspiration. There is no sense of entrepreneurship.

"We are all racist. It's embedded in us. You can't blame [white working class constituents]. Immigration really impacts them, and that's what the BNP exploited: legitimate anxieties and a lack of investment in public infrastructure. But people don't understand the real BNP agenda, and a lot of the people have naturally Conservative views, with a capital 'C.'"

As she took another bite, I asked, "But if the BNP exploits constituents' sentiments, do you ignore them?"

"National politicians are petrified by race," she said, sighing with a hint of exasperation. "So they try to avoid it. When they're forced to engage it, they address it in terms of immigration—something that they can't control—so they fail. When we close one route [of entry], immigrants pop up somewhere else. We were bloody stupid to pretend to be doing something. We need to just acknowledge that migration is a feature of globalization and that it is inevitable. But the people of Barking and Dagenham think it is unfair. And I also think it is unfair."

"Have you told that to your minority constituents?" I asked.

"Yes" she asserted. "Well to some of them, and many agree with me."

In its actions though, Labour has exhibited a sympathetic soft spot for immigrant constituents, and hardness when it comes to white working class claim-making. Alec Edwards from the Council supposed, "If a hypothetical Pakistani family went to Margaret Hodge, they would be listened to more closely than the hypothetical white working class family."

"Why?" I challenged.

"Because it's easier. There is a vestigial guilt about the way people were treated in the British Empire, and that feeling has not been extended to our own. [...] There is an arrogance among the Labour Party. It's class-based. When things are achieved here, it's discounted. Class is deeply ingrained. Inferiority. Superiority. Preference."

When the 12 BNP councilors were elected in 2005, many Barking and Dagenham bureaucrats thought it would shake the national government to attend to the needs of white working class constituents, to invest more in adult skills training, to reduce deprivation and ignorance. In the end, council administrator Ben Bassett says, "The money didn't come because of arrogance in Whitehall, and it was a political calculation to disable the BNP," he says. "There was a concept of the 'Dagenham child' that had a brain that functioned improperly. A declining manufacturing town, but in London. So there are 'new communities' willing to go ten stops to London to get ahead. Among the old communities, there are children who have never ridden the train. It's an insular world here. Meanwhile, among the immigrants, graduates are working in carparks."

YOUNGSTOWN

For decades, Youngstown's city government answered to only an elite cadre of party and business leaders. Officials never built an infrastructure of open consultation and transparency. Even today, City Hall occupies an unassuming, dark building on a side street downtown, and many meetings are closed-door. Consequently, Youngstown's white working class people have always felt a sense of political exclusion. Decisions were made for them—whether in City Hall or in the Golden Dawn restaurant's backroom. And for a long time, this arrangement worked well. Their trash was picked up, the fireman arrived in time, and the wastewater was purified.

"Politicians back then were part of a secret organization, backroom dealings, and ties with organized crime," recalled Gil McMahon. "They called it 'Boom Boom Ballet' or 'Bombtown.' More decisions were made over breakfast at the Hub restaurant downtown than at City Hall. All of them, well 99.9% of them, were involved with organized crime. But living was easier, and people were working. We just didn't know what the hell was going on. People will always have that mistrust because of the background. [. . .] The shadow [of the past's corruption] gives us that old feeling of insecurity and organized crime. It definitely overshadows politics. [. . .] The history of politics in the Mahoning River Valley is a very corrupt old boys club. That distrust is passed down from generation to generation, just by talking."

Now that there is less satisfaction with the quality of their lives, white working class people possess the awareness to talk about government dysfunction, but not the infrastructure to act. Conspiracy theories were threaded through a variety of respondents' statements. The veracity of these theories aside, their prominence suggested a perceived lack of control and transparency.

"You don't confront people or make noise here," said Charlie Johnson, an activist. "There are still names you don't mention in public—[like] Cafaro. You whisper them in the ear of the guy next to you. We haven't engaged them directly in any of our actions, so we don't touch them because there are easier targets than entrenched power brokers. We just have this dead zone where people are scared."

Johnson continued, "The white working class are confused and scared, threatened by the lack of prosperity and how things are getting where they live. A lot of houses are for sale, abandoned, and this time of year, there's a lot of high grass. They come from histories of prosperity, and they have inherent attitudes to trust the police and trust the government. We were doing so well before that you could skim off the top and nobody would notice.

"Now there's a lot of joking about Molotov cocktails, planting yourself in the mayor's office, interrupting government meetings, and that comes from a sense of hopelessness. Many are happy to go to a meeting where [Councilman] Mike Ray hands out charts, gives a presentation, but doesn't actually do anything. Their eyes just glaze over. They are really distrustful of the distant federal government, and I ask them why they can't apply the same skepticism to the government standing in front of them. We also have large groups of people who will never show up to meetings. They're invisible."

White working class political activism is indubitably constrained by reinforced apathy. Youngstown politics were for so long run by backroom negotiations and invisible power brokers that the infrastructure for deliberation and civil society was never well developed. A legacy of complacency has atrophied citizens' claims-making competence and hidden available avenues for activism. Politicians subtly enforce this reticence. It makes their jobs easier.

I attended a Rocky Ridge neighborhood association meeting on the Westside, where members distributed locally harvested maple syrup. Toward the end of the meeting, Councilman Mike Ray offered a City Hall update and solicited queries from the crowd. Annie Lewis, a 65-year-old ex-Air Force nurse, stood up and offered a spirited argument for the regulation of fracking companies: "We have had steel mills here, and when the economy declined, we were left with the scrap metal and contaminated water. The city was left in ruins. Now they intend to lease over land for gas to companies with world domination in mind. These companies will go vertical and horizontal; they will do whatever they want. We should want the right to make a decision, not that somebody else makes another decision for us. Even if the promise is great wealth, here in Youngstown, the people of Youngstown, are we willing to say that our land is precious? Let [Mahoning County Democratic Party Chairman] Dave Betras have a fracking pad underneath his house. He doesn't even live in Youngstown. I think–"

"This is not really the place for those comments," Councilman Ray interrupted. "While I respect your right to think that way, this is not the place."

Lewis quietly sat down and another resident asked a question on a matter Ray found to be more innocuous. While it was unclear where the appropriate place was for Annie's ideas, it was clearly not her councilman's clipboard. At a separate Westside Citizens Coalition meeting that I attended, when the organization's director addressed Ray, the councilman initially failed to respond because he was browsing on his iPad.

I caught up with Annie Lewis shortly after the Rocky Ridge meeting, and asked about the councilman's dismissal. "We don't make any of our own decisions," she says. "It has been so long since we made our own decisions, it's in our heritage. [. . .] Neighborhood associations are all well and good, but we are a bunch of bitties who don't want to rock the boat. They're afraid. They just don't think. They want to preserve their community by making maple syrup."

At a mayoral debate at the Union Baptist Church downtown, organizers from the Mahoning Valley Organizing Collaborative did not solicit a single question for the candidates from an audience of around 300 people. Within the first ten minutes, when a disgruntled resident stood up and complained about new requirements for homeownership, she was escorted out the back doors. The message was clear: attendees were there to listen.

Exiting the debate, I asked an activist why no one insisted on asking further questions. "It's like an abused dog," he replied. "If you've been beaten a bunch of times by someone—I mean, even if you were just beaten one time—you're going to flinch the next time that person comes up to give you a pet. It has a lasting impression."

Compounding the paucity of opportunities to make political claims, the legacy of government favoritism has set a template for activism—one that values connections and bartering more than popular strength and exchanges of ideas. There is a common sentiment that, to exert even a little influence, citizenship is insufficient. Several respondents reported that they were once quite engaged in Youngstown civic affairs, but have since decided to spend their time otherwise:

EVELYN: "The more I saw, the more I realized that money can buy your way out of anything. Then you see your sheriff get indicted, your congressman dishonored, our prosecutor in prison, and a mayoral nominee with a cloud over his head. The Valley has been embroiled in political corruption for a long time, and people just look out for themselves. It makes you sick. You don't see it firsthand, the corruption, but you know it's there."

CALEB: "It's apathy, and a great deal of laziness, but also not getting much of a response or feeling very effective. You feel as if your participation is almost non-consequential."

DIDI: "It matters if you're in the circle. I get along with everyone because I'm not one to run my mouth, but I'm not in anybody's circles. I don't create waves or stand out."

People's capitulation is discernible, even at the highest levels. "None of us are reaching a crowd," said McNally, then the mayoral candidate. "The ten [mayoral] forums we had in the spring, we're talking to the same people. The same places have the same events, the same questions come up, and after going through enough election cycles, nothing new is ever discussed. It's a variation on 'what are you doing for us?' I have a sense of frustration. You don't go to these events excited as a candidate. There's 99% of the city who you're never seeing."

Through this lens, the 2005 election of the BNP in East London, and the continued re-election of Congressman James Traficant in Youngstown between 1985 and 2002, may be understood as acts of desperation. The two anti-system entities gave a voice—a radical voice—to those accustomed to being outside the political discussion. The BNP pandered to xenophobia and racism, capitalizing on distrust of immigrants by blaming them for an economic decline caused by financial deregulation and irresponsibility. Traficant channeled conspiracy theories from the street to the United States Capitol, indulging his voters' sense of helplessness and confusion. He advocated the public flogging of the Internal Revenue Service tax collectors and condemned China at every opportunity. In so doing, each connected with their constituents, but further estranged them from mainstream political parties.

The Union Hangover

Youngstown and East London were regions that were once characterized by exceptionally high social capital. They were strongholds of unions, along with other powerful organizing institutions. Factories placed working class people into direct contact with each other and their sheer size fostered a greater public awareness of working class people, as well as a heightened sense of awareness among the working classes about their shared fate. And yet, in the decades following the collapse of an economic model, their rank and file were rendered incapacitated. Can high levels of networking degrade trust and efficacy?

If corruption left a legacy of secret deliberation that accustomed citizens to their exclusion, unions may have left a legacy of dependency on external entities for a license to agitate. Unions not only handled collective bargaining on behalf of workers; they offered their members a place for advocating, which—given the aloofness of union leadership—may have been a façade. The process of advocacy was frequently left up to a non-consultative labor bureaucracy (Fantasia and Voss 2004: 26, 82–85). The practice of grievance resolution among unions, for example, funneled worker discontent through a long chain of bureaucratic steps that increasingly "remov[ed] the resolution of injustice from its source, spatially, temporally, and socially"; representatives replaced workers as the primary actors for workplace reform (Fantasia and Voss 2004: 85).

Shefter (1986: 197–276) contends that the formation of labor unions in the nineteenth century contributed to the first conceptualization of the American working class in opposition to other sects of society. However, nineteenth-century workers used unions to assert claims against the employer rather than against the state. Shefter argues that the reason for the limited scope of union claim-making lies in the fact that labor mobilization occurred through institutional channels. Company unions, introduced before the onset of the world wars, were effectively used as a means to control worker self-initiative. By placing unions within the context of the company, company unions replaced "working class solidarity" with "company solidarity" (Fantasia 1988: 32, 69–71). Workers would "aid management" rather than act independently for their own interests (ibid.).

By the middle of the twentieth century, while some workers did undertake wildcat strikes, many were lulled into the complacency of waiting for the union to act for them or tell them when to act. Others were lost when the space for activism disappeared with their jobs. This argument complicates established understandings of how associational life improves social capital. Rather than foster networks that were able to subsist in the absence of the association, interview data suggest that unions created institutional dependencies.

"There is a unionist complacency," said Jack Keeley, a railroader from Youngstown's northside. "They get timely raises, improving conditions. Soon it becomes 'the union' instead of 'our union,' with a bigger bureaucracy and the emergence of elite people running it. People feel like their jobs will be protected, and don't want to go to union meetings, so there is some disengagement from unions and also from the government." In Youngstown during the early 1970s, Lynd and Lynd recorded a conversation between union organizers (Lynd and Lynd 2000):

LEWIS: I came to work in 1950. We had a lot of strikes, walkouts in individual departments. Now I think the average steelworker feels that he can't strike. It's in his mind.

MANN: That he'll be fired, that the union will see to it that he'll be fired.

THOMPSON: My plant walked out about a year and a half ago. There were only two people who got time off. Our president got thirty days and our steward got thirty days. [. . .]

LITCH: Doesn't it go back to the old saying that the union is to be with you, and not above you?

MANN: I don't know, from being in it all these years, there's a lot of things that I think I might rather do; but I feel that the union is the best place for a man to express himself. You can talk to people. You can put out leaflets. You can agitate. You can start an organization like RAFT [Rank and File Team]. I can get up on the soapbox in the room and say whatever I please. I still have this freedom. If it gets much results, I don't know. But I still have this freedom, which I don't see white-collar people having.

As Fantasia and Voss (2004) note, unions feature a "strictly top-down hierarchical structure that discourage rank-and-file initiative," promote "closed channels of communication networks at the top that rely on secretive 'backroom' deals" which "create the conditions that produce an ill-informed and passive membership," and support "a unionism that reacts to employer initiatives, rather than acting proactively." Unions, they continue, counter radicalism and are "frequently employed to contain internal political opposition." As a result, unions' rank and file did not realize their clout independent of union structures. While this consolidated unions' power during their heyday, this power disappeared with unions during their decline.

As Youngstown and East London's economies lost their largest employers, society became more atomized. While new corporate giants in fast food, retail, and the service sector have filled in the empty spaces, such businesses tend to be structured as a multitude of loosely connected branches and franchises that foster little collectivism among their employees. Further, such jobs typically do not position employees in circumstances that require a great deal of interdependency and teamwork with the same colleagues. Flexible labor supplies lead to high turnover, and the computerization of basic tasks reduce the importance of bonding with fellow employees. Even after the closure of the steel mills and the deep economic depression of the late 1970s and early 1980s in Youngstown, 34.4% of the region's private sector was still unionized in 1986. That number had dropped as low as 10% in 2010 (CPS, 2012). Comparable statistics are only available for larger regions in Britain. In 1995, 32.4% of the British private sector workers were unionized; by 2013 this number had dropped to 14.4% (Department for Business, Innovation, and Skills 2013).

After Social Capital

Theories of social capital expect dense, crosscutting associations like unions to facilitate the construction of networks between otherwise disconnected citizens. While the organizational locus may serve as the initial link, researchers expect that members will eventually build relationships among each other—fostering norms of reciprocity and understandings of linked fate that promote greater civic engagement and social responsibility outside of associational networks.

Associational architecture appears to matter. The bonds that characterized factories, unions, and mafias were not independent of the institutional locus; they were centralized. So when the institution deteriorated, the links between associates did too. Independent links were hindered because unions reproduced extant ethno-racial and class social divisions.

While Youngstown's and East London's white working class communities have historically thought of themselves as very closely knit, they too were rendered incapacitated. In Youngstown, this was largely because of the secrecy and intrigue surrounding Youngstown's politics. In Barking and Dagenham, it was due to systems of patronage that separated the state apparatus from its citizens. Perhaps equally importantly, both communities lost key hubs of communal relationships with the mass exodus of their white middle and working class in the 1980s and 1990s. Those who remain were less civically connected even in the best of times. And as more people departed, they were replaced by a growing proportion of minorities who were less present in yesteryear's unions.

In interviews in Youngstown, respondents now frequently depict unions as corrupt oligarchies that betray their origins. While it is unclear whether this sentiment is new (unions were known to require under-the-table payments for factory jobs in the 1980s and 1990s), it is nevertheless felt more intensely as the region's economy declines.

"People are misguided that unions are looking out for them," said Caleb Jones, a parking attendant. "Listen, we have had crippling economic woes, but not once has Labor said that they may have had something to do with it. We cannot compete globally when we have to pay people $30 an hour to put in a bolt. But now I don't know that anyone is looking out for the white working class."

Remarkably, such sentiments were often also shared by members and former members of unions themselves. "The unions went too far," said Marge Russell, who was one of the very first women on the assembly line at the General Motors plant down the highway in Lordstown. She began installing batteries and radiators in August 1970. "They got just as powerful and crooked as the companies they fight against. Their philosophy is all about seniority, and they've made it such that even if you're a convict or a drug addict, they will always have your back. The auto industry pays for their counseling and the abuse of the system. People were able to milk the system and it wasn't fair to the clean, hard worker."

"You can't underestimate the importance of organized labor," said Bryant Daniels, a former public official from Youngstown, "because they are the only enterprise with any resources to mobilize voters—to the extent that any remain. There used to be tens of thousands of unionized workers, but now it's mostly just the government employees and some tradesmen who work on fracking-related jobs. [. . .] There's now just less to fight about. The industrial workers are at the mercy of the world economy and the tradesmen are governed by state law, not bargaining agreements. They have nobody else to fight with, and there is no one else to dance with."

So much of organizational politics flows from the identification of an opposition, and the creation of an identity. With the collapse of union power and the collapse of social capital comes the collapse of collective- and self-worth. Manufacturing unions organized a largely homogenous white population in a civic manner independent of their ethnic identity. The white working class now struggles to realize their collective interests otherwise, despite the economic predicament they share with minority groups. When unions collapsed, there was a residue of beliefs and habits that can no longer find purchase. As the next chapter explains, these social boundaries have been redrawn in ways that undermines any sense of cross-ethnic solidarity, any means of collective strength.

"This is the area that founded unions," said Leah Perry, the 29-year-old manufacturing clerk. "People have a chip on their shoulder. They think that they are owed things. They expect the union to do it for you. You'd go to the steel mills, clock in, clock out, collect your pension, and repeat. There are people my age that are still waiting for a union or factory. [. . .] We need an uprising. But if you scheduled one, only three people would show up."

6

Identities

PRISMS OF CULTURE AND CLASS

The ordinary English worker hates the Irish worker as a competitor who lowers his standard of life. In relation to the Irish worker he feels himself a member of the ruling nation and so turns himself into a tool of the aristocrats and capitalists of his country against Ireland, thus strengthening their domination over himself. [...] This antagonism is artificially kept alive and intensified by the press, the pulpit, the comic papers, in short by all the means at the disposal of the ruling classes. This antagonism is the secret of the impotence of the English working class, despite its organization. It is the secret by which the capitalist maintains its power. And that class is fully aware of it.
—Karl Marx, Letter

Institutional explanations set the context for white working class people's political marginality in postindustrial environments. However, they struggle to explain individual-level differences among the populations this book considers. This chapter considers another prominent explanation: namely, that white working class people establish political identities in opposition to ethnic and racial minorities who might otherwise unite with white people as part of an impactful proletariat constituency. Have ethnic and racial divisions truly replaced the powerful economic class identities around which white working class people organized for much of the twentieth century? How have white working class people's immobility and atomization reoriented social and political cleavages? Where are the fault lines of white working class identity and marginality? This chapter will address these questions as they pertain to the residents of Youngstown and East London in order to inform the next chapter's discussion of how these divisions are understood, internalized, and converted into social hierarchies.

I first discuss the reinvigoration of class as a defining social division in Youngstown and East London. I contend that the white working class people I study draw more conventionally understood ethno-racial boundaries on top of contemporaneous class boundaries. Both act as reference groups in their consideration of social hierarchies. However, I observe that class divisions are more salient than ethno-racial divisions for white working class respondents who live in neighborhoods that are predominantly composed of ethnic minority residents. In the end, I argue that it is more accurate to think of white working class political divisions as a matter of social status, which integrates the overlapping divisions of race and class and converts them into narratives that structure people's experiences in the market, society, and political sphere.

Class as Cleavage

Over the past two decades, researchers have considered the changing social position of poor and working class white people, particularly in the United States. Among the most prominent works, researchers have chronicled the endurance of ethno-racial divisions and analyzed their adaptations in the contemporary era. Massey and Denton (1993) noted the continuing presence of racial residential segregation in American society. Maharidge (1996) presented the way demographic changes signal the decline of white ethnic-racial dominance. Kaufmann (2004a; 2004b; 2004c) chronicled the declining dominance of the Anglo-Saxon ethnicity as a result of multiculturalist trends that have championed a liberal-egalitarian ethic. Lipsitz (2006) noted the subtle protection of white advantage vis-à-vis African Americans. McDermott (2006) exposed poor white people's reconciliation of low social position amid expectations of advantage. Massey (2007) analyzed class stratification as a locus of categorical inequality and considered the role that education, race, and gender played in determining class divisions. And Silva (2013) noted the hardening of working class whites as they compete for increasingly scarce jobs and questionable futures in the transition to adulthood. The evidence from case studies of Youngstown and East London hardly disputes these findings. White working class respondents feel estranged from and resentful of ascendant minority groups, who are perceived to receive favor from government and other social institutions. In East London, immigrants are the Other. In Youngstown, where race relations have been anchored in black-white differences, the Other is black, particularly among a white community that maintains a sense of their various ethnic ties.

However, I also witnessed the reinvigoration of class cleavages. Indeed, white working class respondents also feel estranged from white, elite co-ethnics, who exploit working class people in the market, abandon them during economic decline, and side with the social grievances of minority groups. In this way, class does not replace established racial divisions; rather, they are superimposed such that the lines of class consciousness intersect those of ethno-racial difference—cornering white working class people into an ever-shrinking in-group and political constituency. In this way, their marginality is dual.

In interviews, respondents from Youngstown and East London frequently identify both cleavages simultaneously. "Everyone acts like the white people are well off," said Rachel Gibson, a mother of two on Youngstown's Westside. "You're white, so you must be rich. We work two jobs and struggle to get our kids through school. But you're white, you can afford it. You don't need help, no minority loan, no government discount. [. . .] This Westside Citizens Coalition, they're trying to beautify the neighborhood. I don't care how many trees you plant—and they put one in front of my house—that's not going to change the out-of-state landlords who sell to lowlifes."

"There are gang members in that home," she said, pointing angrily next door. "Sitting on their porch, yelling 'nigger-this' and 'nigger-that,' with kids out of school on a weekday, whipping rocks at my house and my dog. Who's going to replace my windows? Not black people. They are running down our neighborhoods. That's why we are getting the hell out."

She threw her cigarette into the grass of her front yard.

"You do not touch, talk to, or threaten a black child," she instructed. "They can say or do whatever they want to a white child though. This place is turning into the Eastside."

Rachel is clearly displeased with and resentful of her black neighbors. However, she assigns the blame for their presence to white, out-of-state landlords who are renting to more ethnically diverse tenants who she believes are altering the nature of her neighborhood. She also expresses a frustration that she is socially grouped with the wealthier white landlords.

"They have a feeling that they've been battered," said Max Greenfield, who has worked for different Youngstown public officials. "A good deal of people hate the rich and successful. There's always jealousy, but here it's more intense. And it's not on the surface. You hear it only after spending a half hour or 45 minutes with them, and I understand it."

In East London, Kieran Turner echoed Rachel's sentiments and blamed white government elites for imposing demographic change, to which wealthy Britons are perceived to be unexposed. "A lot of immigrants moved in, and now the buildings are full of them," he explains. "Why don't you move them in with the politicians and see how they like it? Let them deal with our shit. [. . .] You never see a poor landowner. But I never really go into their neighborhoods. The white working class has had a lot taken away. It used to be the United Kingdom, but it's not that united anymore. [. . .] We used to live all together, and then these fucking Indians came in and the government says that they need to live together. What about us? [. . .] Sometimes I just want to pick up something and destroy it. But somehow I can't. And see, now I'm getting all angry. The rich get richer and the poor get poorer. It makes you want to explode."

For other respondents in East London, cultural divisions actually coincide with class divisions. Lou Griffiths, a lifelong renter now in public housing, groups immigrants together with affluent white antagonists. "The private land-lords are a nightmare. They charge the Earth, they'll cram five families into a one-bedroom, and they don't fix anything. They're taking the piss. You're seeing the divide between working class. But a lot of these landlords are immigrants! The influx blinds people to the inequality. Jobs are the vehicle of inequality. The Eastern Europeans control a lot of the crime, con games, and prostitution." Terry Hammonds said, "In this area, the economy has jobs for Asians, while the English here do the labor. You go for an interview and most of the employers are Asians. Basically, they're discriminating against us, and we were here first. I have some training as a retail sales assistant. But when I've submitted my CV, I've been told that I can't apply because I'm not Asian. [. . .] I feel like I'm beneath them."

Invisibility of Class

Except in these less common cases when blacks and immigrants are associated with wealthy white elites, the targets of class division are typically invisible, in-accessible, and inscrutable. They frequently look like any other white citizen, they live in neighborhoods far removed from the working class boroughs of East London and Youngstown, and respondents are less able to determine reasons for their culpability beyond their material well-being and perceived complicity in the globalization of the economy. The wealthy may understate or veil their affluence and its sources in ways that African Americans may not alter their com-plexion and Lithuanian immigrants may not suppress their accents. "The rich and poor are separated, and the middle people are on the other side," said Oscar Bradley from Barking. "David Cameron concentrates on his type of people, the people who can afford decent homes. And the working class are left to do their own bit. [. . .] I don't see what they do."

The invisibility of class and its antagonists makes working class group identity challenging to forge and mobilize. Given factory towns' exposure to the power of elites, they are more acutely sensitive to elite-imposed inequities. However, in their contemporary day-to-day lives, respondents are rarely—if ever—confronted by the socioeconomic Other the way their grandparents may have encountered the steel barons in previous decades, when cities like Youngstown featured a more diverse class profile. And with the demise of signature compa-nies like Youngstown Sheet and Tube, today's targets of class tension are more dispersed. Without a locus of antipathy—and ever fewer organizations that unite working class people—the expressed class hostility is much less effectively reinforced by white working class discourse in their interpersonal interactions. Class tensions are therefore latent, overshadowed by more concrete and convenient references to racial difference.

In this way, understandings of class have been reduced to a mere material deficiency, rather than the dynamic form of collectivism and mobilization conceptualized by scholars like Malcolm Waters, according to his four propositions of class theory (1990; Pakulski and Waters 1996). First, per Waters, class certainly remains a socioeconomic phenomenon characterized by differential market capacities and property ownership.

Second, counter Waters, class provides respondents with little sense of groupness, as a cleavage in society or the base of conflict when conflicts are increasingly about heritage, authenticity, and entitlement. Respondents in Youngstown and East London expressed some sense of unity with African Americans and immigrants—not as fellow members of the proletariat, but rather as fellow opportunists in a difficult economic climate. "Immigrants are against the system, just like we are," acknowledged Callum Everett, an unemployed 19-year-old from Thamesview in East London. "But we're not going to other countries, working for little money and nicking people's jobs. This is how they do it. They have babies here, so they can say they need to stay here to raise them." Hayden Thomas, a 28-year-old from Barking, said, "Immigrants come over and get everything they want. I don't blame immigrants for it. I'd do the same thing too if I could move somewhere where I got better pay and housing. That's what you want." This sentiment concurs with Standing's observations (2011: 12). "The precariat does not feel part of a solidaristic labour community," he writes. "This intensifies a sense of alienation and instrumentality in what they have to do. Actions and attitudes, derived from precariousness, drift towards opportunism. There is no 'shadow of the future' hanging over their actions, to give them a sense that what they say, do or feel today will have a strong or binding effect on their longer-term relationships. The precariat knows there is no shadow of the future, as there is no future in what they are doing."

Third, counter Waters, class offers fewer behavioral or cultural linkages, as an identity with norms, values, and political preferences. Universal standards of speech and culture conveyed through national media also moderate linguistic and visible differences between rich and poor, particularly in the United States. Class is simply less indicative of an individual's affinities, preferences, or worldview, and therefore must interact with a variety of other factors to be predictive of political behavior. That said, Bennett et. al (2009) find that cultural socialization is strongly correlated with future educational attainment and upward mobility in the United Kingdom. According to Savage et al.'s model (2013) of British class division, Barking and Dagenham workers fall in the "traditional working class," characterized by moderately low capital in all three measures. The immigrant population who has been settling in East London, on the other hand, belongs to what Savage defines as "emergent service workers," characterized by low economic capital, but high social capital and high emerging cultural capital (see also Savage 2005.). This would lead some to question whether working class whites are properly grouped with working class minority groups anyway.

Consequently, fourth and again counter Waters, class has a diminished capacity to mobilize people for the purpose of social transformation when the white working class is silenced, apathetic, and perhaps more importantly, subdivided. "Leaving aside agrarian societies, the globalisation era has resulted in a fragmentation of national class structures," writes Guy Standing (2011: 7). "As inequalities grew, and as the world moved towards a flexible open labour market, class did not disappear. Rather, a more fragmented global class structure emerged." In places like Youngstown and East London, this fragmentation is self-imposed. The English Defence League (EDL) and British National Party (BNP) render a sense of shared moral standards, but in a manner that vilifies immigrants and especially Muslims. They organize around some of working class whites' most basic senses of injustice: terrorism, the armed forces, patriotism, and a sense of priority for Britain's contingency of British people. Harry Carlisle, a 24-year-old BNP member who works for a moving company, said he did not join London's riots, which some construed as a class revolt. "I'm not going to join a bunch of idiots, just to get a pair of trainers," he told me. "If it's about the right thing, I'll be there. Like when British soldiers returned home from the war, and a group of Muslims turned up to call them rapists."

Institutions of Class, Race, and Gender

The incapacity to mobilize around class-based forms of groupness is also a product of Youngstown and East London's civic circumstances. Whereas unions and other working class groups once overcame divisions to pursue professional goals, the deterioration of these organizations and their manifestations in workingman's clubs, union halls, pubs and clubhouses removed a venue for the development of working class consciousness. According to Massey (2007), American labor movements declined as a result of changes made to labor laws in 1947 and 1959. Massey argues that these modifications, coupled with the anti-union policies that the American government pursued in the 1980s, caused de-unionization in the United States. According to the Bureau of Labor Statistics (2013; Vedder et al. 2012), the rate of unionization in Ohio fell from 36.8% of employed wage and salary workers in 1965, to 21.3% in 1989, and to

11.8% in 2013. Nevertheless, Ohio still ranks above the national rate, which was approximately 16% in 1989 and 11% in 2012. In Barking and Dagenham, the Department for Business, Innovation and Skills (2013) reports that trade union density in London fell from 29.8% in 1995 to 21.5% in 2012, which makes it the second least unionized region in the United Kingdom. According to the same report, the national trade union density fell from a peak of 50% in 1980, to 32.4% in 1995, and to 26% in 2012.

Some scholars contend that the lower-class members of majority groups tend to organize around their ethno-racial identity because of a lack of achieved occupational identity. Yiftachel (2000), for example, observes that the economic and social marginalization of Sephardic Jews in Israel has given rise to political movements that emphasize Sephardic Jewishness. Brodkin (1994: 86–89) traces how Jewish immigrants in the United States embraced whiteness as part of their transition into the middle class. Roediger (1991: 137) describes how Irish immigrants in the 1800s came to "insist on their own whiteness and on white supremacy" as a bulwark against association with the black laboring underclass in the United States. Described as "low-browed," "savage," "bestial," and "wild," Irish immigrants depended on the white racial label to secure political rights, keep treasured jobs, and to remain at least one step ahead of their black coworkers on the socioeconomic ladder (133–136). Given the labeling of unskilled white laborers as "white niggers," Irish immigrants heavily relied on the "public and psychological wages" of whiteness to ensure the stability of their social standing (Roediger 1991: 145). Ignatiev (1995: 96) writes along similar lines, tracing the Irish immigrant turn to whiteness as protection against the "slavery" of wage labor. And Vecoli (1995) discusses the socioeconomically advantageous recasting of Italian Americans as whites. Wright (2004: 36) contends that poor or lower-middle-class white Americans continue to glean "vital psychic income" by identifying with those of an upper class who happen to share similar "external characteristics."

It is thought that this reliance on whiteness in the United States as a refuge from association with black co-laborers has evolved out of the realities of colonial life. In his treatise on colonial Virginia, Morgan (1975: 319) reveals how white servants were often described in terms that were also used to describe black slaves. Both were called "shiftless," "irresponsible," "unfaithful," "ungrateful," and "dishonest." It is no wonder, then, that this association between lower-class whites and black servitude prompted a struggle to rely more heavily on an ethno-racial identity rather than a class-based identity. The English reformer William Cobbett once claimed in a similar vein that white workers in English factories were "slaves" under more strenuous conditions than those of the West Indies (cited in Collins 2004: 17). McDermott's (2006: 52–54) account of race relations in Greenfield, Massachusetts illustrates these ideas. She notes how working class whites, viewing whiteness as a badge of superiority, endeavor to physically and socially distance themselves from black co-residents.

However, this may have been less true with the historical presence of trade associations and professional networks. Even today, white working class people who work as police officers, steel workers, flight attendants, firemen, correctional officers, and government employees maintain relatively strong occupational identities. Brattain's (2001: 9) historical account of the textile industry's rise in the American South reveals how definitions of whiteness and blackness were differentially aligned with particular occupations. And Davis's (1986: 26) earlier account of weak working class consciousness also underscores these racial divisions across various professions.

The debilitation of strong bridging organizations has been worsened by the propensity of white working class families to leave their communities after Youngstown's collapse and East London's demographic transformation. In both venues, the choice of white homeowners to flee reinforces common understandings of multiculturalism, whereby diversity is accommodated but accommodated separately. Difference is thus protected, but in the form of seclusion—the creation of space through displacement, rather than the re-creation of space. This is also a product of white people's majority status. During economic decline or civic insecurity, white people have the flexibility to move to suburbs or other cities where they may find suitable communities of co-ethnics. However, ethno-religious minorities do not have this same flexibility if they wish to maintain contact with their cultural in-group. Those who move away may find themselves returning to their original neighborhood for specialty groceries, prayer space, or family gatherings (Gest 2010: 81–82).[1]

The attenuating institutional separation that white people have historically attempted to create between their communities and black or immigrant-origin working class communities parallels the attenuating status that white men historically felt within their households. The Great Recession that began in 2008 disproportionately affected white men's income and employment, because men were more likely than women to be employed in industries such as construction and manufacturing that were exposed to significant fluctuation since 1978 (Hoynes, Miller, and Schaller 2012: 27–48). Women, on the other hand, were more likely to be employed in the service sector and public administration, which are less cyclical in nature. Consequently, women are increasingly their families' breadwinners, compounding white men's sense of political and social disorientation. With the deterioration of unions, white men hold less political sway; with the disappearance of their clubs and associations, white men are less able to separate themselves from other working class communities; and with the loss of their primary means of employment, white men have lost their status as domestic provider.

Default Organizational Identity

The salience of ethno-racial divisions incontrovertibly weakens class mobilization, but it also reorients white people to a much more problematic and weaker source of mobilization: their whiteness. Whiteness in the United States and Britain is framed in society's default negative space. Waters (1990: 146) has observed that European immigrant descendants in the United States tend to subscribe to "symbolic ethnicities" (146). Third and fourth generations selectively associate with distant ethnic options through hyphenated identities such as Irish-American or Italian-American, revealing a need to feel "special and simultaneously part of a community" (Waters 1990: 150). Extrapolation from these findings suggests that whiteness operates as an empty or unfulfilling ethno-racial option. In a biography of the British white working class, Collins (2004: 263) argues that the white working class has never needed to define itself. Kaufmann (2004c: 19) discusses how assimilation of immigrants in the United States followed a trajectory of "Anglo-conformity," where newcomers were expected to increasingly accumulate the attributes of "WASPdom" to ultimately become Americans. Roediger (1991: 6) writes of African-American literary giants such as Cyril Briggs, James Baldwin, and Ralph Ellison, who commented on the tendency of white Americans to define themselves in opposition to the black Other; whiteness, they emphasized, was developed and maintained as a necessary corollary to blackness, rather than a race in and of itself.

Accordingly, though respondents were able to define the ethno-racial Other, they had difficulty defining the in-group. This is a product of compounding factors. One is that the concept of whiteness is an amalgam of European and Eurasian ethnicities. This internal diversity not only reduces the coherency of white norms and culture; its inconsistent boundaries over time weaken the sense of groupness. While whiteness at one point excluded groups like the Irish, Italians, Jews, and Slavs, at its most inclusive, it incorporates all of them along with groups from the Levant and Latin Americans of European descent. Miscegenation among these different groups further entangles their variable cultural lineages, such that whiteness is most generally characterized— at best—by its necessary pluralism, but—at worst—by a cultural nihilism. Whiteness may legitimately mean so many things that it ceases to signify anything in particular.

This weakens the significance of co-ethnicity, and subsequently white people's bonds of cohesion, which otherwise link immigrant groups and more concretely defined minority communities. Despite many subjects' perceptions, whites are not subject to institutional forms of discrimination or disadvantage. Rather, they benefit from an implicit "wage" or a "possessive investment" in whiteness through history. This societal understanding constrains the need for social protection that organizations are built to provide, and this undermines the palatability of their political claims.

To identify a stronger sense of groupness, whites must seek out subcultures related to more distinct identities connected to other social cleavages based on ideology, lifestyle, or sexuality. With fewer resources and their increasing distrust of unions, white working class Americans and Britons actively discard more politically meaningful and more feasible alternatives for group identification. And while middle-class white people can identify with achieved social statuses and therefore invest less in ethnic and racial distinctions, white working class people cannot (Kaufmann 2014).

Neighborhood Composition Effects

Those white working class individuals who assign greater meaning to class boundaries than ethno-racial boundaries tend to live in more diverse neighborhoods in Youngstown and East London. Respondents who reside in areas that are predominantly composed of African Americans or immigrants tend to say they feel closer to their black or foreign neighbors than to white people who left Youngstown and East London for the suburbs. However, white working class people residing in neighborhoods with a small but growing minority population tend to say they feel closer to white people who live in the suburbs than to their black or foreign neighbors. From respondents' statements, this appears to be connected to the passing of perceived social threats. While people living in neighborhoods dominated by members of an ethno-racial minority have acculturated to being outnumbered, uncertainty about the repercussions of demographic change consumes those witnessing the growth of a minority population. While the former have effectively adapted to the status quo (or know no other circumstances), the latter are more likely to note changes and assign blame in the midst of social transformation.

Jimmy Plummer and Wendy Timlin each live in an eastern part of Youngstown's Southside that has featured a larger black population for the past few decades. "I feel closer to the black people in my neighborhood," said Jimmy, a 26-year-old handyman. "It's where I grew up and experienced a lot of things that folks out in the suburbs never seen or experienced. People from [suburbs like] Boardman, Poland, Canfield, they always thought they were better than me. But I wouldn't change a thing."

Wendy is a 55-year-old short order chef at a local bowling alley, who was raised in a public housing project on Youngstown's mostly black Northside. She and her husband live on a street where they are the only white family. "I guess we're just like the black people now. White people, we sell drugs, commit crimes, go on welfare. I grew up in the projects around them, even though we've never been on welfare. We've always had jobs, always worked. We ain't going to depend on no one but ourselves."

"So do you feel closer to your black neighbors or the white people who have left Youngstown?" I asked.

"I feel closer to the black folks. I grew up with them, you know. You meet everyone at the bowling alley, so I get along with everybody except those people next door."

There is also an important and likely selection effect, as those who are less comfortable with the diversification of a neighborhood will tend to move to more homogenously white areas. Put another way, white people who choose to remain in previously white, now minority-dominated neighborhoods may be less bothered by this diversification. A. J. Hardy attended a high school with a student body that was 5% white and 75% black. Now 23 years old, his social circle is integrated among white, black, and mixed friends from Youngstown's almost exclusively black Eastside. "My dad has more black friends than white. [. . .] I've seen photos of him when he was young with a picked afro. Growing up, color was never an issue. My dad's best friend is black, they always called each other 'brother.' I thought they were brothers until I was eight years old. The man slept over enough times in my living room. In high school, when people would fight over race and religion, I would drift into the corner because I didn't know which side to take. When I was going to Rayen High School on the Northside, my dad was driving me to school one time, when a man in a car pulled up along side of us and started yelling, 'You're a nigger too, because you hang out with them!'"

However, the decision to stay in a diversifying neighborhood is not always a matter of choice. Many white residents in minority-dominated neighborhoods lack the resources to move elsewhere. In East London, these individuals tend to be tenants in public housing complexes, who cannot move without Council accommodation. In Youngstown, these individuals may be Section Eight tenants who rent with government support, or private renters who cannot afford elevated suburban prices.

Caleb is a 42-year-old parking attendant and a lifelong resident of Youngstown's upper Southside, which has experienced some of the greatest demographic change in Youngstown over the past 20 years. "I feel closer to the folks who fled the area," he says, acknowledging that he cannot afford to move. "As property values go down, everything around them goes down too. Drops in education, rises in crime, a dilapidated infrastructure. Some people are willing to work out of it. It's about self-preservation. There are reasons for minority representation in the criminal justice and welfare systems, and they're not necessarily blamable reasons. But you can't talk about them because you'll be called prejudiced. People tiptoe around a ton of issues rather than confront them."

Caleb maintains a network of white suburbanites through his Catholic Church, which still attracts departed Southsiders. For this reason he associates the suburbs with other people like himself, despite their ostensible income differences. "Even if you present objective, quantitative data, you're a racist. There has been outrage over the Catholic pedophilia scandals; it's the first thing people mention when you talk about the Catholic Church. But they do not question the Muslims. It's a liberal elitism, from the people who stand on the backs of the poor to get elected."

Generational Effects

In both cases, there is also a further generational effect. Even white youths who live in predominantly white neighborhoods frequently attend schools that are mostly composed of minority students. So while their parents may mitigate their exposure to demographic change, younger generations experience the echo of white birth rates that are decreasing faster than those of ethno-racial minorities. For this reason, across both cases, young white working class respondents felt more comfortable among and affinity with minority populations. Luke Wilkinson is a 25-year-old who works for his father's flooring business in Barking. "We were brought up with different races," he said. "There were just as many nationalities in school as white British students. It's the parents who don't want to adapt." Ashton Roberts is a 24-year-old artist, who has a Jamaican girlfriend and a mixed group of friends in Dagenham. "You got different types of people," he said. "There are people like me who went to diverse schools, and are used to being around people of different backgrounds. But then there are people who are not used to it and need to be. And third, you got some who never met a black person in their lives."

Listening closely to the statements of the youngest interviewees, a sort of post-racist politics is emerging. The newest generation of adults between the ages of 18 and 30 grew up around, attended school with, befriended, and dated people of foreign ethnocultural origins. They have eaten diverse foods, listened to diverse music, and have been directly exposed to a variety of perspectives, tastes, and lifestyle preferences in Barking and Dagenham schools, where two out of every three students are of an ethnic minority background (UK Department of Education 2012). They are more comfortable with ethnocultural difference, and yet they relate to earlier generations' gripes.

However, young adults' politics is not about deporting foreigners. It is not about the transformation of Barking and Dagenham's social landscape. It is not—in short—about maintaining the innate social superiority of white British people. Instead, it is about not being subjected to the casual and institutionalized discrimination that once faced ethnocultural minority groups. It is very much about safeguarding their own rights and entitlements from adversarial government bodies. "There's a sense that people care more about the other ethnic groups," Ashton Roberts continued. "I watched a children's group take about 100 BME [Black Minority Ethnic] kids to a water fun park. And I thought to myself, why don't they do that for us?"

"But what can you do about that?" I asked.

"I was not interested in the BNP because a lot of my friends are not white. My best mates have frequently been black. My girlfriend is black. She's Jamaican. And I hate that the BNP won't tolerate them. [. . .] I know that if I'm dating a black woman, no one can call me a racist. [. . .] I genuinely feel like it's special when different people sing off the same hymn sheet. I think it's brilliant when black and Asian kids feel so close to my culture to make it part of their culture. But because of slavery and colonization, I have to feel guilty for something I've never even seen—something my ancestors could never afford."

Ashton's friend Ollie Marks is a 30-year-old ex-Army soldier, who has been in and out of prison for multiple, separate counts of gross bodily harm—first for a stabbing, and later for attempting to rob an armored bank vehicle. In his youth, he was the victim of a vicious mugging near Dagenham Heathway that left scars across his face and body. "I feel like other people should have the same opportunities as us, but that we should come first," he said. "We should be in the center [of British society], but I feel like I'm on the outside, as far from the center as possible. [. . .] The BNP and the EDL are going the wrong way about it, because they make race the issue. My [2-year-old] son has Caucasian hair, blue eyes, light skin. The only way you can tell he's got a black mother is that he's got a flat nose and big [penis]. If they had their way, they'd fly my kid out of the country. But people think they're only joining them to get a voice."

An alternative politics of race—a purportedly post-racist politics—emerges from these statements. It demands that the government make people of immigrant origin "put in before they take out"—that is, reside and invest in the United Kingdom before receiving access to increasingly scarce entitlements and public services. It demands that equal protection laws consider all forms of discrimination, and that the plight of poor immigrants is not prioritized higher than the plight of equally poor white families. Unlike older generations who have been hesitant to relate to the struggles of ethnocultural minorities and unite over their geographical proximity or working class status, this generation is more integrated. However, now that they perceive the outsider to be an insider, they feel marginal.

Post-racist politics therefore assumes two distinct forms in East London. A first group makes the claims above in order to establish a new social equilibrium, where white and immigrant-origin people are treated equally. They perceive an integrated borough that has progressively diversified to the point that ethnocultural minorities should be of equal status to the working class white community, despite the latter's longevity. Supporters of this agenda are less likely to embellish the centrality of white working class people in years gone by, and more likely to empathize with immigrants' plight. While they acknowledge working class whites' marginality, they have a tempered sense of entitlement.

A second group makes the claims above in order to reestablish the earlier social hierarchy. The EDL and BNP have made strides in Barking and Dagenham because they unabashedly articulate these demands. The BNP may use intimidation and exclusivity, and the EDL may use violence; however, they have justified these means as necessary to shake the United Kingdom from its dormancy and return to a rightful social order. Those who pursue the latter agenda and acquiesce to their antidemocratic tactics exhibit a severe discrepancy between where they believe working class whites belong in the British social order, and where they find themselves. "We're outnumbered in a town like this, we're overrun here," said BNP member Harry Carlisle. "We fall outside, but we should be falling right in the middle. But we're not going back to the center without a fight, or we might as well go to another country. You just feel like you're not meant to be here. You feel like you're not wanted in your own country. I've grown up with it and this is my hometown."

Explaining Social Division

These interview data address many observers' confusion about why groups like the British National Party (BNP) and the English Defence League (EDL) emerged only after the departure of much of East London's white population. With their departure, Barking and Dagenham's remaining white working class population was either too poor to join the suburbanites or too elderly and rooted to contemplate moving. Beyond those that were simply comfortable with the demographic change, this process left a white population that was particularly resentful of their neighborhood's social transformation. Furthermore, the depressed housing prices of Barking and Dagenham tended to attract low-income immigrants, many of whom were recent arrivals to the United Kingdom from Eastern Europe, sub-Saharan Africa, and South Asia. This meant that the immigrants who entered Barking and Dagenham were less likely to have acculturated to British life, and more likely to be pressed up against white working class neighbors in concentrated public housing facilities that did not provide the buffered space that suburban life affords.

This evidence renders nuance to hypotheses addressing the causes of xenophobic conflict in urban settings. Benjamin Newman (2012b) underscores the speed of demographic change as a key determinant for intolerance. He identifies differences between communities that experience a rapid influx of minority groups, and those that have already experienced acculturation between different communities. Newman's findings undermine earlier frameworks such as Putnam's "hunkering down" hypothesis (2007) and Blalock's power-threat hypothesis (1967)—according to which intolerance increases as the immigrant population grows larger, because of greater political and economic competition between natives and non-natives. Newman's conclusion also expands upon the intergroup contact theory (see Hewstone and Brown 1986; Pettigrew and Tropp 2006) by accounting for the initial size of the native population relative to the non-native population. In a further study, Jeffrey Denis (2012) studied the group tactics that native and white Canadians deployed when addressing a controversy that pitted one group against the other. The tactics deployed by the dominant non-native group, namely racial prejudice and claims to superiority, mirror the entitlement attitudes that Dagenham and Barking reported to have displayed in the face of increasing immigration. In Youngstown and East London, we witness the enduring salience of ethnoracial boundaries overlaid by emerging boundaries based on class difference among white working class populations that are materially worse off than they were in yesteryear.

A debate receiving increased attention in social science concerns the determinacy of culture versus economic structure over the course of social and political outcomes. In Youngstown and East London, the populations have indeed undergone traumatic economic change that has brought white working class people into direct contact and sometimes intimate connection with people of other ethnic and racial backgrounds. Nevertheless, it is clear that white working class people's sense of groupness is forged at an early age in ways that create meaningful divisions between white people and nonwhite people who occupy the same economic category. As a result, it is more helpful to think of divisions as a matter of social status, which integrates the overlapping divisions described above and converts them into narratives that structure people's experiences in the market, society, and political sphere. The next chapter considers how these narratives explain individuals' sense of disorientation.

7

Deprivations

ALTERNATIVE UNDERSTANDINGS OF SOCIAL HIERARCHY

Hard work is important because, without it, we wouldn't have the
United States. Somebody's got to pick up the slack for the people who don't do
nothing.
—Violet Lammy, 43, recovering crack addict in Youngstown trailer park

The previous chapter presented a clearer understanding of how white working class people establish their sense of identity in East London and Youngstown, as a form of social status that integrates overlapping divisions of class and culture. While this explains the construction of political identities and therefore political constituencies, it does not explain the different ways individuals behave within these constituencies—the primary question of this study. This is because individuals interpret their position in social, economic, and political hierarchies in myriad ways. By investigating variation in these self-understandings, we can build more sophisticated hypotheses about individual political behavior beneath the level of institutions and social boundaries. How do respondents in East London and Youngstown connect the redrawing of social boundaries with the collapse of their respective economies? How do these narratives explain individuals' sense of disorientation and their subsequent political behavior?

In this chapter, I analyze respondents' personal narratives of disorientation and find that the British and American subjects both turn to antecedent symbolic repertoires to explain their contemporary social differences and their marginality. A "symbolic repertoire" refers to the way a group represents shared experiences to explain social identities and social processes. These collective representations are derived from and reinforced by the meanings and values that groups have available to them. While respondents in East London understand their predicament through the prism of nativity and its purported entitlements, those from Youngstown view their economic decline through the prism of a dubious American meritocracy and stereotypes about black people's exploitation of welfare. I contend that subjects use these constructed repertoires to rationalize their plight and inform their political behavior. The remainder of the chapter offers an alternative hypothesis to explain individuals' political behavior. I contend that political behavior can be explained by the extent of individuals' sense of relative social deprivation—that is, the extent to which they have lost social status over time vis-à-vis other groups in American and British society. I find that such deprivation is closely tied to American and British respondents' different symbolic repertoires of their local social hierarchies.

Symbolic Repertoires

In both East London and Youngstown, respondents reveal the presence of a near-constant internal dialogue, which seeks to explain their predicament and the redrawing of social boundaries based on class and ethno-racial difference. Their rehearsal of their ever-evolving personal narratives with fellow citizens consolidates a litany of stories about heartbreak, desperation, disappointment, and betrayal—recounting the tragic steps leading to a world where white working class people have been displaced to their society's periphery. Each story is contextualized in a broader understanding about how the plight of Youngstown and East London fits into the wider American and British social system. To illuminate this dialogue, I solicited each respondent's personal narrative of disorientation. Synthesizing their responses, I find that the British and American subjects both turn to antecedent symbolic repertoires to explain their contemporary social differences and their marginality. The remainder of this chapter examines the nature and endurance of British and American variants.

East London and Heritage

In Barking and Dagenham, class identity is a complex source of pride and limitation. For the British, class is thought to be a matter of heritage in a post-feudal society that is not characterized by America's social egalitarianism. Symbolic repertoires frame class as inherited—a matter of blood, linguistics, geography, and appearance—and therefore subject to entitlement. Despite their families' exodus from the East End, most residents of Barking and Dagenham have maintained strong Cockney accents, characterized by monophthongization, vowel lowering, and glottal stops. Exemplary pronunciations include:

mouth	MAUF	little	LIH—oo
hero	EE—roh	Waterloo	WOH—uh—loo
brother	BRUH—vah	marrow	MAH—rah

Andy Dewhurst is a 31-year-old news editor in Dagenham. "You never class yourself as anything other than working class," he says. "You can keep whatever company you like, and have as much money as you'd like, but you'll always be a product of your working class roots [. . .] a working class boy done good." The idea that class identity is static throughout personal mobility and time is a product of people's comfort with their identity, but also the endurance of the stereotypes and judgment as imposed by others.

In discussing their social position in British society, those interviewed intertwine their social affinities with the sense of rejection by others in superior classes. In his early twenties, Dewhurst was accepted for an internship with London's working class newspaper, the *Sun*. On his first day, he told me, editors segregated interns of working class origins from wealthier interns who were wearing bespoke suits and spoke "proper" English. He and interns from working class Manchester and Bolton were placed on the Images and Photography Desk, while the students from wealthier backgrounds were placed on the more prestigious News Desk. "A working class person needs to work much harder than a middle-class person to get ahead," he said in hindsight. "You'll be offered more chances and get more feet in the door if you're well spoken and your parents know the right people. My dad knows the right people, but only if you want to get into the timber supply business! The working class aren't blameless because we would know more middle-class people if we trusted them more than we do. But if someone speaks well, or wears a suit, people immediately think they're being judged."

This self-awareness among Barking and Dagenham's historical working class has produced a sort of reluctant reverence for those above them, but also complacency about personal aspiration. School headmaster Fred Toulson said that "endemic in British white working class society is a certain anti-intellectualism that is connected to a sentiment that some people were 'born to rule' in the public [elite] schools. There was this sense that there was a ceiling for the 'Dagenham child.' People are reluctant to change the status quo, until there's a famine, and then there's a revolution. So where you come from creates certain expectations that exist for donkey's years. The class system in this country is not based on money. It's based on the way you speak, where you went to school, legacy, where you were born. People will tell you it doesn't exist. But it does. In the United States, you can get by on a meritocracy of cash." Ewan Nickelson, a recently laid-off 22-year-old pipeline worker from Goresbrook, says, "I'm not as important as the prime minister. There's a reason for people to be in power—like the illuminati. Then there are people that run their own businesses, people that have money, famous people. I've been brought up without much money."

Savage (2005) argues that British workers define their class in terms of authenticity and ordinariness. They take pride in being ordinary, authentic individuals because it is what distinguishes them from the middle and upper classes, who act out of social motives rather than naturally. "Even if I got really rich, I'd still have a working class mentality," explains Luke Wilkinson, a 25-year-old who works for his father's flooring business in Barking. "I'd have a nice car and all that, but the people I get along with are here. I can't get along with people from Chelsea. They look down on people who speak like us East End Cockneys. My mate from here started a job in Chelsea, and they are quite stuck up with him over there with all of his 'Allo Darlin!' I think that if I went for the same job against someone from Chelsea, they would get it because of the way I speak and the way I look. They wouldn't wear tracksuit bottoms. You're labeled a 'chav.'" "Chav" is a pejorative label for white working class individuals in Britain, complete with stereotypes of belligerence, stupidity, and low-brow culture (Jones 2011).

Beneath Some, Above Others

Though they are subject to such derogatory labeling outside of Barking and Dagenham, the borough's white working class people create separation between themselves and a would-be underclass of others. This underclass is composed of white people without the dignity of employment, morality, and self-discipline, instead characterized by interviewees as long-term benefit-dependent, criminal, or addicted to alcohol or narcotics. Referring to the Scratton Farms Social Club, local resident Emma Terrington said, "In that social club, half the men are stuffing half the women, and half the women are stuffing half the men. I don't want to watch the drunkards perform or associate myself. I don't want to sound like a snob because I'm not above nobody. I'll talk to anybody. But they're commoner's muck. I've run rougher pubs, but I don't like their language and don't need that anymore." Down the street, Pam Reed, the Mill House Social Club's bartender, said, "Us white people don't get out of bed for work, and some of the foreigners will work for it. I think that's all wrong too. A job's a job, and all the boys on the dole should know that."

This sense of superiority has rendered Barking and Dagenham's white working class a social positionality—beneath some but above others—for centuries. It has contributed to the sentiment that Britain's white working class people, with all their flaws, are central to British society—that there was dignity in their struggle, authenticity in their roots, moral virtue in their culture, and an exclusivity that upwardly mobile minorities could not access. This has informed a sense of class pride and bounded solidarity that has pervaded the borough of Barking and Dagenham since the 1930s.

There are several related historical explanations for this sense of class pride and solidarity in Britain. E. P. Thompson (1963) traces the contemporary working class identity back to the eighteenth century, when ideological and structural changes brought about by the French and Industrial Revolutions caused British workers to become class conscious. Similarly, Laslett's (1971: 53–54) history of social changes in Britain traces this position above some and below others to the preindustrial world, a one-class society that pitted a poor, occupationally diverse group of servants against a prevailing class of elites. In the nineteenth century, Marx (1870) argued that the British aristocracy fomented popular hatred for Irish workers among the English working class to prevent the two oppressed groups from uniting. By perceiving the Irish as competitors, British workers strengthened their own subjection to the landed aristocracy.

Given this rather unique history and heritage-based solidarity, white working class interviewees have been reluctant to admit immigrants of foreign origins to what is clearly a cultural—even while ostensibly class-based—fellowship. Immigrants cannot cite tours of service and sacrifice to the United Kingdom's military. They cannot cite decades of contribution to the welfare state. They are ethnically, linguistically, religiously, and often behaviorally distinct. Many immigrants are not even of humble origins, as London's service sector is increasingly a home for overqualified recession refugees from Eastern and Southern Europe. I encountered a 26-year-old Romanian with a Masters degree in Horticulture shoveling dirt in Creekmouth as a landscape laborer.

Rather than identify with immigrants' parallel struggle, white working class interviewees frame them as competitors for the employment and services of Britain's government. Increasingly, they feel displaced by immigrants; not in material terms—Barking and Dagenham's working class whites have always been of modest means and hardly expect that to change—but rather in positional terms. The presence of immigrants has attenuated working class pride, because the working class perceives less value attributed to their rooted authenticity and nationalist sacrifices. They sense a positional shift to the fringe of British society where they once placed an underclass of addicts, delinquents—and indeed, foreigners.

A False Construction

The idea that white working class people were once closer to the center is a false historic construction. This construction follows naturally from a symbolic repertoire that attributes virtue to nativity (vis-à-vis foreignness). For half a century, there was a carved place for white working class people in Barking and Dagenham's economy and society. Nativity was a currency inside factories where job openings were passed to friends and family members, inside working men's clubs that discriminated according to neighborhood, and inside government offices where Britons were entitled to housing and other benefits.

Though idealized, the British social system of nativist entitlement locked the white working class into their social and economic stratum. It nevertheless connects closely to the imaginaries that the British government has constructed to honor veterans of the world wars in the 1920s and 1950s, to appeal to organized labor in the 1960s and 1970s, and to comfort natives in the presence of increasing numbers of immigrants since the 1990s. The British (and more generally European) politics of assimilation emphasize adaptation by immigrants toward a liberal order and national way of life (Joppke 2007) that flatters the belief that such a thing exists and is worth preserving.

The British government's more blatant disregard for nativity has emerged concurrently with the British economy's shift to an elite-driven, global, capitalist meritocracy that features much greater inequality. Mirroring trends in other parts of the developed world, this capital-intensive economy shifts production to low-rent overseas venues and recruits immigrants to fill the skilled positions that nationals are unqualified to take and the unskilled positions that nationals are unwilling to take—displacing the integral roles once filled by unionized working class white people. Their privileged place in the British economy having disappeared with many of the social protections demanded by unions, nativity has become a value expressed by no one other than white working class people themselves, the few pubs left standing, and the nationalist political parties that appeal to them—defenders of an era that departed, if it ever really existed in the way it is remembered.

Youngstown and the American Dream

In Youngstown, respondents conceive class to be a temporary state in a dynamic economy, despite their actual entrenchment in a particular economic situation. The American Dream is thought to offer an equal opportunity to succeed to people of all backgrounds, reward hard work with upward mobility, and render individuals a sense of agency over the direction of their lives. Accordingly, white working class people understand their historically dignified, blue-collar position as the product of Youngstown's meritocracy (see DiTomaso 2012). For a century, Steeltown attracted destitute and ambitious immigrants from all corners of

Europe and the Levant, who sought to take control of their lives and invest their labor in an industry that offered stability and better quality of life for their families. The symbolic repertoire of agency, self-sufficiency, and mobility endures in respondents' propensity to place blind faith in the continuation of an economic reality that deteriorated with the steel mills in the 1980s.

The American Dream occupies a space in people's rhetoric reserved exclusively for the likes of Jesus Christ and George Washington. Many respondents bend their harsh realities to exhibit the Dream's endurance in trying times. Others bend their interpretation of the American Dream to align it with their own experience. Most respondents are worse off than their parents despite their best efforts. Many work for companies on flexible contracts and earn incomes that afford little long-term stability and qualify them for few public benefits. Many are one misfortune away from a life of poverty and can do little to ensure that their children's future is not predetermined to follow a similar, if not worse, course. Despite weighty evidence to the contrary, most insist that the American Dream exists or that hard work pays off, albeit with caveats. Frequently, these caveats would otherwise be quite damning to the American Dream they construct. Some examples follow:

EVELYN: Hard work and pride pays off. You may not get a $300,000 house, but you respect yourself. You give your employer 100% from nine-to-five, they give you money, and from there, it's your life. I don't think everyone has an equal shot though. It's by birth, and some people start with more money or intelligence than others.

PAUL: The American Dream exists but only to an extent. Not sure how far you can go. It's easier to come from old money.

TIMMY: People still respect hard work, but luck and relationships play a role.

MARGE: I want to say that hard work matters, but I firmly believe that it is not enough. The American Dream works because people are busting into this country to live that dream.

TANK: Hard work pays off because I can look at different jobs I did and say "You know what? I built that." Manny calls me his right hand man. A little pat on the back makes all the shit worth it. This shit wasn't built by God.

RALPH: In some instances, hard work pays off, but in others, it gets you scorn from other workers.

NELLY: Hard work pays off if you're working for yourself, but not if you're working for somebody else. I think that the American Dream exists if you have family stability, a good education, and faith. But not if you're brought up on welfare. Then I don't think you have a chance. You're just too focused on meeting your basic needs.

Respondents are reluctant to count out the possibility of Youngstown's res-urrection. Many presage Youngstown's rebirth as a national fracking hub, and in doing so, renew their faith in the existence of the American Dream and its provision of opportunity, agency, and mobility. However, the fracking industry emerges in an era that features a more mobile labor force and weaker unions to promote worker safety, provide fair compensation, and prevent environ-mental hazards. Rather than rebuild the civic infrastructure that facilitated the earlier corporate responsibility that most Americans now view as voluntary, Youngstown's white working class views the American Dream as an ever-present actuality that exists independent of oversight, standards, and popular mobiliza-tion. Capitalism gave, and capitalism hath taken away.

From interviews, respondents were unlikely to identify structural reasons for Youngstown's predicament. Indeed, those who understand the economy as naturally promoting upward mobility correspondingly blame themselves. John Avery, age 46, worked as a foreman at a window factory for 24 years, but was laid off in 2008. Now a laborer in a smaller metal shop, he has a 9-year-old daughter with his estranged girlfriend and currently lives in the Austintown suburb with his parents. "Everyone knows where Youngstown is," he said. "We're known as the steel capital of the world and that brings people back. There are still a few mills kicking and it's because of that history. They closed down before and it was because the workers exploited the companies. They didn't know how good they had it. The companies gave them everything they could want, the unions, everything, until the jobs were gone. This generation will be more grateful." Like other respondents, John views companies' earlier provisions as voluntary rather than required by a civic infrastructure that lev-eraged commercial dependencies on local labor into social protections and benefits.

John's tendency to blame the individual worker aligns with McDermott's (2006: 38–49) determination that whiteness can function as a "burden" or "mark of inferiority"; when working class whites believe that they have fallen short of the meritocratic yardstick traditionally attributed to their more success-ful middle- and upper-class counterparts, their self-esteem and self-evaluation plummets. Sharone (2013) finds similar trends among white-collar workers who are prone to self-blame. He argues that a conventional focus on personal-ity, fit, and interpersonal connections above skills and qualifications makes the unemployed think "there's something wrong with me" as opposed to "there's something wrong with the system."

Fantasia and Voss (2004: 9) attribute the loose organization of Americans around class as the result of an individualist ideology that stymies labor soli-darity. This assignment of social self-worth is confirmed by the beliefs of middle-class compatriots. Dudley (1994: 73–79) documents the "meritocratic individualist" view of the educated middle-class in deindustrialized Kenosha, Wisconsin. Middle-class professionals, contrary to the sentiments of the working class, see deindustrialization as the inevitable result of prolonged incompetence; the working class worker, in this sense, was deemed to be at the heart of economic, social, and even political failure (73–79).

Public officials concur. Democratic Party official Rick Hanley said, "America is still rough and tumble, where the fittest survives. Just because I strive to get everyone a fair shot doesn't mean they get one. They still gotta try [. . .] The cold reality of America is that you got to look out for yourself. You gotta work hard, have a little bit of luck, then you'll be okay. If you don't want to, then you'll be wherever your lot takes you."

But even in the best of times, Youngstown's economy was not as meritocratic as it is remembered to have been. Unions, mafias, and the Democratic political machine were engaged in cronyism, corruption, and an elaborate system of favors. And each institution was as bigoted as the steel manufacturers they attempted to keep in check. However, to suggest that the white working class's backbreaking work and extended hours on the job were not what secured their stable lifestyle is to desecrate the labor they glorify. Like nativity in the United Kingdom, Youngstown's white working class can claim little else to ensure their future prosperity. With depressed levels of civic engagement, if they cannot believe in the virtue and determinacy of labor, there is little else to believe in.

A Matter of Faith

As measures of mobility drop precipitously from generation to generation and the American economy is characterized by wider inequality, the American Dream is increasingly a matter of faith. The United States is now developing a class of people who effectively inherit poverty or working class status. According to recent OECD statistics, the US Gini coefficient has increased from 0.316 in the 1970s to 0.357 in the 2000s, which makes America one of the most unequal developed countries in the world. Recent studies also reveal levels of economic mobility that are much lower than the interviewees' perception. According to a Pew Charitable Trust study (2013), 70% of Americans who are raised in the two lowest income quintiles never make it to the middle quintile.

A variety of research emphasizes the deterioration of social ladders and social cohesion. Massey (2007) points to an increasingly less progressive American tax structure. Reardon (2011) points to the widening achievement gap between children from high- and low-income families, although he attributes this trend to a higher association between income and achievement rather than to greater income inequality. Also noting that the American intergenerational mobility rate has remained roughly flat, Mazumder (2012) argues that the widening class gap in children's academic performance is another alarming sign from the standpoint of economic mobility. Putnam et al. (2012) attribute low mobility to the growing class gap in social trust, educational achievement, and extracurricular involvement among youth, all of which are strong predictors of personal success. Considering this growing class discrepancy, Putnam et al. conclude that America is becoming more and more of "a caste system," where children inherit their social standing from their parents.

The alarming economic mobility predictions defy the ideal of the American Dream in which Youngstown residents so strongly believe. The respondents' optimism, however, is consistent with national trends. According to the 2013 Pew Charitable Trust report on economic mobility, in fact, 40% of Americans consider it common for a person born to a poor family to work their way up the economic ladder. In 2011, 54% of Americans believed they would be better off in 10 years.

Cracks in the Façade

Now, even in Youngstown, some respondents are taking notice. "There are a lot of people who are living charmed lives who haven't worked hard but knew the right people thanks to how they grew up and where they're from," said Leah Perry, the 29-year-old manufacturing clerk. "I mean, what year is it? Nepotism is still very much at play. And anyone who says it's not is full of shit. The American Dream that me and my parents were sold has become impossible. It's impossible to buy a house, to get a raise, there's a huge disparity."

The 42-year-old flea market stall owner, Gillian McPhee, said, "The American Dream works for some people. Other people just live day-to-day. If you do have a dream, this town will find a way to shoot it down. Hard work pays off if you're not under someone else. The harder someone sees you work around here, the more they will take advantage of you. That's this town."

Unemployed 49-year-old mother of three Isabel Crane said, "At this age, we should be so much further along. For two people who've worked all their lives, the only way to have the American Dream is to hit the lottery. That's the new American Dream. We've had setbacks, but we've gotten less support. For the white working class, the American Dream left in the fifties and sixties when companies left to find cheap labor. I'm not asking for wealth, just comfort. I want to pay my bills, pay for my children's education, and put a little money aside."

Thirty-eight-year-old construction worker Tank Schumaker said, "The American Dream died years ago. Greed, loss of religion, liberal political correctness, you can't do anything anymore. People can't get or stay married because it takes so much effort to survive. My ex-fiancée said, 'You're never around.' But I was working to get a better life for us. No one has time for their kids. It's the American Nightmare. The way I see it, you don't have a fucking shot. But it's people like us who make this country go. It's the greed of a few that fuck the masses. I'm a single, white male; I get fucked left and right. [. . .] I should have pursued my dreams, but I was born into a construction family." For the Youngstown respondents who question the American Dream's endurance, it is increasingly difficult to justify their social position according to the capitalist symbolic repertoires their countrymen espouse.

The historical social status of white working class people in the United Kingdom and the United States is not all that different, but one is understood as a product of entitlement while the other is understood as a product of hard work. Though idealized, the British system of entitlement locked white working class people into their status, while the American system of meritocracy really only existed for white workers. In scope, both markets have simply become more open to minority advancement and more difficult to ascend for all. The next section asks: how do these symbolic repertoires and local political institutions connect with observed variation in political behavior between Youngstown and East London's working class white populations?

Expressions of Social Hierarchy

To solicit the personal experiences of interviewees in these hierarchies, I presented each with a set of four concentric circles drawn on paper. I explained that the diagram was a model of their society—that people in the innermost ring were the most central, the most important, the most influential individuals, and that the people in each outward ring were less and less central, less and less important, the farther out the ring was located. I asked each respondent to use their finger to tell me where they believed their place was in this diagram and what kind of people occupied the other circles. I also asked where they thought people like them were situated one or two generations ago.

My objective was to stimulate respondents to visualize and describe the organization of social hierarchies, as they understood them. Their responses stimulated the symbolic repertoires white working class people use to understand their social position. And by referring to their perceptions of the past, this exercise also engaged personal historical narratives and revealed the extent of the social deprivation they feel. In this section, I will document variation in subjects' social hierarchy models across the cases and show how models in Youngstown and East London connect with the symbolic repertoires employed by respondents in the two milieux.

East London

In East London, respondents depicted models that were based on the stratification of social groups (see Figure 7.1). These generally placed Britain's landed or cultural aristocracy in the center. Some made references to Her Majesty "The Queen" and "the Royal Family," while others pointed to "politicians," affluent "bankers," "footballers," and "immigrants." Some actually enumerated a hierarchy of ethnicities that shuffled orders of "Eastern Europeans," "South Asians," "Muslims," "Africans," and others. A few respondents preceded immigrants with a class of professionals that included "solicitors" (lawyers), "doctors," and "people working for the government."

Nearly all placed white working class Britons inside the outermost circle, while some place themselves beyond the bounds of this outermost circle. Notable exceptions were respondents who reserved this out of bounds space for members of an underclass variably composed of "criminals," "addicts," and "gypsies."

"The lowest of the low in this community are the traveler Gypsies, who are looked at with disgust," said Ashton Roberts. "Then just above them, it's us. Then Asian people. Then black people. Then Eastern Europeans. And then comes the middle class, because they're still able to get away from it all. Multiculturalism— that idea is above everything else. They want it to look like everyone gets on. And the price to pay is that some of the worst places in Britain are white working class."

This understanding of the British social hierarchy reflects a symbolic repertoire that construes social positioning as a matter of origin. This model promotes and demotes according to the arbitrary favoring of one heritage over another. From subjects' statements, the favoritism accords with the preferences of a British state, largely framed as a capricious source of incomprehensible power. It is understood to have valued, at one time, the nativity and devotion of white working class Britons, and correspondingly showered them with support and resources in the form of housing, employment, entitlements, and homogeneity. But, it is understood to have inexplicably turned its favor toward immigrants and people of foreign origins, altering the social system to accommodate the needs of the newcomers and deprive natives.

"I can't do nothing," said 30-year-old Ollie Marks. "It's not down to us. It's those people in government, and when I ask myself why they do it, I just have

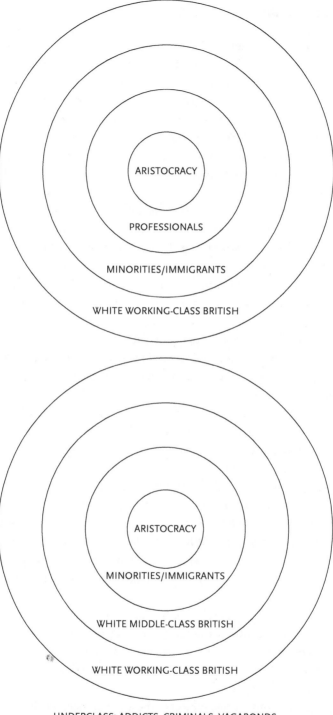

Figure 7.1 BARKING AND DAGENHAM SOCIAL HIERARCHIES. Each interviewee was presented with a set of four concentric circles drawn on paper. They were told that the diagram was a model of their society—that people in the innermost ring were the most central, the most important, the most influential individuals, and that the people in each outward ring were less and less central, less and less important. This figure outlines conventional models among British respondents.

to think it's something sinister. I don't believe in democracy. It's just a covert dictatorship." Still based on heritage, this new model is thought to discriminate against the white working class in the provision of government benefits, in the regulation of borders, and in a grander acquiescence to the European Union that incrementally deprives the British of their self-determination.

Respondents acknowledge a systemic turn toward a meritocracy, but frame this shift as it relates to the relative ascendance of immigrants and ethnic minorities and the relative deprivation of white Britons. Most believe that the British social system was previously meritocratic, insofar as hard work was rewarded inside of each hierarchical circle. Respondents frequently cited the hours invested by family members who exerted themselves on assembly lines, docks, and warehouse floors to earn a living. They are frustrated that the current social system grants immigrants access to the same meritocracy and offers advantages that they believe are not provided to white Britons, such as affirmative action policies, public housing preference, and favoritism disguised as antiracism platforms.

"The Council [bureaucrat] said, if you're not black, Asian, a lesbian or pregnant, you can't get a flat," said 23-year-old Lexie Browning, who has asked to be relocated by the council. "I feel like I'm on the outside. I'm so depressed. I feel like I'm always begging."

"If there's a job interview and an immigrant doesn't get it, they'll say the employer is racist," said 22-year-old Nicki Josephs. "I feel like they're taking our jobs, homes, and everything that the government is trying to do for English people, they're getting it first."

Because of the rigidity with which Britain has historically understood class divisions, respondents do not believe that immigrants will ever enter the ranks of the aristocracy. No matter how wealthy someone becomes, he or she is thought to always maintain class origins. White working class people therefore have trouble envisioning a meritocracy in which people may move from one circle to the next; they see only a static system of entitlement that has unfathomably shifted loyalties.

"[Asians] walk around like they're higher than us, when we were the ones who welcomed them into our country," said 18-year-old Terry Hammonds. "Everyone is really annoyed with it. I feel like I'm on the outside looking inside to the immigrants. We can't communicate with them. We can't do nothing. We just sit here and let it happen."

Younger generations are less subject to these beliefs because they do not have the longitudinal perspective to acknowledge the relative ascendance of immigrants vis-à-vis the antecedent position of the white working class. They balance family members' idyllic depictions of the past with their existence in a meritocracy that is concerned less with origins and more about the bottom line.

Some acknowledge this new reality. "A lot of people blame foreigners, but everyone's got an equal opportunity at the end of the day," said Ewan Nickelson, a 22-year-old, laid-off construction worker who is taking courses in plumbing. "And yeah, a lot of foreign people do get jobs over English people, but I have a lot of Asian and black friends. I was replaced by cheaper Polish painters, but my time will come. I get along with people. I was brought up with diversity. And besides, there's nothing you can do about it except change the government."

Others reproduce their parents' and grandparents' sense of deprivation. "You just feel like you're not meant to be here," said Harry Carlisle, a 24-year-old mover. "It'll take one big thing to spark it all off. And once it starts, it ain't going to stop. You can feel the tension. It will be released, and in such a way that the whole country's going to have to do something about it. How long are people going to put up with it? I blame my parents and their generation because they just swallowed the change and accepted it. They just went about it the wrong way. They were pretty racist. It should not be about color; it should be about work ethic and the nature of the system."

As I did in field interviews, this book's survey of British respondents presented a set of four concentric circles as a model of status in society and asked respondents to place themselves among the rings—a measure of abstract social centrality. The descriptive results in Table 7.1 shows that, on average, working class people place themselves further to the fringe. The results also show that—contrary to British white working class perceptions—there is effectively a sliding scale of social self-placement according to class and income. These results reflect a more American conception of social hierarchy—one driven by income, rather than birthright or heritage.

Youngstown

In Youngstown, respondents constructed models that were based on the stratification of income groups (see Figure 7.2). These generally presented a sliding scale of wealth from the center outward. An important exception are those respondents who interrupted this sliding scale with welfare recipients who were referred to as "people on welfare," "long-term benefits," "welfare queens," and "the whining poor." Those whose scaled hierarchies were interrupted by welfare recipients invariably placed this group immediately outside the central circle occupied by "the wealthy," "politicians," "the rich," and the "people making six and seven figures." Respondents generally placed themselves outside a circle reserved for the middle class. Depending on where welfare recipients were situated, white working class people were therefore either inside the outermost ring or inside the penultimate ring.

Table 7.1 **Perceived Social Centrality**

	United Kingdom Mean	**United States Mean**
Education		
University Education	2.29	2.73
No University Education	2.17	2.48
Age		
18–24	2.25	2.44
25–39	2.21	2.62
40–59	2.24	2.49
60 +	2.22	2.68
Self-reported Social Class		
Upper	2.35	3.02
Middle	2.24	2.67
Lower Middle	2.20	2.35
Working	2.05	2.75
Gender		
Male	2.28	2.56
Female	2.18	2.54
Working Class		
White Working Class	2.17	2.48
All Other Whites	2.28	2.73

British and American respondents were asked to report how central they are to their society by placing themselves on one of the four concentric circles shown in this chapter. 4 indicates that the respondent feels people like them are most central and important to society, 1 indicates least central and important. Working class is here is defined as having no college education. Note that Americans have different understandings of "working class," which skews the self-reported class data.

"Education and money drive power differences," explained Will Macmillan, a 48-year-old union electrician. "The days when being white could get you closer to the center are over. And I'm glad they're over. We're outside but we're not on the far outside, because I still feel like things could get worse. There was a time when a man could work 40 hours of honest labor and let his wife stay with the kids, own his home, give children the choice of whether or not to go to college. But something has happened."

"I feel like I'm on the outside," said Leah Perry. "But that is based on my choices. I didn't have to have a baby at 21. I didn't have to take the job I have. But

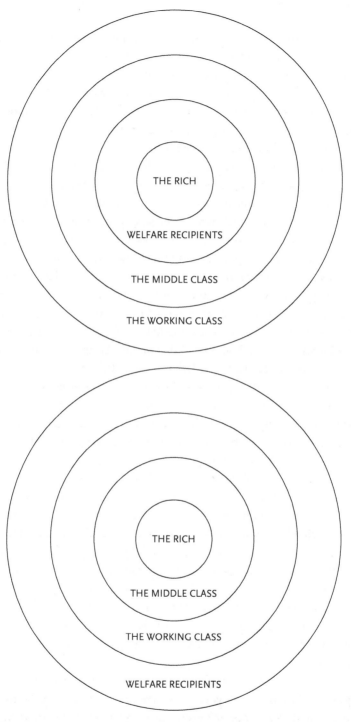

Figure 7.2 Youngstown Social Hierarchies. Each interviewee was presented with a set of four concentric circles drawn on paper. They were told that the diagram was a model of their society—that people in the innermost ring were the most central, the most important, the most influential individuals, and that the people in each outward ring were less and less central, less and less important. This figure outlines conventional models among American respondents.

we benefit the least from the government. You're not living in a society where the less fortunate are getting a hand—or at least a hand that is helpful. The wealthy are getting protected. I'd take welfare if I qualified. Shit, you pay into it. It's like, are you also too proud to drive on the streets that your taxes built, pave, and light? It's a caste system based on wealth. It doesn't matter to them if food stamps got cut, if insurance premiums go up, if a factory they don't own closes. There's not that much of a difference between us on the outside. Just because I don't qualify for welfare doesn't mean that I can afford to pay my bills any easier."

This understanding of the American social hierarchy reflects a symbolic repertoire that construes social positioning as a matter of material wealth. This model promotes and demotes according to the possession of resources. From subjects' statements, this structure corresponds to a system predicated on mobility—an economy that offers equal opportunity to succeed and renders individuals a sense of agency over the direction of their lives. Such dynamism reflects respondents' belief in the persistence of the American Dream, which understands the concentric circles as milestones rather than rigid boundaries. According to Lamont (2000: 97–116), the importance that workers attribute to the American Dream also contributes to their ambivalent attitude toward the upper classes. On the one hand, they acknowledge that the material wealth of the upper classes is the result of their ambition and intelligence—skills that the interviewees admire. On the other hand, however, working class whites draw a clear moral boundary between themselves and the upper classes. They reject middle-class values such as competitiveness, the quality of their social relationships, all while emphasizing their own working class values, like integrity and responsibility.

In their reflections about how the American economy has changed, Youngstown's white working class construes their higher status from the 1950s and 1960s as a matter of higher incomes, rather than a matter of structural advantages provided by unions and a social system that discriminated according to race. This finding corroborates McCall's (2013) suggestion that Americans calibrate their understandings of inequality based off of "a tolerable level of inequality" or "any level [of inequality in pay between those at the top and bottom] that is compatible with widespread opportunities for a good job with fair pay for most workers" (11). The presence of the "undeserving rich" (ibid.) and an "underserving poor" frame the social positionality of Youngstown's white working class.

"The Cafaros are in that middle circle with the very wealthy," explained Timmy Butler. "Then you get your politicians and business owners, me on the third circle, and the very poor on the outside who nobody cares about. My family probably felt closer to the middle when my grandfather was a steelworker and foreman, and there were a lot of them in Youngstown. [. . .] My grandfather's life, from an orphanage to a sixth-grade education to forming a successful family and working at a management level, that'll never happen again. I've plateaued. I'm basically a laborer."

The working class white American is increasingly caught between what Sennett and Cobb (1972: 23) call the "contradictory codes of respect in the America of their generation." People like Timmy feel that they have lost the industriousness of their father and mother while simultaneously falling short of the "cultured" ideal espoused by the American meritocratic ideology. Timmy brands himself as "a laborer" without the dignity of his forebears or the means to ascend among the ranks of his own generation.

Given the meritocratic equality that characterizes respondents' depictions of the American past, many were frustrated by the government's provision of welfare benefits to people they believe are undeserving (see DiTomaso 2012). Respondents conventionally frame welfare as a matter of morality and dignity— a choice that individuals make when they are unwilling or too indolent to pursue employment—even while many of these respondents accepted welfare provisions to supplement low incomes. Lamont (2000: 131–141) writes that a majority of American working class whites attributes the misfortunes of the poor to their moral worth rather than to structural conditions. In doing so, they draw a net and unequivocal class boundary between themselves and "the people below" by appealing to an ideal of self-sufficiency. However, many Youngstown respondents did not believe that such self-sufficiency was valued by society, which they accused of favoring the pleas of welfare recipients over the silent industry of the working class.

Respondents' moralizing pronouncements on welfare align with the general tendency in the United States to distinguish the deserving poor from the undeserving (Steensland 2008).[1] This connects to a general perception that "welfare" refers exclusively to cash payments, rather than food stamps, unemployment, housing, or disability benefits. Given low hourly minimum wage standards in Ohio ($7.25 for small businesses and $7.85 for large businesses), cash payments are perceived to rival the incomes of low-wage workers who "work for a living."[2]

Though many respondents described their frustration with welfare recipients in general terms, some suggested that welfare recipients were disproportionately African American. This corroborates what Kinder and Kam (2009: 182–191) suggest is an ethnocentric inclination among whites to support means-tested welfare cuts; unlike social insurance and programs investing in human capital (e.g. Head Start), whites disproportionately associate means-tested welfare programs with black recipients. Brown (1991) similarly contends that the American welfare system reproduces the color line, casting relief-program recipients as black and Social Security recipients as white. The association of government-supplied welfare with African-American recipients effectively confuses the symbolic status of working class whites within the American social structure. Welfare operates as a contradictory "symbol of status" (Gusfield 1963: 15).

Whereas working class white people view welfare depreciatively, they also recognize that government support symbolizes a certain badge of respect. The perception that minorities receive governmental support to a greater extent than struggling whites effectively strips working class whites of their sense of deservingness. The perceived status of poor whites is, in this sense, called into question. "The minorities that get me are the ones that are uneducated, that realize they have no future, so they get knocked up [pregnant] and collect," said Fran. "Not all of them do it; many work. But I think that if you're black or Hispanic, you can get almost anything. Meanwhile, I go to the welfare office, and get looked at like 'Why aren't you working?' They come in on drugs and get free food stamps, medical, and unemployment. They know you can only get welfare for a child for the first five years. So they have babies every five years. The squeaky wheel gets all the oil. I've always been one to take care of my own. We're hardworking poor people."

However, because cash payments (and all other forms of government benefits) are perceived to be equally available to white individuals, respondents do not depict a social system that is structurally discriminatory. They acknowledge their own capacity to solicit government support. "A lot of people like to link welfare to race, but that's not entirely true," said Iggy Nagy, an electrician. "Yeah there are a lot of black people abusing the system, but there are some white people who do the same thing. They do it with worker's compensation claims too."

Rather, castigation of African Americans is in the more gratuitous interest of establishing moral superiority in the absence of institutionalized superiority. Unlike their British counterparts, very few Youngstown respondents suggested that white Americans are entitled to greater government support. This is partially because African Americans can compete with white peoples' claims of heritage, but also because most respondents in Youngstown were quick to acknowledge their own immigrant roots. In light of this history as the ostracized Other, they view their ancestors' social ascendance past the ranks of African Americans as a matter of industry, not prejudice.

Social Deprivation and Political Behavior

The previous section describes the way respondents in Youngstown and East London characterize the organization of social hierarchies and demonstrates how these depictions are informed by symbolic repertoires of class position. This section will elaborate how these hierarchies structure respondents' senses of deprivation, and consequently, their political behavior. By asking respondents to evaluate their position vis-à-vis that of white working class people from previous generations, we may more accurately measure this deprivation, where it exists. Each respondent was simply asked to locate where people like them were situated on the same diagram of concentric circles one or two generations ago.

There was a good deal of variation in respondents' perceived gaps between where they belong in the social order and where they believed themselves to be today, as measured by their self-reported placements on the concentric circle diagram. Those whom I determine to identify a "large gap" between their expected and experienced social position pointed to a two-circle difference—meaning that they moved from one of the middle ranks of the social order to the outer circle or beyond. Those whom I determine to identify a "small gap" between their expected and experienced social position pointed to a one-circle or more marginal difference. And finally, those whom I determine to identify "no gap" between their expected and experienced social position expressed no difference, or a gain in status. I maintained this system of classification across all social hierarchy depictions and across both cases.

Responses suggest a strong relationship between senses of social deprivation and observed habits of political behavior. Those respondents who reported significant regression or "large gap" in the social hierarchy were more likely to participate in anti-system political behavior that used undemocratic tactics to express political preferences. This group of "large gap" respondents also often joined peaceful protest movements. Those respondents who reported a "small gap" or "no gap" at all were more likely to engage in democratic activities or be complacent. Finally, those respondents who understood their social position to be peripheral—and to have always been peripheral—were more likely to be politically withdrawn.[3] These trends are summarized in Figure 7.3. In the remainder of this chapter, I will explain how these different self-understandings may predict variation in political behavior.

	PRO-SYSTEM	ANTI-SYSTEM
ACTIVE	ENGAGEMENT *Small or moderate gap* between expectations and perceptions of centrality in social hierarchies	REBELLION *Large gap* between expectations and perceptions of centrality in social hierarchies
PASSIVE	SITTING OUT *Small or moderate gap* between expectations and perceptions of centrality in social hierarchies	WITHDRAWAL *Very low expectations* of centrality in social hierarchies

Figure 7.3 Hypotheses Explaining Variation in Political Behavior.

East London

With hierarchies defined by rigid social divisions, East London respondents' powerful sense of deprivation was derived from their perceived displacement— from a valued position in the middle of the social order to its periphery. Conventionally, respondents sensed that they would have severe difficulty regaining their antecedent position because it was occupied by people of foreign origins, a group they could and would never join. Similarly, they believed that their origins also prohibited them from ascending to the social ranks of the white middle or professional classes, because class was conceived as a bloodline. The visible and audible attributes that differentiate working class whites substantiate this static understanding of class position, which is compounded by growing economic inequality and immobility in the United Kingdom. However, rather than yearn for this ascent to elevated class categories, most respondents were more concerned to recover their favor from upwardly mobile minority groups, who are thought to replace white Britons in working class jobs, public housing, and the social order.[4]

Given British respondents' symbolic repertoires of class position, the rigidity of these inherited social categories entrenches white working class people into their perceived place in the social hierarchy and creates a widespread sense of determinacy. Most respondents expressed neither a sense of agency over their fate nor a sense of efficacy over the political choices of government officials. This helplessness became problematic among those with the greatest sense of deprivation, because they saw few ways to alter the state of affairs without coercion. Those respondents who identified the largest gaps are also the most likely to participate in anti-system behavior and join anti-system organizations like the BNP or the EDL. With their radical tactics that circumvent peaceful channels of claim-making, these groups reflect their members' frustration with democratic processes and their sense of helplessness in their dealings with government. And the more rigid the social order appears, the more drastic action appears to be required.

While not all respondents who identified large gaps engaged in active, anti-system behavior, all respondents who engaged in active, anti-system behavior identified large gaps—suggesting a necessary, but not sufficient, causal relationship. Respondents who perceive a more meritocratic economy (often despite some setbacks) are less bothered by large gaps in social hierarchies. For them, the meritocracy overrides disadvantages created by extant boundaries. Such a perspective indicates that, for these respondents, institutionalized social advantages are embedded and therefore moderated by a fairer economy. These respondents acknowledge their own agency and self-determination, but lament the greater obstacles that face white working class Britons. They were often democratically active.

Among the remainder of respondents, those who are resigned to a peripheral position on the social hierarchy's outer bounds are more likely to be deliberately withdrawn from the political system. Each of the passive, anti-system respondents communicated very low expectations of their social centrality. They were doubtful about their ability to alter this state, and were doubtful about the government's interest in their sentiments.

Those respondents with small or marginal gaps do not believe that white working class people had been so displaced from their earlier social centrality in Britain. Many complain that minority groups and immigrants were structurally advantaged in their society. However, these respondents do not believe that these advantages reflected an alteration of the social hierarchy. They believe that white working class Britons maintain a special place in the British social order, or they construct social hierarchies that are less defined by ethno-racial boundaries and more defined by wealth disparities.

Youngstown

In Youngstown, social hierarchies are conventionally based on material wealth, which is understood to be dynamic even in the face of growing inequality. As a result, a drop in status is not conceptualized to be nearly as permanent as it is understood to be in East London, where social position is considered a matter of inheritance. The prospect—or myth, some may contend—of mobility rationalizes respondents' peripheral positions and perceived loss of status. So when their hierarchy is shuffled, the British feel a greater sense of loss because they view their place in the hierarchy more rigidly than Americans, who subscribe to the indefatigable American Dream.

Moreover, Youngstown respondents were much less likely to have ever perceived themselves higher up in the American social hierarchy. They do not acknowledge a historically institutionalized advantage, but rather a history of labor struggles. Youngstown's white working class respondents peer through the lens of factory workers who had to endure grueling work and fight for rights and social protections. While they promote a self-image as the reliable backbone of the American economy, they have few illusions of wider recognition by elites. At best, they sense broader dignity in their pursuit of the American Dream to one day reach such recognition.

For these reasons, few of Youngstown's white working class respondents perceive a history of higher status from which they have fallen. Nearly all acknowledge that their city and their families were better off in the 1960s and 1970s. Some are frustrated by the government's support of welfare recipients and minorities. However, they understand the changes to be less structural, and more cyclical—less political, and more personal. Consequently, Youngstown respondents are more likely to assign blame to themselves or their peers. Most respondents identify small gaps between their expected and their experienced social position, and are politically complacent. And those respondents who identify a large gap between their expected and their experienced social position believe that they are one big break away from a recovery.

The primary exceptions are found among older interviewees, who sense the permanency of their drops in status much more than young people. Respondents over age 60 were the most likely to perceive large gaps, and were also more likely to believe that minorities now hold a privileged place in the social hierarchy in the United States, as in the United Kingdom. "I felt closer to society when I was in the military and working for GM," said Mo Kerrigan, a Southside retiree. "But now, I'm meaningless. I don't do anything to promote the good of the community. I'm supposed to lay down and die, rather than suck up all the resources—that's what all the people in the inner circle think of me. Be seen and not heard. Mind your own business. Outside the circle, we are the minority. It doesn't matter what color you are. Money is power and influence, so I don't have anyone at my side or at my back. If I had trouble as a black man, I can call the NAACP. If I had trouble as a Jewish man, I can call the Jewish Defense League. As a white man, I have the KKK. They protect us like the others but they have to hide . . . and they hate Catholics [like me]. We have laws and equal justice for all, but on a sliding scale."

However, Mo and other elderly respondents remain an exception. As long as the American Dream persists alongside perceptions of social mobility, Youngstown respondents will maintain lower levels of deprivation. The absence of observed active anti-system behavior in this case venue is as much a product of this lack of deprivation as it is a product of the paucity of anti-system organizations. Indeed, the aforementioned sovereign citizen movement, patriot groups, and Ku Klux Klan are all known to exist in Youngstown's surroundings, but they have yet to establish a foothold among citizens who see no reason for drastic action. However, as Hochschild's (1995) analysis of disaffected African Americans reveals, a gradual turn away from the American Dream could open up space for "alternative ideologies" (257). Depending on the circumstances and individual experiences, these "alternative ideologies" could realize anti-system behavior (258). Most Youngstown respondents identify small gaps, or they have always found themselves so far to the periphery that they are politically withdrawn anyway. In scope, to predict individuals' political behavior, interview data exhibit the importance of deprivation as it is perceived through lenses tinted by symbolic repertoires of social hierarchies.

8

Measuring Marginality

AMERICAN AND BRITISH SUPPORT FOR THE
RADICAL RIGHT

The frustration-aggression mechanism is ... analogous to the law of gravity.
Men who are frustrated have an innate disposition to do violence to its source
in proportion to the intensity of their frustration, just as objects are attracted to
one another in direct opposition to their relative masses and inverse proportion
to their distance.
—Ted Robert Gurr

The preceding chapters depict two white working class communities, composed of individuals who nearly unanimously attest to a dramatic social, political, and economic decline over the past several decades. At this juncture, we have a solid understanding of East London and Youngstown's histories and contexts, and the variety of political behaviors their transformations have inspired. We have a strong grasp of the role that identity politics and various political institutions have played (and have not played) during this time period. We also have a set of understandings about how individuals' senses of deprivation led to different types of political behavior.

To recap these understandings, interview data point to a strong relationship between senses of deprivation and observed habits of political behavior. As depicted in Figure 7.3, those respondents who reported significant regression or "large gap" in the social hierarchy were more likely to participate in anti-system political behavior that uses undemocratic tactics to express political preferences. Those respondents who reported a "small gap" or "no gap" at all were more likely to engage in democratic activities or be complacent. Finally, those respondents who understood their social position to be peripheral—and to have always been peripheral—were more likely to be politically withdrawn.

These findings tweak my initial hypotheses—grounded in my earlier research on Muslim minority political behavior—in an important way. On the one hand, they reinforce the argument that perceptions of relative deprivation are a key determinant of individual-level political behavior, in particular whether actors will be pro-system or anti-system in orientation. On the other hand, the findings demonstrate that deprivation is not exclusively related to power differences. White working class respondents not only yearn for greater political influence; they yearn to restore a sense of their lost centrality in their countries' and communities' social hierarchy. Their sense of deprivation is therefore as much a matter of power as it is a matter of social stratification. This chapter seeks to apply these concepts, and measure their capacity to explain political behavior among a much broader sample than qualitative research permits.

Using an analysis of survey data that controls for a range of demographic characteristics, I find that social and political forms of deprivation drive people's support for the radical right in Britain and the United States. However, I also find that such deprivation drives people's engagement in peaceful, inclusive, and democratic political behavior. In attempting to distinguish between those who express their deprivation in radical and non-radical ways, I find that supporters of the radical right are disproportionately white, young, lower class, male, without a university education, and ideologically conservative. Those who fit this profile are significantly more likely to back radical parties and candidates. Probing further, I find that those people who are socially or politically deprived and perceive the ascent of historically disadvantaged groups are much more likely to support the radical right than those who are not deprived or do not perceive such an ascent. The data show that senses of social and political deprivation drive white working class people in Britain and America to support the radical right to address what they perceive to be a changing social hierarchy.

Measurement Challenges

Because of the fringe nature of rebellion and radicalism, hypotheses about radical political behavior are rarely measured quantitatively. Indeed, it is a challenge to measure marginality. The withdrawn, the disenchanted, the isolated, and others at society's fringe are—by definition—often challenging to locate, let alone survey. Likewise, those who are politically active but affiliated with illegal or radical groups are often reluctant to report these affiliations. This is a principal reason that ethnographic fieldwork is typically a more effective instrument for developing a complete understanding of the marginalized and developing hypotheses about their behavior and character. However, to establish a broader understanding of these phenomena, polling research is necessary.

The United Kingdom offers an opportunity to conduct such polling about rebellious political behavior and the role of social, economic, and political deprivation. In particular, British politics features a well-known and reasonably established far right flank. The British National Party, the English Defence League, and the English National Alliance are rebellious groups that pursue xenophobic agendas with often-violent tactics. While notorious, their prominence in British public discussion means that, when surveyed, people will be less reluctant to reveal their support for them. The survey for this book was fielded just before the 2015 national election.

Some scholars argue that the United States now features an analogously prominent and more palatable far right, embodied by the antiestablishment Tea Party (Parker and Barreto 2013) and the radical, populist presidential candidacy of Donald Trump (Mudde 2015). However, in order to create a more reliable equivalent in the United States, I also asked American respondents to report their support for a hypothetical third party that was dedicated to "stopping mass immigration, providing American jobs for American workers, preserving America's Christian heritage, and stopping the threat of Islam"—the BNP's platform adapted to the United States. This allows for a more "apples and apples" comparison, though I also collected data about support for the Tea Party and Donald Trump's candidacy, all just before the 2016 primary elections in the United States.[1]

To validly measure people's sense of deprivation, I simply applied interview techniques from the field. Using a scale of 1 to 10, I asked individuals how financially well off they are today, and how financially well off "people like you" were thirty years ago. I asked how much power they have today, and how much power people like them had 30 years ago. And I asked how much politicians care about people like them today, and how much they cared about people like them thirty years ago. The discrepancies in their financial states and political states produced a measure of deprivation (or a lack thereof).

Similarly, to measure people's social deprivation, the surveyed individuals were presented with a concentric circle diagram—identical to that which was presented to people in Youngstown and East London. Using this as a model of social centrality, respondents placed themselves today and placed themselves (or people like them) thirty years ago. I refer to this as a measure of "abstract" centrality. As in the field, I also asked individuals to place a range of other social groups today, including Muslims, women, young people, immigrants, the wealthy, white working class people, nonwhite working class people, and the elderly. As it did in the field, this approach allowed respondents to visualize their social position, their movement over time, and the context of other reference groups' positions (Blumer 1958; Masaoka and Junn 2013). I refer to this as a measure of "contextualized" centrality.

Taken together, these techniques permit a better grasp on a number of questions inspired by this book's fieldwork:

- Does deprivation affect people's support for the radical right?
- Does deprivation affect people's democratic engagement?
- How does deprivation affect people differently?
- How does deprivation relate to perceptions of immigrant centrality?

The remainder of the chapter addresses each question in turn.

Does Deprivation Affect People's Support for the Radical Right?

Before addressing the question of what causes support for a radical right movement or party, it is first worth determining if people who report a willingness to engage in, or prior engagement in, radical right support are more likely to experience greater levels of deprivation than people who would never support the radical right. In other words, is there even a correlation here? In Britain, I classified people as supportive of the radical right if they have voted or would vote for or participate in the activities of the British National Party, the English Defence League, or the English National Alliance—about 7.5% of the sample. I also asked respondent how strongly, on a scale of 0 to 10, they have considered voting for UKIP. Those who reported 5 or higher—indicating serious consideration or inclination—made up 37% of the sample. In the United States, I classified people as radical right if they strongly or somewhat strongly supported Donald Trump (38% of the sample), the Tea Party (35% of the sample), or the hypothetical third party—a whopping 64.5% of the sample.[2]

Ultimately, across all British and American respondents, I found that those who are willing to or have supported the radical right are more likely to have experienced greater deprivation of each type and measure. Radical right respondents reported greater political deprivation as a measure of *political power*, greater political deprivation as a measure of *politicians' care*, greater economic deprivation as a measure of *financial well-being*, and greater *social deprivation* as well. These results hold whether one classifies radical right support in the American context as support for a third party, Donald Trump, or the Tea Party, and in the British context as support for the BNP, EDL, or UKIP. Across every measure of deprivation, those who support the radical right are more deprived than those who do not.

While this substantiates my findings from the field, this analysis does not provide us with much insight into how deprivation actually works, as the difference in deprivation could be explained by any number of other factors. This finding is also descriptive, rather than causal; we merely have seen that those who

Table 8.1 **Impact of Deprivation on Support for the Radical Right**

Deprivation Measure	UKIP Support	UK BNP/EDL Support	US Trump Support	US Tea Party Support	US Hypothetical Radical Right
Politicians Care	+40	+9		+25	+50
Political Power	+35	+5*			+28
Social Centrality	+22	+7			
Social Context				+15*	
Economic Deprivation	+23		+37		

Each number indicates the change in the predicted probabilities of engaging in or expressing a willingness to support the Radical Right, given a movement from minimum levels of deprivation to maximum levels of deprivation with all other factors held at their means. The first differences with stars are significant at p = 0.10 and unlabeled cells are not statistically significant.

support the radical right are more likely to experience deprivation. The question is whether deprivation drives support for the radical right even after controlling for alternative categorical explanations like class, gender, and ideology.

To account for this range of other factors, I tested the impact of all deprivation on support for the radical right, while controlling for ideology, age, college education, gender, home ownership, marital status, and class.[3] As displayed in Table 8.1, the British analysis shows that the individual who perceives the most political deprivation (as a matter of politicians' care) is about 9 percentage points more likely to support the BNP or EDL than someone who perceives no deprivation whatsoever, holding all other variables constant. Similarly, the individual who perceives the most political deprivation (as a matter of self-reported power) and the most social deprivation (as a matter of personal centrality as placed on the concentric circle diagram) is about 5 and 7 percentage points, respectively, more likely to support the BNP or EDL than someone who perceives no deprivation whatsoever. Correspondingly, it seems reasonable to say that the economic deprivation and the contextualized social deprivation measures are not significant factors here. From this analysis, it is clear that Britons who perceive the greatest political and social deprivation are more likely to support the BNP and EDL than those who perceive no deprivation. Economic deprivation appears to have no noticeable impact. This finding concurs with work by other scholars (Sniderman, Hagendoorn, and Prior 2004; Hainmueller and Hopkins 2014) which finds that economic disadvantage or deprivation fails to drive support for the far right or hostility to immigration. White people appear to respond to a cultural threat—the re-ordering of social hierarchies and associated losses of political power.

In the United States, the individual who perceives the most social deprivation (as contextualized by the centrality of immigrant-origin groups) is 15% more likely to support the presidential candidacy of Donald Trump, and 12% more likely to support a hypothetical radical right party (though the latter narrowly misses standard levels of statistical significance), holding all other variables constant. As in the British case, those white Americans who perceive the greatest political deprivation (in terms of politicians' regard for their views) are also more likely to support the radical right, in the form of the Tea Party and the hypothetical third party. Interestingly, a sense of economic deprivation is only significant in explaining support for Donald Trump.

Does Deprivation Affect People's Democratic Engagement?

Running the same type of analysis,[4] I was also able to test the impact of deprivation on peaceful, inclusive, democratic participation, while controlling for demographic factors. I classified respondents as democratically engaged if they reported partaking in at least one voluntary participatory activity, and reported no interest in the radical right. These participatory activities include signing a petition, attending a neighborhood meeting, voting, joining a community association, joining a union, and participating in a peaceful protest or strike. How might differences in deprivation alone (controlling for all other potential factors) impact the probability that a person will participate in peaceful, democratic ways?

As we see in Table 8.2, my analysis of British respondents shows that the individual who perceives the most political deprivation (as a matter of politicians' care) is about 16% more likely to engage in at least one democratic activity than someone who perceives no deprivation whatsoever, holding all other variables constant. The effect of political deprivation as a measure of self-reported power also drives democratic behavior, but less strongly at 9%. Correspondingly, we can say that the economic deprivation and social deprivation measures are not significant factors here. In fact, abstract social deprivation may even decrease the probability of democratic engagement.

From the British analysis, we see that economic deprivation has no noticeable impact on the probability of engaging in either democratic or radical political behavior, while social deprivation is only associated with support for the radical right. People who feel socially deprived do not perceive democratic means of recourse. This is an important finding. As recorded in interviews, many of my respondents in East London felt helpless about their movement to Britain's social periphery. Sensing their dismissal by mainstream, democratic outlets, they opt for alternative means of achieving their social agendas.

Table 8.2 **Impact of Deprivation on Democratic Activism**

Deprivation Measure	UK Democratic Activism	US Democratic Activism (excluding Third Party support)
Politicians Care	+16	
Power	+9*	
Social Centrality		
Social Context		+25*
Economic		+44

Each number indicates the change in the predicted probabilities of engaging in democratic activities, given a movement from minimum levels of deprivation to maximum levels of deprivation with all other factors held at their means. The first differences with stars are significant at p = 0.10 and the unlabeled cells are not statistically significant. In the US, democratic activism is defined as any reported democratic activity without support for a Radical Right entity (Trump, Tea Party, or the third party). Some may consider support for Trump or the Tea Party as consistent with democratic activism. Accordingly, I also show results for an analysis that only excludes those supportive of the Radical Right third party.

Meanwhile, political deprivation motivates both democratic engagement and—per the earlier results—support for the radical right in Britain. This result suggests the shiftiness of political capital, which leads people to take both democratic and radical action. Indeed, those who feel politically deprived are the most politicized actors surveyed in Britain. They are not only associated with intense expressions of rebellion, but also the most intense democratic activism. Looking just at those who move 7 points or more on the 10-point deprivation scale, those who are severely politically deprived tend to engage in more democratic participation than others who are less deprived or not deprived at all. None of the other forms of deprivation show strong patterns. These results suggest that deprivation effectively cuts both ways—the same intensity that produces model democratic activists also produces, or turns them into, radicals. In the United States, various expressions of deprivation cut both ways, depending on the form of political participation.

Among British democratic activists, however, we see that political deprivation produces a specific kind of activist, one that uses extra-institutional means of pursuing an agenda. Looking at each measure of political participation in Table 8.3, we see that both measures of political deprivation are significant predictors of actors' membership in a union and signing of a petition. Political deprivation (as a matter of power) significantly predicts participation in peaceful protests. All of these activities are important forms of democratic engagement, but forms that seek to influence the state from outside its institutions—they are forms of protest.

Table 8.3 **Effects of Deprivation on UK Political Participation**

	Political Deprivation (politicians)	Political Deprivation (power)	Social Deprivation (abstract)	Social Deprivation (contextual)	Economic Deprivation	
Neighborhood Meeting			–	–		Institutional
Vote for Different Party				–		
Community Association	+					
Petition	+	+			+	Protest
Union	+	+		+	+	
Peaceful Protest		+			–	
British National Party			+			Anti-System
English Defence League or English National Alliance	+	+	+			
UKIP	+	+	+		+	

Plus signs and minus signs indicate statistically significant and direction of relationship (at or above 90% level) for the deprivation measure in each model with full controls. Plus signs indicate that deprivation is positively associated with the behavior. Minus signs indicate a negative association.

Table 8.4 **Effects of Deprivation on US Political Participation**

	Political Deprivation (Politicians)	Political Deprivation (Power)	Social Deprivation (Abstract)	Social Deprivation (Contextual)	Economic Deprivation	
Neighborhood Meeting						Institutional
Vote for Different Party						
Community Association	−		−		−	
Petition	+				+	
Union						
Peaceful Protest	−	−			−	Protest
Hypothetical Third Party	+	+				
Trump Candidacy				+		Anti-System
Tea Party Support	+				+	

Plus signs and minus signs indicate statistically significant and direction of relationship (at or above 90% level) for the deprivation measure in each model with full controls. Plus signs indicate that deprivation is positively associated with the behavior. Minus signs indicate a negative association.

More established means include voting, membership in organized associations, and community meetings. Of these three institutional means of participation, only community meetings are an outlet for British people who sense exclusively political deprivation. Instead, the data show that a *lack* of social deprivation (in both measures) is what leads people to join associations or express their frustration by voting.

In the United States (Table 8.4), political deprivation (as a matter of politicians' care and political power) has a stronger association with far-right behavior than institutional means of participation. While it does increase the likelihood that one will sign a petition, it is also associated with support for the hypothetical far-right party and the Tea Party. A lack of political deprivation is associated with a higher likelihood of both institutional and protest democratic behaviors, increasing the likelihood that an individual will join a community association and/or attend a peaceful protest.

Social deprivation (contextualized with other groups) is associated with Tea Party support in the United States. Similarly, economic deprivation is associated with support for Donald Trump. Economic deprivation is associated with a higher probability of signing a petition. A lack of all kinds of deprivation is associated with a higher likelihood of community association involvement.

When I separated those people who reported severe social deprivation (a decline of 3 points or more) from those respondents who reported minor deprivation (a decline of less than 3 points), the results were even more dramatic. Those who reported support for the radical right are twice (200%) as likely to be severely socially deprived (as measured abstractly), 100% more likely to be severely politically deprived (politicians' care), and 70% more likely to be severely politically deprived (power) than those who reported no radical inclinations. What remains confounding is that the same sense of political deprivation mobilizes some to engage democratically and others to rebel. What separates these two groups of individuals: those who engage and those who rebel?

How Does Deprivation Affect People Differently?

The above tests of deprivation on support for the radical right are, in some ways, very conservative. Given the stability of partisanship (Campbell et al. 1960), it is less likely that perceived deprivation will drive left-wing partisans to support the radical right. In this section, I first look at the heterogeneous effects of deprivation on just those who self-identify as Republicans (in the United States) or Conservatives (in the United Kingdom). I then consider demographic attributes to calculate the predicted probability that a "profiled" radical will support the Radical Right.

Table 8.5 **First Differences Min–Max Deprivation for Interaction Models (Republicans/Conservatives Only)**

	US Tea Party	US Trump	US Third Party	UK BNP/EDL	UKIP
Social (Abstract)	46.5		37.6	10.6	45.2
Social (Contextual)	46.7		30.1		28.1
Political (Politicians)	44.1	37.8	50.6	14.4	72.3
Political (Power)	50.1	41.1	65.9	10.2	67.9
Economic	48.6	66.9	41.7		47.9

Predicted first differences and 95% confidence intervals moving each deprivation from its minimum value to its maximum value for each DV for Republicans (Conservatives in UK) only in interaction models.

In Table 8.5, I display the change in probability of supporting the radical right given a change from minimum levels of deprivation to maximum levels of deprivation among Republicans and Conservatives with all other covariates held at their means.[5] I find, not surprisingly, that deprivation has a much stronger effect on this target subgroup than either of the full samples. Some notable patterns emerge. Political deprivation remains a strong and consistent predictor of support for the radical right in all models. Indeed, its effect is downright enormous when it comes to American support for the Tea Party, the hypothetical third party, and British support for UKIP. Moving from minimum to maximum levels of political deprivation is associated with a 68 and 72 percentage point increase in support for UKIP. Social deprivation emerges as a similarly stronger predictor of support for the Tea Party, the hypothetical third party, and UKIP. Finally, economic deprivation becomes a significant predictor of support for the Tea Party and the hypothetical third party. These results are remarkably consistent across the two samples.

To distinguish democrats from radicals, I also considered their demographic attributes. Those respondents who expressed a willingness to support, or a record of support for, the radical right were disproportionately white, young, lower class, male, without a university education, and ideologically conservative. While this describes the "profiled" radical, it does not reveal how much these demographic attributes drive the differential impact of social and political deprivation on individuals' behavioral choices.

To do this, I asked the probability that a so "profiled" deprived, conservative, working class, 24- to 39-year-old, white male without a university degree would support the radical right. According to the demographic breakdown, such an individual should be highly likely to support the radical right. I then compared him to an "average" white British male—that is, a white British male whose demographic characteristics are all set to their means (a moderate ideology score, of average class, age, and educational attainment, and average levels of political deprivation). The difference is substantial.

Figure 8.1 summarizes the extent to which the "profiled" individual—subject to different forms of deprivation—is more likely to support the radical right in the United Kingdom and the United States. While all effects are quite strong, some stand out. In Britain, I found that the "profiled" individual who is socially deprived (as a matter of abstract centrality) is about 51% more likely to support the BNP or EDL. The same profiled individual is 67% more likely to support UKIP. In the United States, similar effects exist across almost every type of deprivation. In particular, the profiled individual who is socially deprived (as a

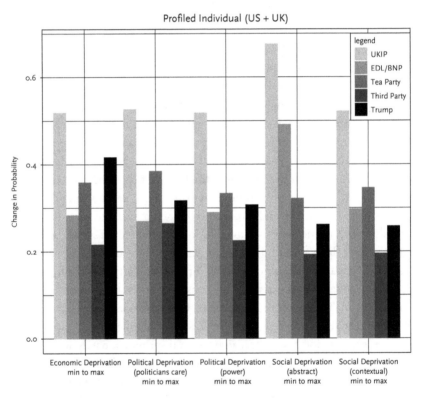

Figure 8.1 Profiled Individual United States and United Kingdom. Bars indicate the change in the predicted probabilities of engaging in or expressing a willingness to engage in anti-system activities given a movement for an average white male with minimum levels of deprivation to a "profiled" white male with maximum levels of deprivation in both the United States and United Kingdom. All estimates were statistically significant.

matter of contextualized centrality) is about 26 percentage points more likely to support Trump, 34 percentage points more likely to support the Tea Party, and 20% more likely to support the third party. The demographic characteristics that are significant indicators of democratic activism are age, education, ideology, gender, and class. Older, more liberal, female, college-educated, and middle- or upper-class individuals are more likely to engage democratically.

The British and American data therefore both suggest that while political and social deprivation mobilizes most people to become democratically engaged in the political system, this deprivation drives white working class Britons and Americans toward the fringe of the public sphere. The qualitative data suggest two important reasons for this. First, radical right groups offer a source of heritage-based political identity for white working class Britons who have lost sources of occupational identity, and now try to distance themselves from association with immigrant origin minorities. And second, radical right groups serve as a refuge or an antiestablishment alternative to mainstream political parties that white working class individuals believe have adopted the cause of immigrant-origin minorities at the expense of native constituents. In this logic, wealthier, more educated, and more liberal people who also feel a sense of political deprivation are better able to find a democratic outlet for their views. These two proposed reasons presume that individuals who support the radical right perceive the ascendance of immigrant-origin minorities in their society—a presumption worth examining.

How Does Deprivation Relate to Perceptions of Immigrant Centrality?

If an individual perceives deprivation and believes that other historically marginalized groups are becoming more central to society, does this increase the probability that he or she supports the radical right? Put another way, are people who perceive the relative ascendance of historically marginalized groups—namely Muslims, immigrants, and nonwhite working class people—more likely to support the radical right than those who believe these historically disadvantaged groups are still disadvantaged?[6]

In Britain, the results show that people who sense that they are socially deprived (as a matter of contextualized centrality) or politically deprived (as a matter of power) and perceive the ascent of historically disadvantaged groups are much more likely to support the radical right than those who are not deprived or do not perceive such an ascent. Interactions with other measures of deprivation do not demonstrate significant effects.

In the United States, we see far more robust results. Those who are economically, socially, or politically deprived *and* perceive historically disadvantaged groups as central to society are more likely to support the Tea Party or Donald Trump than those who are deprived but also see historically disadvantaged groups as deprived.

An alternative way to analyze this phenomenon is by comparing an individual's self-placement on the provided concentric circles with where they place other groups. If an individual were to place herself closer to the center than historically disadvantaged groups, would she be less likely to express support for the radical right?[7] In Britain, I find no difference. This confirms that it is the perceived centrality of historically disadvantaged reference groups that matters, rather than the relative position of the white working class. In the United States, we find another strong pattern. Those who place themselves on the periphery of social centrality, but place historically marginalized groups in the center, are 32% more likely to support the Tea Party.

Competing Extremisms

These results offer unique measurements of white working class marginality and the way marginality motivates the contentious and occasionally extreme political behavior surrounding immigration, multiculturalism, and Islam. Indeed, the radical right parties discussed in the British survey would not exist if it were not for the demographic change and subsequent Muslim politics of contemporary Britain. And in many cases, white working class people's extremism competes with the extremism exhibited by certain members of the historically disadvantaged minorities they resent. Violence has erupted when radical right groups have interrupted British Muslim demonstrations in favor of shariah, or when Muslim extremists have sought to publicly attack British soldiers returning from tours of duty in Afghanistan and Iraq. More conventionally though, far-right radicals and Muslim radicals compete quite separately, in the seclusion of their own living rooms, against the constructed imaginaries of their alter ego reference group—each other. Both sets of radicals receive disproportionate publicity relative to the peaceful, adaptive, and tolerant majority of their democratic co-ethnics.[8]

In earlier research of Muslim political behavior (Gest 2010), I noted the similar sense of deprivation detected by British Muslims. While white working class people express their marginalization in terms of lost social and political status, the British Bangladeshis I interviewed in London's East End described the way they feel disqualified from the rights, freedom, and membership that other Britons enjoy in the United Kingdom. In this light, both groups refer to unfulfilled senses of entitlement, closely tied to the politics of heritage stimulated by immigration, diversity, and the challenges of coexistence. Many white working class individuals are frustrated by their eviction from positions of advantage, their lost sense of centrality in the societies they once defined. As shown in this chapter, I found this feeling of social and political deprivation to clearly predict a higher probability of support for radical right groups.

Meanwhile, many British Muslims are frustrated by the prejudice that underpins their entrenched disadvantage, and the perceived impossibility of ever achieving centrality in the only society they know. The British survey suggests that such frustrations motivate both democratic and extreme political behavior. The survey does not test for radicalism among historically disadvantaged groups. The sample has a disproportionately small number of nonwhite respondents, and I do not solicit respondents' engagement with extremist organizations, or causes that appeal specifically to Muslims or other minorities.

For the white British and American people, I find that political and social frustrations, respectively, create a form of transferable political capital—one that is directed at extra-institutional means of democratic engagement, but also support for the radical right. In scope, these are both forms of protest politics. The data suggest that while the wealthier, the educated, and the older opt for peaceful means of protest, younger white working class men are more likely to pursue anti-system activity. Driving this radicalism is not merely a measurable sense of political deprivation, but evidently a profound sense of social displacement—a shift to the periphery of British society.

Given the large sample of respondents, these data corroborate a number of key dynamics that this book discusses, particularly the effect of relative deprivation on political behavior. They also demonstrate the parallels between the ways that white working class people and visible minority groups may understand their marginality, their minoritization. The analysis here permits a more confident discussion of how to mitigate marginality and the radical political behavior it inspires.

9

The Untouchables

They don't care about what you know, until they know that you care.
—Quotation hanging on the locker room office wall of then-Youngstown
State University Head Football Coach Jim Tressel (attributed to his father,
Lee Tressel, but also to US President Theodore Roosevelt)

There was a time when the white working class defined American and British politics. Today, few politicians know what to do with them. While white working class voters make up a major portion of the electorate, especially in Rust Belt regions, many elected officials are baffled about how to reach them—or at least how to do so in a postindustrial economy without alienating other crucial components of their respective electoral coalitions. In Britain, the United Kingdom Independence Party (UKIP) has emerged as a third party by making a direct play for white working class votes, and Jeremy Corbyn has returned Labour to its socialist roots. But there is no exact equivalent in the United States, which is constrained by a two-party landscape. Rather, in the more candidate-driven American system, individual campaigns have made populist appeals to white working class voters, and have attempted to pull their parties to the far reaches of the political spectrum.

After offering a prospectus of the partisan landscape in the United Kingdom and the United States, this chapter traces how history has shaped the white working class's tense relationships with political parties—with special emphasis on the emergence of UKIP and the 2016 presidential candidacy of Donald Trump, the Republican nominee. In the end, I offer insights for any political organization or candidate who attempts to bring the white working class back into the political fold.

A UKIP Future in Britain?

In the United Kingdom today, UKIP has already capitalized on the attitudes discussed in this book. After not contesting the 2010 general election, UKIP claimed 12.6% of the national vote in 2015 (BBC News 2015). Because of Britain's first-past-the-post system, this only translated into one Parliamentary seat. However, the popularity of its anti-immigration platform and skepticism of the European Union made UKIP a potent factor during the campaign and the subsequent referendum on British membership in the European Union. In the 2015 Parliamentary election, the Conservatives felt pressured to cover their right flank, and ultimately, UKIP challenged Labour for the votes of disaffected Liberal Democrats on the left. In Barking, UKIP garnered 22.2% of the vote, which was largely comprised of BNP supporters who backed Nick Griffin in 2010. In Dagenham, UKIP received 29.8% of the vote, taking a good number of voters from both the Tories and Liberal Democrats (*Telegraph* 2015).

A formal political party, UKIP renders antiestablishment and working class voters a peaceful, democratic means of expressing their frustration with the direction of British society. Emboldened by its results, UKIP is now poised to poach further support from both Labour and the Conservatives, having already absorbed a substantial number of Liberal Democrat voters since 2010. UKIP appeals to the isolationist (and often former unionist) far left and also the nativist far right, which had been reluctant to support the more profane and overtly racist BNP. UKIP promises a reduction in foreign aid provisions, an increase in National Health Service spending, and no tax on low-wage workers. Until UKIP's emergence, Labour struggled to unite urban cosmopolitans and ethnic minority blocs with its historically unionist base. Meanwhile, the Tories worried that nativist rhetoric might alienate moderates, and were largely distrusted by unionists after decades of antagonism anyway. With the establishment of UKIP, the British political landscape may shift, leaving fewer voters for whom Tories and Labourites may compete.

With the Tories' enduring Euroskepticism placating many on the far right, Labour responded to their 2015 defeat by appointing socialist Jeremy Corbyn as their leader and, in so doing, sought to reclaim the far left and its historically working class base. However, the move represents precisely the gamble that Democrats and Republicans in the United States have been unwilling to take. It opened an opportunity for Prime Minister David Cameron to monopolize the British center with his progressive approaches to environmentalism, gay rights, and the minimum wage. However, Cameron was soon undone by the EU referendum he long promised to nationalist Tory backbenchers. With his Brexit loss and subsequent resignation, both parties are now being tugged to their fringes, leaving the center wide open and increasingly precarious. In many ways, the British case will serve as a useful experiment for American politicians of both parties. How will the Tories respond to their internal division? Will Labour be able to hold any space in the center of the political spectrum? Will Labour actually be able to appeal anew to white working class people wooed by UKIP and thus far estranged from Labour for its support of minority rights? In any case, UKIP will endure as the kind of party which would emerge were the United States not constrained by its traditional two-party structure. Instead, American parties have been reluctant to adopt the positions and strategies that might mobilize greater white working class engagement.

Personality Contests in America

Three weeks before the 2012 general election, Republican vice presidential candidate Paul Ryan made a campaign stop at the St. Vincent De Paul Society's soup kitchen in Youngstown, Ohio. The dining hall was largely empty. Its mostly homeless patrons had eaten, the servery had been cleaned, and many volunteers had left. En route to the airport, Ryan and his staffers rushed into the kitchen for a fifteen-minute photo-op, touting those who give back. The candidate was presented to the volunteers who remained, and he was handed clean dishes to re-wash for the photographers, according to charity workers (Montopoli 2012).

There was a time when every American presidential candidate stopped by Youngstown to appeal for support. In its Steeltown days, Youngstown was one of the United States' key manufacturing hubs. Ever since, Youngstown has seen plenty of politicians promise to spruce things up. Yet in the minds of those who live here, little gets cleaned.

Though they are dispersed countrywide, there is a significant concentration of white working class people in postindustrial regions like Youngstown throughout the Upper Midwest and Great Lakes—encompassing a number of swing states in national elections. These include Pennsylvania, West Virginia, Ohio, Indiana, Michigan, and Wisconsin. According to a variety of studies that understand the white working class in different ways, the group makes up about 53% of the electorate in Michigan, 55% in Pennsylvania, 58% in Wisconsin, 62% in Ohio, 66% in Indiana, and nearly 70% in West Virginia (Judis 2007; Democratic Strategist 2011; Olsen 2010). As a result, this subset of the American electorate is a key determinant of electoral outcomes, but alas, one that has been misunderstood and under-mobilized. In recent elections, white working class people have had low turnouts relative to their share of the US population (CNN 2008; 2010). This is true despite the fact that white Americans are disproportionately of voting age vis-à-vis non-white Americans, who on average are younger.

While Republicans continue to expand upon their support among white working class people in the American South, Democrats have salvaged a nearly split vote among this group in the North and Upper Midwest—bolstering their recent electoral victories in those states and nationwide (Edsall 2012). But the reflexive Democratic affiliation which was founded in deep ties to unions is eroding, and now, both political parties are perplexed about how to attract white working class support in the Rust Belt region, and how to balance that support with that of their traditional bases.

Researchers, campaigners, and locals alike wonder whether Youngstown's voters are permanently withdrawn, having lost all faith in government. However, the evidence suggests that the citizens of Youngstown—and many other post-traumatic cities in the American Rust Belt—have merely been waiting for parties and organizations to mobilize them. Youngstown does not have a shortage of civic-minded individuals; those individuals simply do not feel comfortable entering a political sphere that has long been character-ized by corruption and dysfunction. Today's working class, Rust Belt voters are disenchanted by what they perceive to be a political and economic cul-ture of exploitative greed and gridlock, and are waiting for someone to adopt their cause.

Jimbo Democrats

It is precisely this sense of abandonment, coupled with a general distrust of gov-ernment, that softened the ground for Youngstown's most popular politician, the late Congressman Jim Traficant—the nine-term member of the House of Representatives who evaded FBI prosecution for two decades before being con-victed on ten counts of racketeering and corruption in 2002. Even though he was expelled from Congress and imprisoned for his misdealings, he remains revered by many Youngstown residents, as described in Chapter 4. Despite his unscru-pulous behavior, Traficant gave white working class voters a sense of representa-tion, a sense of identification with someone who finally spoke truth to power. As many respondents emphasized, "he cared." Indulging working people's griev-ances but also their conspiracy theories, Traficant laid out a basic blueprint for attracting white working class votes: earn working class credentials; employ working class language; and engage in working class actions with voters—not just for them. Voters in Youngstown were so desperate for such a candidate, and such candidates were so rare, that they overlooked Traficant's criminality, mania, and legislative inaction, because he was perceived to be one of the last white working class people in national public office.

Traficant also channeled a political outlook that has otherwise confused na-tional political parties. Like Traficant, Youngstown's citizens have been reliably affiliated with the Democratic Party for decades, but their political preferences frequently run counter to party prerogatives. So Democrats have won due to the absence of a viable alternative. Republicans have historically been viewed as elitist and anti-union—an image that the Obama campaign reinvigorated in 2012 despite its weakening relevance thirty years after Youngstown's mills closed.

Although they cast themselves as the working man's party, the ranks of elected Democrats are just as elite. As I noted earlier, members of Congress are supremely wealthier than their average constituents (Whoriskey 2011) and those who have previously belonged to the working class compose only 2% of Congress overall (Carnes 2012). The influx of money in politics and changing campaign finance rules may be partially to blame, encouraging both parties to rely more heavily on candidates who can self-fund expensive races; the same study found that the average winning House candidate now spends four times as much (in inflation-adjusted dollars) as he or she did in 1976. Even the legendary Jim Traficant had a graduate degree.

Yet despite the social conservatism of Youngstown's white voters, their desperation for economic development, and Democratic elected officials' equal inability to truly reflect the working class electorate, Republicans have made little attempt to capture these voters. And this Republican divestiture from Youngstown has exacerbated the party's problems in this region: because Youngstown's voters have had little exposure to local Republicans who could counter the historical stereotype, the Republican Party remains the representative of the companies, not the workers, to the mostly white voters in Mahoning County and in the Rust Belt more broadly.

In the antiestablishment wave that swept the United States leading into the 2016 general election, Vermont Senator Bernie Sanders competed directly for such voters against the early Democratic favorite, former First Lady, New York Senator, and Secretary of State Hillary Clinton. Sanders spoke directly to many white working class voters seeking a left-wing populism that constrained economic inequality, pursued more protectionist trade policy, and regulated campaign finance. Sanders's endurance in the Democratic primary campaign was a harbinger of the revolutionary sentiment that characterized the complexion of the entire national campaign.

The Trump Experiment

Enter Donald Trump. A self-aggrandizing plutocrat, Trump gained the ear of white working class people with the anti-immigrant, protectionist appeal of his initial June 2015 announcement to run for president in 2016. Trump's entry into the campaign fundamentally altered its style and character. Before his declaration, the early Republican primary polling was led by candidates deeply ensconced in American politics: former Florida Governor and President George W. Bush's brother Jeb Bush, Wisconsin Governor Scott Walker, and first-term Florida Senator Marco Rubio, whom many branded as the face of the Republican Party's future. After the declaration, Bush's campaign entered a tailspin, Walker dropped out, and Rubio would ultimately depart after losing his home state and every other primary except Minnesota. Instead, Trump led the polls over Ohio Governor John Kasich, and the rebellious Texas Senator Ted Cruz—who echoed Trump's scathing perceptions of Washington and the establishment of American politics.

Through the Republican primaries, Trump's meteoric ascendance and ultimate nomination was driven by strong support among white people without university degrees. Though Trump struggled to attract a majority of polled Republican voters before the primaries, these white working class people were numerous enough to give Trump a significant early polling lead in a field that at one point contained sixteen Republican candidates. With many such supporters among so-called "unlikely" voters, he awakened a dormant part of the American electorate, who was otherwise unenthusiastic about either party's candidates or simply withdrawn from participation. The attraction between these strange bedfellows can be understood through the lens provided in this book.

First, in light of party establishments' cagey approach to white working class voters and their subsequent sense of postindustrial abandonment, many are fed up with Washington. "The thing I like about Trump is that both sides hate him," says Bob Campanella, a Youngstown Northsider. This sentiment encompasses much of today's Republican base. A mere 16% of Republicans feel like they are represented in Washington—even though the party currently controls both houses of Congress; those who do not feel represented supported Trump by a sizeable margin (CNN/ORC 2015). Trump's bombastic declarations that his rivals have been corrupted by corporations and donors (like himself) validates the belief among white working class voters that the political system is rigged by the very special interests that abruptly closed American factories, laid off American workers, and invested money overseas to circumvent American wages and taxes.

Second, Trump addresses people who have felt silenced. While Trump does not counterbalance the wealth of American politicians, he validates the views of many ordinary voters as he channels conspiracy theories and whispers from the streets to the stump. Trump's off-color remarks about women and minorities, his frustration with "disgusting" people, and his baseless assertions about Mexico's deliberate exportation of criminals across the US border fit this mold. Much like Jim Traficant in Youngstown, Trump's amplification of these ideas rendered credibility to a subset of voters who feel sidelined. Trump regularly referred to his supporters as the "silent majority."

Third, Trump bluntly acknowledged white working class people's acute sense of loss—the factor that I find best explains radical political behavior. Trump, who talked about economic losses to China, Mexico, and Japan in the manner of an Olympic basketball team on a tour of the United States, communicated his awareness of this lost status in simple, blunt terms. Shamelessly showboating his own successes, Trump promised to spread his winnings around and to punish companies that take their manufacturing overseas—a direct appeal to the Rust Belt. The "Again" in his campaign slogan, "Make America Great Again," plugs into this sense of nostalgia and suggests a return to better times. "I guess I want things back to the way they were," Campanella says in Youngstown. "And in his odd, crude way, he makes sense. I know he's not a woman-hater and he's not going to reverse what liberalism has done for us the last 40 years. He just wants to get our country stabilized and back on track. [. . .] I know it's never going to be like the way it was. But we need to concentrate on this country. We're lowering our standards more than we're raising standards in third world countries. We can't worry about other people's problems."

During his ascent, Trump's support came from a particular, but relatively large, plurality of voters. This group—composed to an important extent of white working class voters—is numerous enough to affect election outcomes, but not large enough to determine them without their integration into a broader coalition. And because many white working class positions are fringe, they are difficult to streamline in combination with more centrist positions. Many registered Republicans said that they would not vote for Trump even after he won the party's nomination; his unfavorability ratings were exceptionally high for a presidential nominee.

Trump's positions very much mirror those of the BNP in the United Kingdom. Indeed, the US-adapted BNP platform that I offered to surveyed American respondents was surprisingly well received. Over 60% of a nationally representative sample of white people said that they were either likely or very likely to support a party that advocated for "stopping mass immigration, providing American jobs for American workers, preserving America's Christian heritage, and stopping the threat of Islam." Consequently, while Trump's rise may have been initially driven by white working class voters who unabashedly backed these once-fringe positions, he appears to have tapped into a latent populism (and distrust of Washington establishment) that has emerged since the global economic crisis and its segmented recovery.

Still, the bombastic Trump remains a product of the candidate-driven nature of American electoral politics. For all his unexpected success, he is unique. Few other candidates can replicate perhaps his most appealing quality—his independence, which he claims renders him the freedom to speak his mind and pursue policies in the interest of those who cannot sway politicians with lobbyists and campaign donations. Combine his wealth with his remarkable impermeability to criticism, and Trump is hardly a blueprint for future candidates of either party hoping to appeal to white working class communities. Nevertheless, the anger of white working class people—which Trump has harnessed—has reinvigorated their role in national politics. Where it was once determinant, it is now disruptive; but white working class people feel like they matter again. Unable to reproduce Trump's personality and wealth, future candidates who seek white working class support will need to become familiar with this otherwise perplexing constituency.

Outlook of White Working Class Americans and Britons

Those who hope to reach the white working class across Britain and America's Rust Belts must first understand the crosscurrents of this group's political outlook.

Economics: Most white working class respondents are antagonistic toward big business. A legacy of their relationship with the manufacturing industry, white working class people distrust the wealthy and are cognizant of elite advantage. They have long memories of labor exploitation and harsh tactics against strikers and in union negotiations.

However, in the United States, they anxiously await the next big industry to rescue their economy. Most Youngstown respondents support the growth of hydraulic fracturing or "fracking," despite its dangerous excavation work, a record of recruiting labor from outside the region, and potential environmental hazards. With fracking, Youngstown has been confronted with a referendum on its past as a factory town, and most citizens would do it all again. They simply can't conceive of another model. While the Britons I interviewed would be pleased to return to the good old days when factories were running, many now look to government to resolve their economic difficulties and facilitate a way forward.

Unions: After the deterioration of unions, many white working class people still rely on such organizations to politically mobilize them. This creates a dependency that has led to low participation rates in many elections. When unions were weakened, so were the principal enablers of working class political expression.

However, few respondents in the United States or the United Kingdom were impressed by contemporary unions anyway. After decades of membership, many working class white respondents believe unions to now be feeble and just as corrupt as the political and business officials they resent.

Immigration: As the descendants of immigrants, nearly all Youngstown respondents are sympathetic to the struggles of American minority groups. On the one hand, working class white Americans are very cognizant and proud of their own immigrant heritages from countries like Italy, Ireland, Slovakia, and Greece. They also admire and acknowledge today's immigrants as hardworking members of society, chasing the American Dream. On the other hand, they are frustrated by the government's leniency about undocumented immigrants, who they believe are likely to work below established wages, driving them down for others.

My British respondents acknowledge no such immigration lineage, even though many have roots abroad. Rather, immigration represents the single greatest issue of political salience in Britain and Europe today. While the flames of this obsession were fanned by the difficult years after the 2008 global recession, the 2015 European refugee crisis ignited them more intensely. Monolithically, they view immigrants as opportunists who will compete for the jobs and benefits to which Britons are entitled, but also a group that profits from sympathy and unfounded favoritism.

However, even many American respondents are convinced of their own emerging minority status. Respondents in both countries feel increasingly outnumbered, in light of both local and national demographic changes. They feel discarded to the periphery of their national psyche, despite a history as the industrial backbone of the country. And they feel subject to discrimination in the form of affirmative action and diversification policies. To express this sense of injustice, respondents have appropriated the language of the civil rights movement (equality).

Culture Wars: Despite their social conservatism, the Americans I interviewed are largely unexcited by culture wars. In Youngstown, many respondents were Catholic parishioners, while others maintain connections with Catholic schools and charities. As a result, they hold relatively conservative views on social issues. However, very few actually vote according to candidates' views on these disputes. Many note that their families have traditionally overlooked culture-war disagreements as long as a candidate aligns with their economic needs. This helps explain how Donald Trump's candidacy maintained momentum despite his wishy-washy statements on abortion, homosexuality, and Christianity. His primary base of supporters is more excited by his nativism and protectionism.

Still, white working class Americans remain wary of welfare recipients whose integrity they judge. A disproportionate number of white working class Americans consume Social Security, food stamps, disability, and unemployment benefits vis-à-vis racial minorities (Jones and Cox 2012), but many white voters in Youngstown understand "welfare" to exclusively mean cash assistance. Consequently, even those who are benefiting from safety-net programs themselves view "welfare" recipients as lazy and disingenuous people, and resent them for receiving a similar amount of money to those who are employed full-time. They frame this matter as a moral, not a racial, issue and emphasize the value of hard work and independence.

The Untouchables

When politicians wish to address white working class people, they must go directly to them on a regular basis. In the United States in particular, few do.

Given the perplexing worldviews of the white working class, Republican and Democratic Party establishments are unclear about how to mobilize white working class voters. So for the most part, they have been left alone. Youngstown has remained a Democratic fiefdom, even though the party's candidates have brought little improvement in citizens' quality of life and economic prospects. If anything, officials have been consumed by corruption and inaction, despite party-unified county and city chambers. As a result, until Trump's emergence, these voters had few options. Neither party has focused recent platforms on working people's needs. And neither party fields very many candidates from working class backgrounds.

The Republican Party is anemic in Mahoning County, and leaders are likely intimidated by the ostensible Democratic monopoly. Even if they recognize that Democrats are winning by default, they are unsure how to appeal to a white working class population without compromising the party's ties to the business lobby.

National Democratic leaders seem to view the region as an enigmatic, troublesome family member—one that they see in November every two years for obligatory reasons but otherwise from which they would prefer to maintain a safe distance. They are confused about how to mobilize greater turnout among people distrustful of big government and harboring more culturally conservative views than much of the Democratic coalition.

This is not a bitter struggle for appeal. Rather, both parties have determined that wooing the white working class risks complicating their established coalitions. While Democrats would benefit the most from the unification of the (white and nonwhite) American working class in the short term, they are reluctant to risk their relationship with more socially liberal and diverse voting blocs who have invigorated their return to power since 2006. More implicitly, they may also be wary of turning off elite moderates who fear the inflammation of class divisions. For now, both party establishments are reluctant to invest in white working class people as a constituency. They are viewed as untouchable.

The candidacy of Donald Trump poses a direct challenge to this logic. Whereas party elites avoided a direct appeal to white working class Americans out of their concern with assembling an electoral majority, Trump has tapped into this neglected set of voters. And while his numbers would not win primary elections in previous years when the Republican Party was unified behind an establishment candidate, Trump benefited from the manner in which the Tea Party has polarized and atomized the right's historic coalition. Early in the anti-establishment 2016 election cycle, populism was the only approach that unified a quorum of Republicans sufficient to lead the presidential campaign.

Appealing to the White Working Class

The result of the difficulties encountered by mainstream American and British political parties is a vast sector of the electorate that has been uninspired, but also largely unsolicited, by political campaigns. White working class people in the American Rust Belt are conventionally thought of as a swing vote, because of their unpredictability and a lack of loyalty to either party at the national level. In both countries, great rewards await the party that finds a way to sustainably re-integrate them as part of a grander coalition. Republicans and Tories seek a new, expanded base of voters to compete with Democrats' and Labour's growing demographic edges. Democrats, in particular, could seal their national dominance by attracting a broader spectrum of working class voters. If any party chooses to make this appeal, there are a number of gaps that a future generation of leaders may fill:

- ***Recruit candidates from the ranks of the non-elites.*** It is not sufficient to hammer the excesses of big business and cast the other side as the keepers of an elitist plutocracy. Working class voters want to see candidates with working class backgrounds. Democrats should not simply assume that their opposition will always be led by a private equity tycoon—a circumstance which made them look working class by comparison in 2012. In fact, the median net worth of Democratic Members of the House of Representatives has

risen substantially, up nearly $200,000 in inflation-adjusted dollars just be-
tween 2004 and 2009 (Center for Responsive Politics 2013). Meanwhile, the
median net worth of Republican House Members was down by nearly the
same amount over that time period, closing the gap between the parties to
less than $100,000 (ibid.). In Britain, election laws allow officials to represent
constituencies in which they do not reside. Barking's Margaret Hodge lives in
a posh neighborhood of Islington, while Dagenham's John Cruddas resides
in Notting Hill. The white working class understands that politicians likely
won't have calloused hands, but they also yearn to see their own reflection
in a representative who understands manual labor. It's not enough to produce candidates who attempt to connect with the middle class based on their
ancestry—for example by indicating that at some point in their family lineage, someone was middle or working class. The African-American, Latino,
and lesbian and gay communities can all see visible representation in party
leadership; the white working class wants no less.

- *Employ working class narratives.* When candidates are not working class
  themselves, they can still show signs of empathy by channeling the language
  and lifestyle of constituents. That means making reference to their realities of
  unstable jobs, declining wages and benefits, and a greater strain on family life
  because of these burdens. It also means emphasizing the common goal that
  everyone should be able to work one job, forty hours a week, and take care
  of their families. Working class voters see the parties doing visible outreach
  to other constituent communities and they want the same consideration and
  thought put toward wooing them. They will listen for language that explicitly
  includes them and lifts them up, favoring politicians who try to earn their vote
  over those who simply assume they have it.

- *Do not conflate the working class with the helpless.* Most working class
  people are not earning the minimum wage, nor do they think of themselves
  as reliant on government welfare programs (even when they are benefiting
  from many of them). They want to be seen as independent, self-sufficient,
  and hard-working, and as such, they won't be satisfied by a candidate or party
  who simply promises to protect or expand poverty assistance programs or
  raise the minimum wage. They want to know that their political leaders both
  understand their struggles, and distinguish them from those of people who
  are another rung down on the income ladder.

- *Do not assume unions are synonymous with the working class.* Times have
  changed, and most white working class people are not unionized anymore.
  Both parties and candidates must eschew shortcuts, address their constituents directly, and stop simply depending on unions as interlocutors—
  especially given that unions' status with many of these voters is questionable
  at best, as this book shows.

- *Challenge nostalgia with hope.* This book has demonstrated the mobilizing power of nostalgia, but also its destructive consequences. No party will ever deliver on promises to turn back the clock, so leaders must seize the challenge to envision a future that incorporates white working class people into the global economy and into coexistence with ethnic minorities. There is an opportunity waiting for leftist leaders who can appeal to white working class voters in these ways, especially if they go hand in hand with pursuing labor standards and strengthening social protections. There is also an opportunity for rightists who believe in an egalitarian meritocracy that rewards hard work and enterprise, especially if they demonstrate a new commitment to ensuring that everyone who works hard can succeed, despite their status at birth.

Ultimately, contrary to conventional portrayals, white working class voters are rational. They seek representatives who care about their grievances. They seek platforms that act on these grievances. And they respond to parties and organizations that invest in them with time, resources, and candidates. This is not different from any other sector of the electorate. The difference is that, in both the United States and the United Kingdom, social and economic forces have isolated the white working class as a political constituency, to the extent that many in this demographic feel like a peripheral afterthought in a country they once defined. A group with a powerful vote has thus been neglected, and populists are beginning to take notice.

Appendix A

METHODS

Research Question

The study's principal research question asks what drives white working class individuals living under similar social and economic circumstances to pursue different intensities and orientations of political activity. This appendix will discuss and explain the methodological choices I make in addressing this question.

Per Figure A.1, four outcomes are of interest. (1) Democratic "engagement" entails peaceful, inclusive political activity that seeks to influence other citizens, elected officials, or institutions of governance. These activities may be institutional in nature (voting, party membership, campaigning, public service, meeting attendance, and other activities within the framework of democratic institutions), or they may be extra-institutional in nature (protest, volunteerism, petitioning, boycotting, associational membership, and other peaceful activities outside the framework of democratic institutions). (2) "Rebellion" entails activity that uses violence, intimidation, or other means to pursue a political agenda in a manner that circumvents democratic channels of peaceful claims making. These activities may include political violence, coercion, corruption, or membership in or support for exclusivist organizations. (3) "Sitting out" entails periods of temporary inactivity by individuals who otherwise support and intend to reengage with the democratic political system, but do not do so. Their disengagement may be due to the pressures of resource (income, skills, time, etc.) shortages, disinterest, or satisfaction. (4) "Withdrawal" entails a commitment to inactivity due a loss of support for the democratic system. Withdrawal is an intentional and indefinite state of inactivity.

The primary hypothesis I build and consider to explain the variation in observed political behavior asserts that the activity and orientation of individuals' political behavior is driven by their variable senses of relative deprivation—that

	PRO-SYSTEM	ANTI-SYSTEM
ACTIVE	(1) ENGAGEMENT	(2) REBELLION
PASSIVE	(3) SITTING OUT	(4) WITHDRAWAL

Figure A.1 VARIATION IN POLITICAL BEHAVIOR.   This is a shorthand edition of the four quadrants modeling observable political behavior. (See Chapter 2.)

is, the discrepancy between their expectation of their status and their subjective perception of its fulfillment. One of the contributions of this research is to consider subjective status deprivation as a matter of economic (H_1), political (H_2), and social (H_3) status attainment. To examine the dynamics of individuals' determination of these forms of status, I undertake two ethnographies that entail 120 interviews in total. This work set out to better understand the contexts, the range of political attitudes, and the range of political behavior in different cases to refine and develop my initial hypothesis. I then undertake an analysis of British survey data. This appendix outlines and discusses these methodological choices and their execution.

Ethnographic Case Selection

To encounter actors in relevant sociopolitical environments, this research required two cases that share (a) similar systems of government and (b) similar socioeconomic environments, while also featuring (c) a significant white working class community in a comparable social position. In addition, as this research is interested in examining comparative cases, the selected population groups in their locality must exhibit a range of political behavior to analyze. (It would be unhelpful to, for example, analyze a region that is almost exclusively democratically engaged, or a region that was almost exclusively withdrawn.)

In light of this study's interest in subjective status deprivation, it was also important to examine cases that featured differing social hierarchies. As I discuss in Chapters 6 and 7 at some length, the United States and the United Kingdom feature divergent histories related to class divisions. Whereas the American system is thought to be more fluid, the British system is thought to be more rigid and inherited. Unlike Britain, the American social hierarchy is also less sensitive to matters of immigrant origin (particularly among white, European-origin immigrants). Therefore, a cross-national comparison offers significant variation in the manner desired, without losing the contextual similarities that enable this study's focus on white working class people in postindustrial spaces (Bloemraad 2005).

Expressions of social and political marginality among working class whites in North America and Europe have been prominent in the early twenty-first century and have significantly influenced national elections and public policy. So there are many communities that feature substantial populations of evidently marginalized working class white people. (See the discussion of post-traumatic cities in Chapter 1.) With this breadth in mind, Youngstown and East London do not represent peculiar cases that enable the examination of a specific trend. Rather, these are two somewhat ordinary cases among many. They take place in historically stable democracies with postindustrial economies severely affected by the global financial crisis. Each group is conventionally thought to be the core ethno-religious constituency of their respective countries, despite an era of increasing demographic diversification and low native birth rates. Each group occupies a similar social position within its peri-urban social milieu, which is exogenously characterized by underachievement, ignorance, and simultaneously, cultural authenticity.

I am nevertheless sensitive to the various differences between postindustrial Ohio and East London. Several variables exist and must be acknowledged as potential reasons for variations in political attitudes and behavior. The East London borough of Barking and Dagenham is on the outskirts of a global city that epitomizes the great social, demographic, and economic transformations of contemporary times. East Londoners have both witnessed these changes, and been directly impacted by them. Many are Cockneys who once defined life in London's East End, just ten miles to the west. They lost jobs as the East End's textile and automotive factories closed and moved overseas; they lost political clout as unions dissolved and industries were privatized; and they lost control of the East End's streets and social identity as growing numbers of immigrants settled into council estates and altered communal life. Nearly all of the "original" East Enders have since fled further eastward. Subsequently, many have been mobilized by the xenophobia, isolationism, and economic populism of the British National Party—an openly racist, secular organization, the members of which have been known to use violence. The United Kingdom also features a more generous and accessible welfare state, a more interventionist local government sector, and a shorter, less acknowledged history of immigration.

Youngstown and the Mahoning Valley were once at the center of the United States' Rust Belt, stretching from Chicago, Illinois to Erie, Pennsylvania. The region's surrounding hills and hollows also once supplied much of America's coal, timber, and clay commodities. As the industrial core of the country deteriorated with the resources of the foothills, the region is now more closely situated at the edge of American consciousness. Ohio's cities are today shrinking at rapid rates, and the surrounding region is increasingly dependent on government welfare and the illicit drug trade—the echoing effects of global transformations. Similar to East Londoners, Ohioans have subsequently been susceptible to political populism and the xenophobia of "patriot group" militias. However, rather than vilified by a changing society, this population appears to be ignored. They exist far from the churning change of America's coastal cities, and even while embracing inactivity, the marginalized rhetorically celebrate "democracy" as the cornerstone of their often Christian, American identity. They have only limited contact with the diversity, atheism, and elitism they lament. Still, Americans are never far removed from their own immigration history. And unlike Britain, American government provides fewer public resources in support of the mobility it purports to champion.

I acknowledge these variables, keeping in mind that case studies are undertaken to explain differences in political perceptions and political behavior between comparable cases, and therefore conditional on any other factors that might also have an effect. Despite these differences, it is worth noting that the marginality of working class white people in Ohio remains quite typical of similar populations in North America, while alienation among those in Barking and Dagenham remains typical of similar populations across Western and Northern Europe.

Interview Subject Selection

Representative sampling is an unattainable standard for two qualitative case studies. Instead, I entered the field—cognizant of existing differences in political behavior—and interviewed a total of 120 subjects representing a broad variation on the study's dependent variable: political behavior (King, Keohane, and Verba 1994: 129, 141). Indeed, as this study seeks to make both descriptive and correlative inferences about different forms of political behavior among white working class individuals, it was necessary to ensure that I interviewed and observed a selection of subjects who collectively exhibited a spectrum of political behavior—from democratic activism to complacency, from rebellion to withdrawal—none of which fails to exist outside the selected cases.

To address the corpus-theoretical paradox (Bauer and Gaskell 2000: 29–31), I used pilot investigations and secondary-source research to identify the range of outcome variation—that is, the different forms of democratic and anti-system behavior. I also relied on my earlier research on European Muslims, which informed the range of outcomes I considered. I also narrowed the subject pool to fit within my interest in examining native-born, white, working class individuals in Youngstown and East London. I understood any individual who self-identified as phenotypically white as such. While this was relatively straightforward in East London, in Youngstown this included individuals who were of various ethnic origins (e.g., Irish, Italian, Greek, Slovak, Hungarian, and even Palestinian or Lebanese). As a category, "working class" is more subjective, as it may be a matter of subjectively understood and inherited class (as was often the case in East London). However, it may also be more measureable in terms of annual income, educational attainment, or work in manual labor. To be inclusive, I interviewed individuals who qualified as working class in any of these ways. Occasionally, this meant including someone like a university-educated individual who was a grocery store cashier.

The case studies took place between April and June 2012 (East London) and between May and July 2013 (Youngstown). In both locations, subjects were examined using complementary, in-depth interviews and observation. In all cases, subjects were notified that I was present for the purpose of research and observation. Before each interview, participants were reminded of this and explained that all statements would be noted but remain unattributed to them. All names used in the study are aliases, with the exception of Youngstown mayoral candidate (now Mayor) John McNally and Barking MP Margaret Hodge, who agreed to speak on the record.

Interviews were structured according to a topic guide, built to discipline the collection of pertinent data required to make descriptive and correlative inferences. The structure of interviews was kept consistent across units and across venues to produce two congruent examinations. Repetition of questions was followed to ensure the reliability of the procedure (King, Keohane, and Verba 1994: 25). However, questions were asked in variable sequences and fashions, tailored to subjects' responses and reported behavior. This fostered the most outwardly casual approach, and permitted further inquiry into fruitful threads of discussion.

To encounter subjects, I employed multidirectional snowball networking. In both East London and Youngstown, I began by reaching out to well-networked individuals and by visiting hubs of community life. In East London, I attended Tenants and Residents Association meetings and local fairs, and spent time in worksites, train stations, and visited bakeries, community centers, and libraries. To reach individuals less likely to be connected with these hubs and well-networked individuals, I also spent an enormous amount of time at pubs (awkward for a researcher who does not drink beer). In Youngstown, I similarly attended community meetings, flea markets, visited metal shops, community centers, diners, and spent a good amount of time at the Youngstown YMCA, the Defend Youngstown store, and the Greyland vintage shop.

Data from both case studies were recorded by hand, in the interest of placing subjects at ease. Because interviews regularly touched on issues of race, prejudice, money, and family, I was concerned that audio recorders would stimulate certain subconscious and conscious defense mechanisms and mitigate subjects' candidness.

Observation was made possible by full immersion into both communities on a daily basis. In the case of Youngstown, I lived on the Northside on Madera Avenue. Observations were made by integrating myself in local life. In East London, this entailed commuting daily to council estates and local pubs.

Ethnography and Replication

The replication of this study is not as simple as with quantitative research, nor as straightforward as qualitative research focusing on targeted elites (for a discussion see King, Keohane, and Verba 1994: 26–27; and for critiques see Brady and Collier 2004).[1] However, it is nevertheless reasonable to expect that a similarly structured study would encounter similar results. There are two principal impediments to precise replication. First, while the target group of subjects was selected according to the plan above, individuals were often encountered randomly. Second, nearly all participants were ensured anonymity (non-attribution) due to the nature of the subject matter, and the extraordinary level of some individuals' distrust and suspicion. Anonymity was also granted to political and community leaders, to facilitate their free speech without concern for electoral or popular backlash after publication, except in the case of elected officials including Barking MP Margaret Hodge, and Youngstown Mayor John McNally—both of whom kindly spoke to me on the record, as it would have been impossible to conceal their identities given the nature of their statements.

Statistical Analysis

I designed a unique survey that was administered to a sample of British respondents in May 2015, and a sample of American respondents in December 2015. Respondents were asked a variety of questions as part of a broad wave of Internet-based polling research conducted by YouGov and SSI, respectively. This survey applied three of this study's key ideas.

First, I sought to measure respondents' senses of deprivation—economically and politically. To do so, respondents were asked to use a 10-point scale to describe:

- How financially well off do you consider yourself?
- How much power do people like you hold?
- How much do politicians care about people like you?

In order to ascertain senses of deprivation, respondents were then asked the same questions, but as they applied to "people like you 30 years ago." This approach allows the respondent to define who "people like you" may be, and solicits respondents' sense of lost economic or political status. The provided 10-point scale allows a more precise measure of deprivation.

Second, I sought to measure respondents' senses of social deprivation, based on the notion of social centrality I developed in my fieldwork. As I did in field interviews, the surveys presented a set of four concentric circles as a model of status in society and asked respondents to place themselves among the rings—a measure of abstract social centrality. Later, the same diagram was presented and I asked respondents to place themselves along with a variety of other groups:

- Muslims
- women
- young people
- immigrants
- the wealthy
- white working class people
- nonwhite working class people
- the elderly
- people like you 30 years ago

This is a measure of contextualized social centrality. As it did in the field, this approach allowed respondents to visualize their social position, their movement over time, and the context of other reference groups' positions (Blumer 1958; Masaoka and Junn 2013). This permits an analysis of individuals' social deprivation, while accounting for the relative placement of others.

Third, I sought to measure political behavior in a variety of forms to better understand what determines the courses individuals take. I presented a list of conventional political acts and asked which of them respondents "have done in the last 12 months to demonstrate your frustration with the way politicians work in your interests or political preferences." The selection includes:

- sign a petition
- attend a neighborhood meeting
- abstain from voting
- vote for a different party
- join a community association
- join a union
- participate in a peaceful protest or strike
- vote or campaign for the British National Party (UK only)
- take part in an English Defense League or English National Alliance protest/demonstration (UK only)

This approach embeds anti-system behavioral choices among pro-system alternatives to reduce social desirability bias—that is, respondents' misrepresenting their true behavior out of concern for palatability or self-incrimination. Respondents are also given the option to note that they "have done in the last 12 months," "haven't done but would do in the future," or "would never do." For my purposes, reporting a willingness or openness to anti-system behavior is effectively as important as performing such an act, and renders respondents a further way to couch their radical right inclinations.

In the United States, respondents were asked to what degree they support or do not support the Tea Party and, separately, the presidential candidacy of Donald Trump. American respondents were also asked how likely they would be to support a hypothetical third party that mirrored the platform of the British National Party—one that advocated for "stopping mass immigration, providing American jobs for American workers, preserving America's Christian heritage, and stopping the threat of Islam."

The survey was administered to 4,742 British adults from April 27 to May 6, 2015, and to 1,005 American respondents from December 16 to January 1, 2016. The British fielding immediately preceded the 2015 general election in the United Kingdom, while the American fielding took place a month before the start of presidential primary elections—times of heightened politicization. While such an environment may frustrate and sensitize some respondents to their marginality, others may receive a unique amount of attention from politicians appealing for their support. As the survey was administered before the (unpredictable) election results were released, respondents were primed neither to feel disappointed or vindicated.

About 93% of the British sample identifies as white. While 51% of the sample is female, 28% identifies as working class, and 42% have a college degree. The average respondent is 49 years old with a standard deviation of about 16 years. The US sample was entirely white, 50% female, and 29% college educated. The average respondent is 46 years old with a standard deviation of about 17 years. It was not possible to analyze individuals who report being "withdrawn" or "sitting out" from political participation, because this survey does not discern between the two groups—one of which is committed to political inactivity, while the other is more complacent or otherwise occupied.

Appendix B

REGRESSION TABLES

Table B.1 **Regressions for Table 8.1**

			Dependent Variable		
			Anti-System UK		
	(1)	(2)	(3)	(4)	(5)
Pol dep (power)	−0.044*				
	(0.025)				
Pol dep (politicians)		−0.077***			
		(0.023)			
Soc dep (abstract)			−0.219***		
			(0.078)		
Soc dep (context)				0.020	
				(0.077)	
Economic deprivation					−0.011
					(0.024)
Conservative	0.353***	0.374***	0.443***	0.424***	0.377***
	(0.055)	(0.055)	(0.064)	(0.062)	(0.055)
Age	−0.485***	−0.496***	−0.515***	−0.403***	−0.497***
	(0.087)	(0.089)	(0.106)	(0.100)	(0.088)

Table B.1 (**Continued**)

	Dependent Variable				
	Anti-System UK				
	(1)	(2)	(3)	(4)	(5)
College	−0.591***	−0.574***	−0.505***	−0.472***	−0.588***
	(0.149)	(0.151)	(0.175)	(0.167)	(0.151)
Female	−0.123	−0.189	−0.407**	−0.364**	−0.110
	(0.134)	(0.135)	(0.162)	(0.153)	(0.135)
Owns home	−0.206	−0.127	−0.342*	−0.419**	−0.323**
	(0.155)	(0.157)	(0.183)	(0.173)	(0.156)
Married	0.019	−0.020	0.132	0.058	0.069
	(0.145)	(0.145)	(0.174)	(0.165)	(0.146)
White	−0.139	−0.190	−0.341	−0.313	−0.076
	(0.284)	(0.285)	(0.302)	(0.285)	(0.293)
Class	−0.160**	−0.140**	−0.127*	−0.121*	−0.152**
	(0.063)	(0.063)	(0.074)	(0.070)	(0.063)
Constant	−1.571***	−1.725***	−1.736***	−1.838***	−1.624***
	(0.428)	(0.430)	(0.481)	(0.462)	(0.440)
Observations	3,265	3,231	2,363	2,569	3,239
Log Likelihood	−837.170	−829.739	−597.041	−661.759	−832.034
Akaike Inf. Crit.	1,694.340	1,679.479	1,214.082	1,343.517	1,684.068

Note: Point estimates for logistic regression coefficients. Standard errors in parentheses. * p < 0.1; ** p < 0.05; *** p < 0.01.

	Dependent Variable				
	Support Trump				
	(1)	(2)	(3)	(4)	(5)
Pol dep (power)	−0.018				
	(0.030)				
Pol dep (politicians)		−0.024			
		(0.029)			

Table B.1 (**Continued**)

	Dependent Variable				
	Support Trump				
	(1)	(2)	(3)	(4)	(5)
Soc dep (abstract)			0.018		
			(0.073)		
Soc dep (context)				0.023	
				(0.065)	
Economic deprivation					−0.088***
					(0.028)
Conservative	0.349***	0.349***	0.350***	0.350***	0.356***
	(0.035)	(0.035)	(0.034)	(0.034)	(0.035)
Age	0.007	0.007	0.007	0.007*	0.006
	(0.004)	(0.004)	(0.004)	(0.005)	(0.004)
College	−0.491***	−0.490***	−0.504***	−0.505***	−0.435***
	(0.168)	(0.167)	(0.167)	(0.167)	(0.169)
Female	−0.397***	−0.393***	−0.391***	−0.389***	−0.410***
	(0.145)	(0.144)	(0.144)	(0.145)	(0.145)
Owns home	0.400**	0.402**	0.398**	0.395**	0.432***
	(0.164)	(0.164)	(0.164)	(0.164)	(0.166)
Married	0.230	0.233	0.237	0.237	0.260
	(0.159)	(0.159)	(0.160)	(0.159)	(0.161)
Constant	−2.216***	−2.214***	−2.223***	−2.232***	−2.309***
	(0.251)	(0.251)	(0.251)	(0.254)	(0.255)
Observations	1,004	1,004	1,004	1,004	1,004
Log Likelihood	−611.172	−610.923	−611.296	−611.352	−606.742
Akaike Inf. Crit.	1,238.343	1,237.845	1,238.592	1,238.704	1,229.484

Note: Point estimates for logistic regression coefficients. Standard errors in parentheses. * $p < 0.1$; ** $p < 0.05$; *** $p < 0.01$.

Table B.1 **(Continued)**

	Dependent Variable				
	Support Tea Party US				
	(1)	(2)	(3)	(4)	(5)
Pol dep (power)	−0.029 (0.030)				
Pol dep (politicians)		−0.060** (0.029)			
Soc dep (abstract)			−0.069 (0.073)		
Soc dep (context)				−0.108* (0.066)	
Economic deprivation					−0.043 (0.028)
Conservative	0.319*** (0.035)	0.318*** (0.035)	0.321*** (0.035)	0.321*** (0.035)	0.323*** (0.035)
Age	−0.011** (0.005)	−0.011** (0.005)	−0.010** (0.005)	−0.011** (0.005)	−0.010** (0.005)
College	−0.085 (0.167)	−0.071 (0.167)	−0.094 (0.166)	−0.087 (0.166)	−0.068 (0.168)
Female	−0.546*** (0.145)	−0.542*** (0.145)	−0.538*** (0.145)	−0.550*** (0.145)	−0.546*** (0.145)
Owns home	0.458*** (0.166)	0.467*** (0.166)	0.460*** (0.166)	0.475*** (0.166)	0.468*** (0.166)
Married	0.377** (0.161)	0.380** (0.161)	0.376** (0.161)	0.371** (0.161)	0.395** (0.161)
Constant	−1.619*** (0.243)	−1.614*** (0.244)	−1.608*** (0.244)	−1.562*** (0.246)	−1.659*** (0.245)
Observations	1,004	1,004	1,004	1,004	1,004
Log Likelihood	−605.482	−604.138	−605.537	−604.717	−605.268
Akaike Inf. Crit.	1,226.964	1,224.276	1,227.073	1,225.435	1,226.537

Note: Point estimates for logistic regression coefficients. Standard errors in parentheses. $^*p < 0.1$; $^{**}p < 0.05$; $^{***}p < 0.01$.

Table B.1 **(Continued)**

	Dependent Variable				
	Support Third Party US				
	(1)	(2)	(3)	(4)	(5)
Pol dep (power)	−0.065**				
	(0.030)				
Pol dep (politicians)		−0.123***			
		(0.030)			
Soc dep (abstract)			−0.083		
			(0.071)		
Soc dep (context)				−0.092	
				(0.064)	
Economic deprivation					−0.051*
					(0.028)
Conservative	0.251***	0.249***	0.253***	0.253***	0.256***
	(0.034)	(0.034)	(0.034)	(0.034)	(0.034)
Age	0.0004	−0.001	0.001	0.001	0.001
	(0.004)	(0.004)	(0.004)	(0.004)	(0.004)
College	−0.372**	−0.361**	−0.396**	−0.395**	−0.369**
	(0.158)	(0.158)	(0.157)	(0.157)	(0.158)
Female	−0.024	0.001	−0.0003	−0.007	−0.005
	(0.141)	(0.142)	(0.141)	(0.141)	(0.141)
Owns home	0.167	0.176	0.166	0.178	0.176
	(0.160)	(0.161)	(0.160)	(0.161)	(0.161)
Married	0.513***	0.524***	0.514***	0.513***	0.536***
	(0.158)	(0.159)	(0.158)	(0.158)	(0.159)
Constant	−0.584**	−0.565**	−0.570**	−0.540**	−0.635***
	(0.231)	(0.232)	(0.231)	(0.233)	(0.232)
Observations	1,004	1,004	1,004	1,004	1,004
Log Likelihood	−623.692	−618.183	−625.134	−624.653	−624.829
Akaike Inf. Crit.	1,263.383	1,252.367	1,266.269	1,265.305	1,265.657

Note: Point estimates for logistic regression coefficients. Standard errors in parentheses. * $p < 0.1$; ** $p < 0.05$; *** $p < 0.01$.

Table B.2 **Regressions for Table 8.2**

	Dependent Variable				
	Pro-System UK				
	(1)	**(2)**	**(3)**	**(4)**	**(5)**
Pol dep (power)	−0.021				
	(0.015)				
Pol dep (politicians)		−0.034**			
		(0.014)			
Soc dep (abstract)			0.061		
			(0.045)		
Soc dep (context)				−0.020	
				(0.045)	
Economic deprivation					0.004
					(0.014)
Conservative	−0.207***	−0.199***	−0.221***	−0.217***	−0.209***
	(0.031)	(0.031)	(0.036)	(0.035)	(0.031)
Age	0.129**	0.133**	0.234***	0.265***	0.108**
	(0.052)	(0.052)	(0.061)	(0.058)	(0.052)
College	0.196**	0.185**	0.188*	0.243***	0.206**
	(0.082)	(0.083)	(0.096)	(0.092)	(0.082)
Female	−0.125	0.012	0.036	0.022	0.022
	(0.188)	(0.187)	(0.202)	(0.192)	(0.186)
Owns home	0.176**	0.138*	0.164*	0.180**	0.115
	(0.077)	(0.077)	(0.090)	(0.086)	(0.077)
Married	0.014	0.014	−0.111	−0.121	0.045
	(0.096)	(0.096)	(0.112)	(0.107)	(0.097)
White	−0.083	−0.042	−0.031	−0.070	−0.049
	(0.083)	(0.083)	(0.098)	(0.094)	(0.083)
Class	0.036	0.052	0.047	0.080**	0.047
	(0.036)	(0.036)	(0.042)	(0.040)	(0.036)
Constant	0.817***	0.535**	0.390	0.122	0.685**
	(0.268)	(0.268)	(0.297)	(0.284)	(0.271)
Observations	3,011	2,978	2,177	2,366	2,985

Table B.2 **(Continued)**

	Dependent Variable				
	Pro-System UK				
	(1)	**(2)**	**(3)**	**(4)**	**(5)**
Log Likelihood	−1,954.128	−1,941.769	−1,426.041	−1,557.329	−1,948.576
Akaike Inf. Crit.	3,928.257	3,903.539	2,872.082	3,134.657	3,917.152

Note: Point estimates for logistic regression coefficients. Standard errors in parentheses. * $p < 0.1$; ** $p < 0.05$; *** $p < 0.01$.

	Dependent Variable				
	Pro−System US (exclude third party)				
	(1)	**(2)**	**(3)**	**(4)**	**(5)**
Pol dep (power)	−0.061				
	(0.048)				
Pol dep (politicians)		−0.078			
		(0.049)			
Soc dep (abstract)			−0.033		
			(0.115)		
Soc dep (context)				−0.185*	
				(0.111)	
Economic deprivation					−0.097**
					(0.047)
Conservative	−0.100*	−0.095	−0.107*	−0.107*	−0.097
	(0.059)	(0.060)	(0.059)	(0.059)	(0.060)
Age	0.013*	0.013*	0.014*	0.012	0.014*
	(0.007)	(0.007)	(0.007)	(0.007)	(0.007)
College	0.036	0.056	0.019	0.022	0.078
	(0.250)	(0.251)	(0.249)	(0.250)	(0.252)
Female	−0.205	−0.229	−0.218	−0.226	−0.190
	(0.222)	(0.223)	(0.222)	(0.222)	(0.223)
Owns home	−0.134	−0.119	−0.122	−0.079	−0.114
	(0.263)	(0.263)	(0.263)	(0.265)	(0.264)

Table B.2 **(Continued)**

	Dependent Variable				
	Pro–System US (exclude third party)				
	(1)	(2)	(3)	(4)	(5)
Married	0.136	0.124	0.139	0.127	0.142
	(0.254)	(0.254)	(0.253)	(0.254)	(0.254)
Constant	−0.127	−0.153	−0.083	−0.002	−0.250
	(0.364)	(0.365)	(0.361)	(0.366)	(0.371)
Observations	348	348	348	348	348
Log Likelihood	−235.596	−235.103	−236.366	−235.009	−234.149
Akaike Inf. Crit.	487.193	486.207	488.732	486.018	484.298

Note: Point estimates for logistic regression coefficients. Standard errors in parentheses. * p < 0.1; ** p < 0.05; *** p < 0.01.

Regressions for Tables 8.3 and 8.4

Each cell of these tables are individual regressions. Because space is limited, the individual regression results are available upon request of the author.

Table B.3 **Regressions for Table 8.5**

	Dependent Variable				
	Tea Party Interaction				
	(1)	(2)	(3)	(4)	(5)
Soc dep (abstract)	0.064				
	(0.098)				
Soc dep (context)		0.014			
		(0.089)			
Pol dep (politicians)			0.073*		
			(0.044)		
Pol dep (power)				−0.024	
				(0.043)	
Economic deprivation					0.025
					(0.040)

Table B.3 (**Continued**)

	Dependent Variable				
	Tea Party Interaction				
	(1)	(2)	(3)	(4)	(5)
Republican	1.382***	1.414***	1.165***	1.314***	1.309***
	(0.146)	(0.146)	(0.161)	(0.157)	(0.151)
Age	−0.012**	−0.012***	−0.011**	−0.012***	−0.012**
	(0.005)	(0.005)	(0.005)	(0.005)	(0.005)
College	−0.148	−0.129	−0.141	−0.124	−0.125
	(0.166)	(0.166)	(0.167)	(0.166)	(0.167)
Female	−0.498***	−0.520***	−0.486***	−0.512***	−0.517***
	(0.145)	(0.146)	(0.146)	(0.145)	(0.146)
Owns home	0.424**	0.436***	0.435***	0.444***	0.446***
	(0.168)	(0.168)	(0.168)	(0.167)	(0.168)
Married	0.374**	0.363**	0.367**	0.383**	0.405**
	(0.162)	(0.162)	(0.163)	(0.162)	(0.162)
Soc dep (abstract)*Repub	−0.378**				
	(0.150)				
Soc dep (context)*Repub		−0.302**			
		(0.132)			
Pol dep (politicians)*Repub			−0.198***		
			(0.062)		
Pol dep (power)*Repub				−0.074	
				(0.058)	
Economic deprivation*Repub					−0.135**
					(0.058)
Constant	−0.802***	−0.779***	−0.785***	−0.833***	−0.827***
	(0.212)	(0.214)	(0.211)	(0.212)	(0.213)
Observations	1,004	1,004	1,004	1,004	1,004
Log Likelihood	−601.315	−601.211	−599.294	−601.766	−601.626
Akaike Inf. Crit.	1,220.630	1,220.422	1,216.589	1,221.531	1,221.251

Note: Point estimates for logistic regression coefficients. Standard errors in parentheses. * $p < 0.1$; ** $p < 0.05$; *** $p < 0.01$.

Table B.3 **(Continued)**

			Dependent Variable		
			Trump Interaction		
	(1)	**(2)**	**(3)**	**(4)**	**(5)**
Soc dep (abstract)	−0.054				
	(0.096)				
Soc dep (context)		−0.013			
		(0.087)			
Pol dep (politicians)			0.044		
			(0.042)		
Pol dep (power)				0.027	
				(0.042)	
Economic deprivation					−0.020
					(0.038)
Republican	1.568***	1.558***	1.412***	1.452***	1.472***
	(0.145)	(0.145)	(0.160)	(0.155)	(0.151)
Age	0.007	0.007	0.006	0.006	0.005
	(0.004)	(0.005)	(0.005)	(0.005)	(0.005)
College	−0.562***	−0.566***	−0.550***	−0.544***	−0.493***
	(0.167)	(0.168)	(0.168)	(0.168)	(0.168)
Female	−0.366**	−0.362**	−0.348**	−0.367**	−0.381***
	(0.145)	(0.145)	(0.146)	(0.145)	(0.146)
Owns home	0.375**	0.372**	0.371**	0.377**	0.399**
	(0.166)	(0.166)	(0.166)	(0.166)	(0.168)
Married	0.229	0.233	0.223	0.238	0.270*
	(0.160)	(0.160)	(0.161)	(0.161)	(0.162)
Soc dep (abstract)*Repub	0.100				
	(0.147)				
Soc dep (context)*Repub		0.051			
		(0.130)			
Pol dep (politicians)*Repub			−0.122**		
			(0.060)		

Table B.3 (**Continued**)

	Dependent Variable				
	Trump Interaction				
	(1)	(2)	(3)	(4)	(5)
Pol dep (power)*Repub				−0.104*	
				(0.058)	
Economic deprivation*Repub					−0.151***
					(0.058)
Constant	−1.408***	−1.407***	−1.354***	−1.367***	−1.400***
	(0.216)	(0.218)	(0.215)	(0.215)	(0.219)
Observations	1,004	1,004	1,004	1,004	1,004
Log Likelihood	−606.556	−606.759	−604.670	−605.023	−597.790
Akaike Inf. Crit.	1,231.113	1,231.517	1,227.341	1,228.047	1,213.580

Note: Point estimates for logistic regression coefficients. Standard errors in parentheses. * p < 0.1; ** p < 0.05; *** p < 0.01.

	Dependent variable				
	Third Party Interaction				
	(1)	(2)	(3)	(4)	(5)
Soc dep (abstract)	−0.021				
	(0.082)				
Soc dep (context)		−0.067			
		(0.075)			
Pol dep (politicians)			−0.010		
			(0.035)		
Pol dep (power)				−0.073**	
				(0.037)	
Economic deprivation					−0.018
					(0.033)
Republican	1.297***	1.292***	1.086***	1.172***	1.222***
	(0.162)	(0.161)	(0.169)	(0.166)	(0.162)

Table B.3 **(Continued)**

			Dependent variable		
			Third Party Interaction		
	(1)	(2)	(3)	(4)	(5)
Age	0.0002	0.0001	0.0002	−0.001	0.001
	(0.004)	(0.004)	(0.004)	(0.004)	(0.004)
College	−0.428***	−0.425***	−0.412***	−0.395**	−0.406***
	(0.157)	(0.157)	(0.157)	(0.158)	(0.157)
Female	0.018	0.002	0.011	0.007	0.006
	(0.142)	(0.142)	(0.143)	(0.143)	(0.142)
Owns home	0.112	0.130	0.119	0.129	0.129
	(0.161)	(0.162)	(0.161)	(0.162)	(0.162)
Married	0.506***	0.503***	0.506***	0.522***	0.539***
	(0.159)	(0.159)	(0.159)	(0.160)	(0.159)
Soc dep (abstract)*Repub	−0.377** (0.166)				
Soc dep (context)*Repub		−0.152 (0.144)			
Pol dep (politicians)*Repub			−0.185*** (0.068)		
Pol dep (power)*Repub				−0.178*** (0.069)	
Economic deprivation*Repub					−0.115* (0.062)
Constant	0.028	0.037	0.016	0.015	−0.031
	(0.201)	(0.203)	(0.201)	(0.202)	(0.202)
Observations	1,004	1,004	1,004	1,004	1,004
Log Likelihood	−615.289	−617.240	−612.895	−606.910	−616.284
Akaike Inf. Crit.	1,248.577	1,252.480	1,243.790	1,231.819	1,250.568

Note: Point estimates for logistic regression coefficients. Standard errors in parentheses. * $p < 0.1$; ** $p < 0.05$; *** $p < 0.01$.

Table B.3 (**Continued**)

	Dependent variable				
	British RR Interaction				
	(1)	(2)	(3)	(4)	(5)
Soc dep (abstract)	−0.063				
	(0.121)				
Soc dep (context)		0.295**			
		(0.117)			
Pol dep (politicians)			−0.024		
			(0.035)		
Pol dep (power)				0.003	
				(0.037)	
Economic deprivation					0.002
					(0.034)
Republican	0.823***	0.745***	0.666***	0.705***	0.645***
	(0.189)	(0.156)	(0.159)	(0.143)	(0.135)
Age	−0.437***	−0.331***	−0.476***	−0.450***	−0.455***
	(0.100)	(0.095)	(0.084)	(0.083)	(0.083)
College	−0.747***	−0.685***	−0.852***	−0.866***	−0.860***
	(0.176)	(0.168)	(0.152)	(0.150)	(0.150)
Female	−0.374**	−0.320**	−0.191	−0.125	−0.119
	(0.158)	(0.151)	(0.133)	(0.132)	(0.132)
Owns home	−0.420**	−0.480***	−0.178	−0.270*	−0.332**
	(0.176)	(0.167)	(0.150)	(0.149)	(0.149)
Married	0.018	−0.076	−0.060	−0.032	0.0003
	(0.172)	(0.164)	(0.144)	(0.143)	(0.144)
Soc dep (abstract)*Repub	−0.102				
	(0.157)				
Soc dep (context)*Repub		−0.300*			
		(0.155)			
Pol dep (politicians)*Repub			−0.052		
			(0.046)		

Table B.3 **(Continued)**

	(1)	(2)	(3)	(4)	(5)
	\multicolumn{5}{c}{*Dependent variable*}				
	\multicolumn{5}{c}{**British RR Interaction**}				
Pol dep (power)*Repub				−0.055 (0.049)	
Economic deprivation*Repub					−0.031 (0.046)
Constant	−0.826*** (0.298)	−0.974*** (0.281)	−0.788*** (0.253)	−0.811*** (0.243)	−0.702*** (0.244)
Observations	2,235	2,426	3,084	3,115	3,092
Log Likelihood	−629.606	−689.731	−875.430	−881.268	−884.607
Akaike Inf. Crit.	1,277.213	1,397.461	1,768.859	1,780.536	1,787.215

Note: Point estimates for logistic regression coefficients. Standard errors in parentheses. * $p < 0.1$; ** $p < 0.05$; *** $p < 0.01$.

Regressions for Figure 8.1

Predicted probabilities were generated using point estimates from regressions in Table 8.1.

Table B.4 **Regressions for Interaction Models in Chapter 8**

	(1)	(2)	(3)	(4)	(5)
	\multicolumn{5}{c}{*Dependent Variable*}				
	\multicolumn{5}{c}{**Anti-System**}				
Pol dep (power)	0.094 (0.087)				
Pol dep (politicians)		−0.134* (0.078)			
Soc dep (abstract)			−0.325 (0.229)		

Table B.4 **(Continued)**

	(1)	(2)	(3)	(4)	(5)
			Dependent Variable		
			Anti-System		
Soc dep (context)				0.410*	
				(0.231)	
Economic deprivation					0.003
					(0.080)
Marginal central	−0.108**	−0.063	−0.022	−0.060*	−0.075**
	(0.042)	(0.045)	(0.044)	(0.035)	(0.038)
Conservative	0.428***	0.475***	0.426***	0.402***	0.435***
	(0.067)	(0.067)	(0.065)	(0.063)	(0.066)
Age	−0.601***	−0.575***	−0.555***	−0.430***	−0.557***
	(0.109)	(0.109)	(0.108)	(0.101)	(0.109)
College	−0.506***	−0.483***	−0.459***	−0.412**	−0.527***
	(0.178)	(0.179)	(0.176)	(0.169)	(0.179)
Female	−0.285*	−0.346**	−0.370**	−0.329**	−0.218
	(0.165)	(0.165)	(0.164)	(0.156)	(0.163)
Owns home	−0.321*	−0.277	−0.291	−0.398**	−0.448**
	(0.187)	(0.186)	(0.185)	(0.176)	(0.185)
Married	0.060	0.032	0.143	0.067	0.078
	(0.175)	(0.175)	(0.176)	(0.167)	(0.175)
White	−0.134	−0.203	−0.351	−0.279	−0.195
	(0.325)	(0.326)	(0.303)	(0.292)	(0.324)
Class	−0.104	−0.080	−0.126*	−0.117	−0.097
	(0.075)	(0.075)	(0.075)	(0.072)	(0.076)
Pol dep1 X marg cent	−0.027**				
	(0.013)				
Pol dep2 X marg cent		0.004			
		(0.012)			
Soc dep1 X marg cent			0.015		
			(0.034)		

Table B.4 **(Continued)**

	(1)	(2)	(3)	(4)	(5)
			Dependent Variable		
			Anti-System		
Soc dep2 X marg cent				−0.064*	
				(0.034)	
Econ dep X marg cent					−0.004
					(0.012)
Constant	−0.923	−1.585***	−1.458**	−1.382***	−1.104*
	(0.579)	(0.596)	(0.567)	(0.531)	(0.582)
Observations	2,214	2,208	2,275	2,466	2,202
Log Likelihood	−569.459	−571.636	−581.922	−640.834	−573.743
Akaike Inf. Crit.	1,162.919	1,167.272	1,187.844	1,305.668	1,171.486

Note: Point estimates for logistic regression coefficients. Standard errors in parentheses. * $p < 0.1$; ** $p < 0.05$; *** $p < 0.01$.

	(1)	(2)	(3)	(4)	(5)
			Dependent variable		
			Trump Support (interaction model)		
Pol dep (power)	−0.046				
	(0.090)				
Pol dep (politicians)		−0.070			
		(0.091)			
Soc dep (abstract)			0.013		
			(0.234)		
Soc dep (context)				0.387*	
				(0.204)	
Economic deprivation					−0.217**
					(0.086)
Marginal central	0.042**	0.045**	0.040**	0.040**	0.049***
	(0.017)	(0.018)	(0.016)	(0.016)	(0.017)

Table B.4 **(Continued)**

	Dependent variable				
	Trump Support (interaction model)				
	(1)	**(2)**	**(3)**	**(4)**	**(5)**
Republican	0.349***	0.349***	0.350***	0.349***	0.359***
	(0.035)	(0.035)	(0.035)	(0.035)	(0.035)
Age	0.007	0.007*	0.008*	0.007	0.007
	(0.005)	(0.005)	(0.005)	(0.005)	(0.004)
College	−0.491***	−0.491***	−0.502***	−0.520***	−0.440***
	(0.168)	(0.168)	(0.168)	(0.168)	(0.169)
Female	−0.411***	−0.418***	−0.410***	−0.404***	−0.435***
	(0.145)	(0.145)	(0.145)	(0.146)	(0.146)
Owns home	0.395**	0.395**	0.393**	0.414**	0.428**
	(0.165)	(0.165)	(0.165)	(0.166)	(0.166)
Married	0.243	0.239	0.243	0.218	0.279*
	(0.160)	(0.160)	(0.160)	(0.161)	(0.162)
Pol dep1 X marg cent	0.002				
	(0.006)				
Pol dep2 X marg cent		0.004			
		(0.006)			
Soc dep1 X marg cent			−0.001		
			(0.015)		
Soc dep2 X marg cent				−0.027**	
				(0.013)	
Econ dep X marg cent					0.010
					(0.006)
Constant	−2.836***	−2.887***	−2.814***	−2.771***	−3.024***
	(0.362)	(0.369)	(0.354)	(0.351)	(0.368)
Observations	1,004	1,004	1,004	1,004	1,004
Log Likelihood	−607.177	−607.209	−607.666	−605.489	−602.112
Akaike Inf. Crit.	1,234.354	1,234.419	1,235.333	1,230.977	1,224.225

Note: Point estimates for logistic regression coefficients. Standard errors in parentheses. * $p < 0.1$; ** $p < 0.05$; *** $p < 0.01$.

Table B.4 **(Continued)**

	(1)	(2)	(3)	(4)	(5)
			Dependent variable		
			Tea Party Support (interaction model)		
Pol dep (power)	−0.032				
	(0.092)				
Pol dep (politicians)		−0.049			
		(0.094)			
Soc dep (abstract)			−0.332		
			(0.243)		
Soc dep (context)				−0.176	
				(0.205)	
Economic deprivation					−0.189**
					(0.089)
Marginal central	0.050***	0.055***	0.057***	0.057***	0.063***
	(0.017)	(0.018)	(0.016)	(0.016)	(0.017)
Republican	0.320***	0.321***	0.324***	0.323***	0.328***
	(0.035)	(0.035)	(0.035)	(0.035)	(0.035)
Age	−0.011**	−0.010**	−0.010**	−0.011**	−0.010**
	(0.005)	(0.005)	(0.005)	(0.005)	(0.005)
College	−0.067	−0.080	−0.075	−0.079	−0.072
	(0.168)	(0.168)	(0.168)	(0.168)	(0.169)
Female	−0.567***	−0.572***	−0.569***	−0.580***	−0.580***
	(0.146)	(0.146)	(0.146)	(0.147)	(0.147)
Owns home	0.462***	0.453***	0.448***	0.474***	0.466***
	(0.167)	(0.167)	(0.167)	(0.168)	(0.168)
Married	0.388**	0.386**	0.389**	0.381**	0.416**
	(0.162)	(0.162)	(0.162)	(0.163)	(0.163)
Pol dep1 X marg cent	−0.002				
	(0.006)				
Pol dep2 X marg cent		0.001			
		(0.006)			
Soc dep1 X marg cent			0.016		
			(0.016)		

Table B.4 **(Continued)**

	Dependent variable				
	Tea Party Support (interaction model)				
	(1)	**(2)**	**(3)**	**(4)**	**(5)**
Soc dep2 X marg cent				0.003	
				(0.013)	
Econ dep X marg cent					0.011*
					(0.006)
Constant	−2.364***	−2.434***	−2.476***	−2.393***	−2.592***
	(0.361)	(0.367)	(0.353)	(0.348)	(0.363)
Observations	1,004	1,004	1,004	1,004	1,004
Log Likelihood	−598.478	−599.792	−599.093	−598.428	−598.039
Akaike Inf. Crit.	1,216.957	1,219.583	1,218.186	1,216.856	1,216.078

Note: Point estimates for logistic regression coefficients. Standard errors in parentheses. * $p < 0.1$; ** $p < 0.05$; *** $p < 0.01$.

	Dependent variable				
	Third Party Support (interaction model)				
	(1)	**(2)**	**(3)**	**(4)**	**(5)**
Pol dep (power)	−0.143				
	(0.092)				
Pol dep (politicians)		−0.087			
		(0.090)			
Soc dep (abstract)			−0.073		
			(0.226)		
Soc dep (context)				−0.082	
				(0.193)	
Economic deprivation					−0.153*
					(0.084)
Marginal central	0.009	0.010	0.010	0.012	0.014
	(0.016)	(0.017)	(0.016)	(0.016)	(0.016)

Table B.4 **(Continued)**

			Dependent variable		
		Third Party Support (interaction model)			
	(1)	**(2)**	**(3)**	**(4)**	**(5)**
Republican	0.249***	0.251***	0.253***	0.253***	0.257***
	(0.034)	(0.034)	(0.034)	(0.034)	(0.034)
Age	−0.001	0.001	0.002	0.001	0.002
	(0.004)	(0.004)	(0.004)	(0.004)	(0.004)
College	−0.363**	−0.373**	−0.397**	−0.395**	−0.375**
	(0.158)	(0.158)	(0.157)	(0.157)	(0.158)
Female	−0.002	−0.028	−0.004	−0.012	−0.009
	(0.142)	(0.141)	(0.141)	(0.141)	(0.141)
Owns home	0.173	0.165	0.164	0.176	0.174
	(0.161)	(0.160)	(0.161)	(0.161)	(0.161)
Married	0.525***	0.513***	0.512***	0.511***	0.542***
	(0.159)	(0.158)	(0.159)	(0.159)	(0.159)
Pol dep1 X marg cent	0.002				
	(0.006)				
Pol dep2 X marg cent		0.002			
		(0.006)			
Soc dep1 X marg cent			−0.001		
			(0.015)		
Soc dep2 X marg cent				−0.001	
				(0.013)	
Econ dep X marg cent					0.008
					(0.006)
Constant	−0.705**	−0.736**	−0.711**	−0.704**	−0.830**
	(0.333)	(0.336)	(0.327)	(0.325)	(0.333)
Observations	1,004	1,004	1,004	1,004	1,004
Log Likelihood	−617.880	−623.443	−624.813	−624.232	−623.958
Akaike Inf. Crit.	1,255.760	1,266.887	1,269.626	1,268.463	1,267.917

Note: Point estimates for logistic regression coefficients. Standard errors in parentheses. * $p < 0.1$; ** $p < 0.05$; *** $p < 0.01$.

Appendix C

INTERVIEW TOPIC GUIDE

[Consent to being a research subject]

[Introduction and Demographics]

What do you like about living in [East London/Youngstown]?

What would you change about living in [East London/Youngstown]?

What was [East London/Youngstown] like when you were growing up?

How has [East London/Youngstown] changed?

What has been driving that change?

What would you do to improve this state of affairs?

Have you suggested this idea to anyone else? Have you tried to change this state of affairs? What [political activities] have you done?

Why not?/Did you feel like you had an impact? Why [not]?

I'm going to draw a diagram. Think of these circles as a model of [East London/Youngstown] society. The people who are in the center circle are the most important, the most influential, and those on each outer circle are less and less central. Where would you place yourself?

Where would you place someone like you 30 years ago?

Who do you think occupies these other rings?

What makes you say that?

Do you think there is such a thing as [upward mobility/The American Dream]?

Do you think the democracy works?

NOTES

Preface

1. "Working class" is a term that has been variably employed with pride, humility, and as a rhetorical tool of mobilization and vilification. Zweig defines classes based on "the degree of authority and independence [employees] typically [have] on the job" (2000: 28). He labels those with the power to "organize and direct production" as capitalists, while the larger group of workers who have "almost no authority" are termed the working class (3). Even so, there is an inconsistency in whether "working class" refers to those without a university degree (Abramowitz and Teixeira 2009)—a modern construction reflective of an increasingly educated labor market—or more classic understandings of those in manual labor and the manufacturing sectors that once formed the core of Western economies. Ultimately, I focus on those white individuals without a university degree, acknowledging that purely economic understandings ignore powerful ethnocultural boundaries of race, religion, age, and regional affinity within the working class, and treat it as an undifferentiated whole. To account for this, I interview and solicit survey responses from a broad variety of "working class" individuals in a manner that accounts for their self-perceptions.

Chapter 1

1. Related prominent theories have pointed to differences in individual personality (Milbrath 1965), rationality (Green and Shapiro 1994), and institutional opportunity structures (see McAdam 1999; Meyer 2004). Relevantly, explanations related to political opportunity have been criticized for ignoring the variability in individual actors' capacity to recognize and take advantage of political opportunities (see Tarrow 1998).
2. East London and Youngstown are largely typical of the post-traumatic regions this chapter underscores. While they are unique in certain ways discussed in Chapters 3 and 4, the samples of respondents I recruit are not intended to be representative of white working class people anyway. It is unrealistic to expect any one case to embody the range and balance of attributes found across its kind. These ethnographies seek to build testable hypotheses that I may apply to subsequently collected survey data from nationally representative samples of white people in the United Kingdom and the United States.

Chapter 2

1. Cited in Skeggs 2004: 88.
2. Three theories are advanced in the literature to explain this trend. First "in-group out-group theory" explains how humans have a propensity to classify others relative to themselves as either members of a common group (in-group members) or members of a different group (out-group members). People are more likely to discriminate against and distrust out-group members. Second, "neo-Darwinian theory" follows a similar logic but makes the concrete assumption that people instinctively prefer members of their own ethnocultural group. Third, "reciprocal altruism" theory proposes that people will in turn cooperate and help people that have cooperated or helped them in the past. Several authors (Gilens 1999; Van der Waal et al. 2011) support the reciprocal altruism hypothesis, without dismissing the role of racial stereotypes in the construction of white working-class identity. Gilens (1999: 173) concludes that the violation of reciprocal altruism, or the belief that welfare recipients are undeserving, is the key factor underlying opposition to welfare in the United States. He goes on to argue that white opposition to welfare programs is reflective of widespread perceptions that African Americans are the largest recipients of welfare and negative stereotypes that African Americans are typically lazy and therefore undeserving (Gilens 1999: 113). Similar results can be found in Europe (Van der Waal et al. 2011: 16; Lamont 2000). In countries with the most generous unemployment benefits, the unemployment level of immigrants is positively related to the welfare chauvinism of natives. The perception that ethnic minorities do not put in what they take out of the welfare system is the dominant explanation for opposition to welfare. Interestingly, Van der Waal et al. find that neither a country's proportion of non-Western immigrants nor its proportion of less-educated immigrants is correlated with levels of welfare chauvinism. They therefore conclude that neither the ethno-racial composition nor educational background of a population has any effect on public opinion (2011: 13–14).
3. This state of affairs can again be traced back to conceptions of racialized poverty. When race is used as a proxy for socioeconomic status it is assumed that the white working-class individual benefits from the same advantages as whites in the upper echelons of society. Indeed, it is imagined that they share in a form of "cross-class alliance" (Olson 2002: 395) that maintains their privileged status. And yet, when this proves not to be the case, the white working-class individual may be left with little opportunity for recourse and great capacity for resentment.

Chapter 3

1. Like all narratives, this collective memory of the remaining few forms a cohesive body of past experiences to define a path for future action (or inaction). (See Lamont, Daniel, and Arzoglou 2011: 304.)

Chapter 4

1. Arguably, the most prominent socioeconomic linguistic distinction in the United States is in Boston, where poorer communities tend to feature what is colloquially known as a Southie accent. Though middle-class communities conform more closely to a Northern or New England standard, there is a distinct "Cape" or "Hyannis" accent which is spoken by certain members of the older aristocracy. Linguistic scholars also commonly study New York City for socioeconomic divisions. Other American examples include Chicago, Charleston, and Baltimore.
2. The presence of such "high" and "low" dialects (also known as "diglossia") is frequently accompanied by code-switching, whereby individuals—particularly politicians or

salespeople—with "elaborated" forms of language adapt to the tendencies of their "restricted" listeners.

Chapter 5

1. It is worth noting that the discussion of nonparticipation and passivity in the context of "political behavior" complicates how we conventionally conceive of "behavior." Indeed, the term connotes an affirmative nature. However, I think it is reasonable to consider abstention, withdrawal, and rejection to be just as behavioral as more activist forms. Indeed, if actors must choose to participate, then they must also choose to abstain. Volition is still entailed.

2. Note that the distinction here is not about whether an individual accepts the public goods and provisions afforded by the political system, like health services, welfare, education, or housing. Consumption does not indicate support or participation as much as it suggests instrumentalism.

3. A complication arises when individual actors occupy more than one classification simultaneously. These borderline examples include:

    Type I/III an actor who is democratically active about some issues and complacent about others;

    Type I/II an actor who engages in both active democratic engagement and active anti-system behavior (such as an activist who occasionally uses violence); and

    Type III/IV an individual who is universally passive, envisions future action in some respects, but is otherwise withdrawn.

    Such cases are hardly anomalies; indeed, they are conventional. In these cases, it is useful to suggest the key triggers of classification. Any actor who exhibits active anti-system behavior (Type I/II) should be considered actively anti-system, because their choice to rebel against or circumvent the system corrupts any other activity within it. Any actor that is ever actively democratic and not actively anti-system (Type I/III) may be classified as actively democratic, as this reflects a (very common) form of selective activism. Passive democratic engagement may be characterized by universal passivity with openness to one-day engaging (Type III/IV), while passive anti-system behavior is characterized by withdrawal without any intention to take part in one-day engagement.

Chapter 6

1. The argument of Sniderman and his coauthors (2000, 2004, 2007) that xenophobic sentiment is more a product of a cultural threat than an economic threat suggests that if ethnoracial lines were transcended, barriers to class integration would be less problematic. Intolerance today, he argues, generates more intolerance down the line (2000: 143–144). Newman (2012a) argues that the perception of cultural threat can be explained by noneconomic concrete threats like language barriers, rather than objective measures like income, employment, and field of occupation.

Chapter 7

1. According to a study by Newman (2013), people with financially struggling friends are more likely to support income redistribution.

2. However, by comparing pre-taxation and post-taxation levels of inequality in industrialized countries, Massey (2007) shows that redistribution in the United States achieves very little in terms of promoting equality.

3. It is worth noting that many respondents were not always sure how to represent the social hierarchies of the past. They located the position they or people like them occupied in the concentric circle diagram, but many were uncertain about the positions of other groups in previous decades.

4. A recent study shows that, in the United Kingdom between 1986 and 2008, the gap between income groups in attitudes toward the wealthy remained stable, whereas attitudes toward welfare recipients converged on the conservative end. Contrary to what political scientists have documented, the gap between income groups in attitudes toward redistribution has not increased over time, in spite of growing inequality (Cavaille and Trump 2012).

Chapter 8

1. Because the manifestations of the radical right in the United States are more mainstream and palatable in public discourse, the American effects I find are larger than those I identify in Britain. One may argue that UKIP could be included in a class of radical right parties, but their platform is more protectionist and nativist than overtly exclusivist or racist. They are also not militant in the manner of the BNP or EDL. Further, the hypothetical third party that I test on American respondents does not possess the stigma and condemnation associated with its BNP counterpart. This stigma can lead to social desirability bias, when respondents are reluctant to share unpopular views. Social condemnation also suppresses real support. Were such a party to emerge in the United States (and perhaps the Trump candidacy was the test balloon), it would likely be subject to similar stigmatization.

2. It is worth emphasizing that this third party is hypothetical. That means that while it espouses similar views to those of the British National Party, it will not possess the BNP's public associations with racism and public disapproval. On the one hand, one may consider this a truer test of support for such policy platforms—cleansed of judgment, as it were. On the other hand, such a third party is free of the media checks and public scrutiny that would accompany it were it to exist in a competitive party landscape.

3. Class is measured using the British NRS social grade scale, which features four categories: AB (higher and middle); C1 (lower middle); C2 (skilled working); and DE (working and non working).

4. I use a logistic regression to regress democratic engagement on each measure of deprivation independently. Again, I then use a simulation to measure and estimate the effects of hypothetical changes in each deprivation measure on the probability of engaging in participatory acts.

5. First differences were calculated by simulation using point estimates from a model that interacts a Republican/Conservative dummy variable with each deprivation measure. Full regression results are in Appendix B.

6. To measure perceived centrality of other groups, I create an index where the perceived location of Muslims, immigrants, and nonwhite working class people (historically disadvantaged groups) are added together into a scale. The lowest value on the scale indicates that the individual placed all three groups on the outermost circle of centrality. The highest value indicates that the individual placed all three groups at the center of society. The hypothesis supposes that deprived individuals who also place all other groups at the center will be most likely to support the radical right. I again use a logistic regression to estimate the impact of deprivation on radical right support. This time, however, I interact this measure of centrality for historically disadvantaged groups with each measure of deprivation.

7. In this measure, I take respondents' self-placement and subtract it from their placement of historically disadvantaged groups. If the score is positive, the individual perceives herself to be more central. If it is negative, she perceives herself to be more marginal.

8. To determine just how fringe these groups are, I use survey weights and calculate the distribution of respondents' attitudes. In Britain, among white respondents, a mere 8.4% of individuals expressed their support for radical right groups; a separate 59.5% reported their engagement in democratic activism. This chapter has shown the manner in which political and social deprivation drive political behavior choices. However, 27.4% and 20.3% of white respondents reported negative movement in the abstract and contextualized social centrality measures, respectively. And 35.8% and 45.8% of white respondents reported political deprivation as a function of lost power or politicians' care, respectively. So clearly, many of these individuals managed democratic engagement anyway. These forms of deprivation therefore constitute an important and largely necessary, but not a sufficient, condition for radical right support among white respondents.

In the United States, 38% of white American respondents support Trump, 35% support the Tea Party, 65% support the hypothetical radical third party, and 14% report participating in democratic political activities (and no support for the various radical right alternatives). Thirty percent of white American respondents reported a sense of social deprivation as measured by their abstract social centrality, but 27% reported a sense of deprivation as framed by the centrality of immigrant-origin groups and minorities. A further 48% and 52% of white American respondents reported senses of political deprivation, as measured by perceptions of power and politicians' care. Finally, 46% reported a sense of economic deprivation.

Appendix A

1. Adapted from Gest 2010.

WORKS CITED

Abrajano, Marisa, and Zoltan L. Hajnal. 2014. *White Backlash: Immigration, Race, and American Politics*. Princeton, NJ: Princeton University Press.

Abramowitz, Alan, and Ruy Teixeira. 2009. "The Decline of the White Working Class and the Rise of a Mass Upper-Middle Class." *Political Science Quarterly* 124 (3): 391–422.

Ackroyd, Peter. 2000. *London: The Biography*. London: Vintage.

Alibhai-Brown, Yasmin. 2007. "The View from India: Horror at these Barbarians." *The Independent*, January 22, http://www.independent.co.uk/voices/commentators/yasmin-alibhai-brown/yasmin-alibhaibrown-the-view-from-india-horror-at-these-barbarians-433136.html.

Allgren, James M. 2009. "Youngstown's Fortunes Rose and Fell with the Steel Industry." In *Remembering Youngstown: Tales from the Mahoning Valley*, edited by Mark C. Peyko, 35–40. Charleston, SC: The History Press.

Bartels, L. M. 2008. *Unequal Democracy: The Political Economy of the New Gilded Age*. Princeton: Princeton University Press.

Bauer, Martin W., and George Gaskell. 2000. *Qualitative Researching with Text, Image and Sound*. London: Sage.

BBC News. 2015. "2015 Election Results." http://www.bbc.com/news/election/2015/results.

Bennett, Tony, Mike Savage, Elizabeth Bortolaia Silva, Alan Warde, Modesto Gayo-Cal, and David Wright. 2009. *Culture, Class, Distinction*. New York: Routledge.

Bishop, Bill. 2008. *The Big Sort: Why the Clustering of Like-Minded America is Tearing Us Apart*. New York: Houghton Mifflin.

Blake, William. 1808 (1998). "Jerusalem." *Milton, a Poem*. Princeton, NJ: Princeton University Press.

Blalock, Hubert M. 1967. *Toward a Theory of Minority Group Relations*. New York: Wiley & Sons.

Bloemraad, Irene. 2005. "Of Puzzles and Serendipity: Doing Research with Cross-National Comparisons and Mixed Methods." In *Research Methods Choices in Interdisciplinary Contexts: War Stories of New Scholars*, edited by Louis DeSipio, Sherrie Kossoudji, and Manuel Garcia y Griego, XX–XX. XXX: SSRC.

Blumer, Herbert. 1958. "Race Prejudice as a Sense of Group Position." *The Pacific Sociological Review* 1 (1): 3–7.

Bourdieu, Pierre, and Jean-Claude Passeron. 1977. *Reproduction in Education, Society and Culture*. London: SAGE Publications.

Brady, Henry, and David Collier, eds. 2004. *Rethinking Social Inquiry: Diverse Tools, Shared Standards*. Oxford: Rowman and Littlefield.

Brattain, Michelle. 2001. *The Politics of Whiteness: Race, Workers, and Culture in the Modern South*. Princeton, NJ: Princeton University Press.

Brodkin, Karen. 1994. "How Did Jews Become White Folks?" In *Race,* edited by Steven Gregory and Roger Sanjek, 78–99. New Brunswick, NJ: Rutgers University Press.

Brown, Michael K. 1991. *Race, Money, and the American Welfare State.* Ithaca, NY: Cornell University Press.

Brownstein, Ronald. 2011. "Eclipsed: Why the White Working Class is the Most Alienated and Pessimistic Group in American Society." *The National Journal,* May 26, http://www.nationaljournal.com/columns/political-connections/white-working-class-americans-see-future-as-gloomy-20110526.

Bruno, Robert. 1999. *Steelworker Alley: How Class Works in Youngstown.* Ithaca, NY: Cornell University Press.

Bureau of Labor Statistics. 2013. "Union Membership in Ohio—2012." http://www.bls.gov/ro5/unionoh.htm.

Bureau of Labor Statistics. 2015. "Union Members Summary." http://www.bls.gov/news.release/union2.nr0.htm.

Buss, Terry F., and F. Stevens Redburn. 1983. *Shutdown at Youngstown: Public Policy for Mass Unemployment.* Albany, NY: State University of New York Press.

Campbell, Angus, Philip E. Converse, Warren E. Miller, and Donald E. Stokes. 1960. *The American Voter.* New York: John Wiley & Sons, Inc.

Carnes, Nicholas. 2012. "Does the Numerical Underrepresentation of the Working Class in Congress Matter?" *Legislative Studies Quarterly* 37 (1): 5–34.

Case, Anne, and Angus Deaton. 2015. "Rising Morbidity and Mortality in Midlife among White Non-Hispanic Americans in the 21st Century," *PNAS* 112 (49): http://www.pnas.org/content/112/49/15078.full.pdf.

Cavaille, Charlotte, and Kris-Stella Trump. 2012. "Redistributive Attitudes in Hard Times." Presented at "The State and Capitalism since 1800" workshop. Cambridge, MA: Harvard University.

Center for Responsive Politics. 2013. "Millionaire Freshmen Make Congress Even Wealthier." http://www.opensecrets.org/news/2013/01/new-congress-new-and-more-wealth/.

Chetty, Raj, Nathaniel Hendren, Patrick Kline, Emmanuel Saez, and Nicholas Turner. 2014. "Is the United States Still a Land of Opportunity? Recent Trends in Intergenerational Mobility." NBER Working Paper 19844. http://www.equality-of-opportunity.org/images/mobility_trends.pdf.

Closed Pubs. 2012. "The Lost Pubs Project." http://www.closedpubs.co.uk/essex/barking.html.

CNN. 2008. "Exit Polls." http://www.cnn.com/ELECTION/2008/results/polls/#val=USP00p1.

CNN. 2010. "Exit Polls." http://www.cnn.com/ELECTION/2010/results/polls/#val= USH00p1.

CNN/ORC. 2015. "Poll August 18, 2015." http://i2.cdn.turner.com/cnn/2015/images/08/17/rel8a.-.gop.2016.pdf

Cobain, Ian. 2006. "Exclusive: Inside the Secret and Sinister world of the BNP." *The Guardian,* December 21.

Collins, Michael. 2004. *The Likes of Us: A Biography of the White Working Class.* London: Granta Books.

Corak, Miles. 2013. "Income Inequality, Equality of Opportunity, and Intergenerational Mobility." *Journal of Economic Perspectives* 27 (3): 79–102. http://pubs.aeaweb.org/doi/pdfplus/10.1257/jep.27.3.79.

CPS. 2012. "Union Data Compilations from 2012." http://www.unionstats.com/.

Dancygier, Rafaela. 2010. *Immigration and Conflict in Europe.* New York: Cambridge University Press.

Davis, Mike. 1986. *Prisoners of the American Dream: Politics and Economy in the History of the US Working Class.* London: Verso.

Dawson, Michael. 1995. *Behind the Mule: Race and Class in African-American Politics.* Princeton, NJ: Princeton University Press.

Demie, Feyisa, and Kirstin Lewis. 2010. *Raising the Achievement of White Working Class Pupils: Barriers and School Strategies.* London: Lambeth Council.

The Democratic Strategist. 2011. "Teixeira on Obama's White Working Class Threshold." http://www.thedemocraticstrategist.org/strategist/2011/06/teixeira_on_obamas_white_worki.php.

Dench, Geoff, Kate Gavron, and Michael Young. 2009. *The New East End: Kinship, Race and Conflict*. London: Profile.

Denis, Jeffrey S. 2012. "Transforming Meanings and Group Positions: Tactics and Framing in Anishinaabe—White Relations in Northwestern Ontario, Canada." *Ethnic and Racial Studies* 35 (3): 453–470.

Department for Business, Innovation & Skills. 2013. "Trade Union Membership 2012." https://www.gov.uk/government/uploads/system/uploads/attachment_data/file/204169/bis-13-p77-trade-union-membership-2012.pdf.

DiTomaso, Nancy. 2012. *The American Non-Dilemma: Racial Inequality without Racism*. New York: Russell Sage Foundation.

Douthat, Ross, and Reihan Salam. 2008. *Grand New Party*. New York: Doubleday.

Dudley, Kathryn Marie. 1994. *The End of the Line: Lost Jobs, New Lives in Postindustrial America*. Chicago: The University of Chicago Press.

Edsall, Thomas B. 2012. "White Working Chaos." *The New York Times*, June 25, http://campaign-stops.blogs.nytimes.com/2012/06/25/white-working-chaos/.

European Parliament. 2015. "Results of the 2014 European Elections." http://www.europarl.europa.eu/elections2014-results/en/country-introduction-2014.html.

Fantasia, Rick. 1988. *Cultures of Solidarity: Consciousness, Action, and Contemporary American Workers*. Berkeley: University of California Press.

Fantasia, Rick, and Kim Voss. 2004. *Hard Work: Remaking the American Labor Movement*. Berkeley: University of California Press.

Fenton, Peter Tyler, Sanna Markkanen, Anna Clarke, and Christine Whitehead. 2010. "Why Do Neighbourhoods Stay Poor? Deprivation, Place and People in Birmingham: A Report to the Barrow Cadbury Trust." Cambridge, UK: The Cambridge Center for Housing and Planning Research.

Ford, Robert. 2015. "Where the Votes Switched and Why: The Key Lessons for Parties." *The Guardian*, May 9, http://www.theguardian.com/politics/2015/may/10/election-2015-where-the-votes-switched-and-why.

Ford, Robert, and Matthew Goodwin. 2010. "Angry White Men: Individual and Contextual Prediction of Support for the British National Party." *Political Studies* 58: 1–25.

Ford News. 2011. "100 Years: Celebrating Ford's Centenary in Britain: From the Model T at Trafford Park to Today's UK Market Leader." *Ford News*, March, http://www.at.ford.com/news/Publications/Publications/2009_FOE/112/@Ford112%20-%20March%202011%20-%20Fordnews.pdf.

Freeman, Gary. 2009. "Immigration, Diversity, and Welfare Chauvinism." *The Forum* 7 (3): Article 7.

Gaventa, John. 1980. *Power and Powerlessness: Quiescence and Rebellion in an Appalachian Valley*. Champaign: University of Illinois Press.

Gelman, Andrew. 2009. *Red State, Blue State, Rich State, Poor State: Why Americans Vote the Way They Do*. Princeton, NJ: Princeton University Press.

Gest, Justin. 2010. *Apart: Alienated and Engaged Muslims in the West*. New York: Columbia University Press.

Gest, Justin. 2015. "Pro- and Anti-System Behavior: A Complementary Approach to Voice and Silence in Studies of Political Behavior." *Citizenship Studies* 19 (5).

Gilens, Martin. 2005. "Inequality and Democratic Responsiveness." *Public Opinion Quarterly* 69 (5): 778–796.

Gilens, Martin. 1999. *Why Americans Hate Welfare: Race, Media and the Politics of Antipoverty Policy*. Cambridge, UK: Cambridge University Press.

Givens, Terri. 2005. *Voting Radical Right in Western Europe*. Cambridge, UK: Cambridge University Press.

Goodwin, Matthew. 2011. *Right Response: Understanding and Countering Populist Extremism in Europe*. London: Chatham House Report.

Green, Donald P., and Ian Shapiro. 1994. *Pathologies of Rational Choice Theory: A Critique of Applications in Political Science*. New Haven, CT: Yale University Press.

Gurr, Ted Robert. 1970. *Why Men Rebel.* Princeton, NJ: Princeton University Press.

Gusfield, Joseph R. 1963. *Symbolic Crusade: Status Politics and The American Temperance Movement.* Urbana: The University of Illinois Press.

Hainmueller, Jens, and Daniel Hopkins. 2014. "Public Attitudes toward Immigration." *American Political Science Review* 17: 225–249.

Harris, Cheryl I. 1993. "Whiteness as Property." *Harvard Law Review* 106 (8): 1707–1791.

Held, David. 2006. *Models of Democracy.* Cambridge, UK: Polity.

Hewstone, Miles E., and Rupert Brown, eds. 1986. *Contact and Conflict in Intergroup Encounters. Social psychology and society.* Cambridge, MA: Basil Blackwell.

Hirsch, Barry T., David A. Macpherson, and Wayne G. Vroman. 2001. "Estimates of Union Density by State." *Monthly Labor Review* 124 (7): XX–XX.

Hirschman, Albert O. 1970. *Exit, Voice, and Loyalty: Responses to Decline in Firms, Organizations, and States.* Cambridge, MA: Harvard University Press.

Hochschild, Jennifer L. 1991. "The Politics of the Estranged Poor." *Ethics* 101 (3): 560–578.

Hochschild, Jennifer L. 1995. *Facing Up to the American Dream: Race, Class, and the Soul of the Nation.* Princeton, NJ: Princeton University Press.

Hofstadter, Richard. 1967. *The Paranoid Style in American Politics: And Other Essays.* Vintage Books. http://www.amazon.com/The-paranoid-style-Americanpolitics/dp/B0007EB90E.

Hoynes, Hilary W., Douglas L. Miller, and Jessamyn Schaller. 2012. "Who Suffers During Recessions." NBER Working Paper No. 17951.

Hudson, Paul. 2009. "80 Years of Ford at Dagenham." *The Telegraph,* May 15, http://www.telegraph.co.uk/motoring/classiccars/5318900/80-years-of-Ford-at-Dagenham.html.

Ignatiev, Noel. 1995. *How the Irish Became White.* New York: Routledge.

Inglehart, Ronald, and Christian Welzel. 2005. *Modernization, Cultural Change, and Democracy: The Human Development Sequence.* Cambridge, UK: Cambridge University Press.

Jones, Owen. 2011. *Chavs: The Demonization of the Working Class.* London: Verso.

Jones, Robert P., and Daniel Cox. 2012. "Beyond Guns and God: Understanding the Complexities of the White Working Class in America." Public Religion Research Institute, September 20, http://publicreligion.org/research/2012/09/race-class-culture-survey-2012/.

Joppke, Christian. 2007. "Beyond National Models: Civic Integration Policies for Immigrants in Western Europe." *West European Politics* 30 (1): 1–22.

Joppke, Christian. 2010. "Minority Rights For Immigrants? Multiculturalism Versus Antidiscrimination." *Israel Law Review* 43 (1): 49–66.

Jost, John, and Orsolya Hunyady. 2005. "Antecedents and Consequences of System-Justifying Ideologies." *Current Directions in Psychological Science* 14 (5): 260–265.

Jost, John, Mahzarin Banaji, and Brian Nosek. 2004. "A Decade of System Justification Theory: Accumulated Evidence of Conscious and Unconscious Bolstering of the Status Quo." *Political Psychology* 25 (6): 881–919.

Judis, John. 2007. "Back to the Future." *The American Prospect,* June 17, http://prospect.org/article/back-future.

Katznelson, Ira. 1981. *City Trenches: Urban Politics and the Patterning of Class in the United States.* Chicago: University of Chicago Press.

Kaufmann, Eric P. 2004a. "The Decline of the WASP in the United States and Canada." In *Rethinking Ethnicity: Majority Groups and Dominant Minorities,* edited by Eric P. Kaufmann, 61–83. New York: Routledge.

Kaufmann, Eric P. 2004b. "Introduction: Dominant Ethnicity: From Background to Foreground." In *Rethinking Ethnicity: Majority Groups and Dominant Minorities,* edited by Eric P. Kaufmann, 1–14. New York: Routledge.

Kaufmann, Eric. 2004c. *The Rise and Fall of Anglo-America.* Cambridge, MA: Harvard University Press.

Kaufmann, Eric P. 2014. Personal Correspondence with Author. July 23.

Kelly, Nathan, and Peter Enns. 2010. "Inequality and the Dynamics of Public Opinion: The Self-Reinforcing Link between Economic Inequality and Mass Preferences." *American Journal of Political Science* 54 (4): 855–870.

Kennedy, Liam. 1996. "Alien Nation: White Male Paranoia and Imperial Culture in the United States." *Journal of American Studies* 30 (1): 87–100.

Kinder, Donald R., and Cindy D. Kam. 2009. *Us Against Them: Ethnocentric Foundations of American Opinion.* Chicago: The University of Chicago Press.

King, Vary, Robert O. Keohane, and Sidney Verba. 1994. *Designing Social Inquiry: Scientific Inference in Quantitative Research.* Princeton, NJ: Princeton University Press.

King, Gary, Michael Tomz, and Jason Wittenberg. 2000. "Making the Most of Statistical Analyses: Improving Interpretation and Presentation." *American Journal of Political Science* 44: 341–355.

Kobler, John. 1963. "Crime Town USA." *Saturday Evening Post,* March.

Krouse, Peter. 2010. "State Sen. Capri Cafaro's Dad Admits Making Illegal Contribution to her Unsuccessful Bid for Congress." Cleveland.com, February 22, http://blog.cleveland.com/metro/2010/02/state_sen_capri_cafaros_dad_ac.html

Labov, William. 2006. *The Social Stratification of English in New York.* Cambridge, UK: Cambridge University Press.

Lamont, Michèle. 2000. *The Dignity of Working Men.* Cambridge, MA: Harvard University Press.

Lamont, Michèle, Caitlin Daniel, and Eleni Arzoglou. 2011. "European Workers: Meaning-Making Beings." In *Comparing European Workers Part B: Policies and Institutions,* edited by David Brady, 287–312. Bingley, UK: Emerald Group Publishing Limited.

Laslett, Peter. 1971. *The World We Have Lost.* London: Methuen & Co. Ltd.

Laurin, Kristin, Grainne Fitzsimons, and Aaron Kay. 2010. "Social Disadvantage and the Self-Regulatory Function of Justice Beliefs." *Journal of Personality and Social Psychology* 100 (1): 149–171.

Leith, Dick. 1997. *A Social History of English.* London: Routledge.

Levison, Andrew. 2013. *The White Working Class Today: Who They Are, How They Think, And How Progressives And Regain Their Support.* Democratic Strategist Press.

Linkon, Sherry Lee, and John Russo. 2002. *Steeltown U.S.A.: Work and Memory in Youngstown.* Lawrence: University Press of Kansas.

Lipsitz, George. 2006. *The Possessive Investment in Whiteness: How White People Profit from Identity Politics.* Philadelphia: Temple University Press.

London Borough of Barking & Dagenham. 2013. "Local Council Elections."

London Borough of Barking & Dagenham. 2011a. "Joint Strategic Needs Assessment—Educational Attainment 2011."

London Borough of Barking & Dagenham. 2011b. "Joint Strategic Needs Assessment Summary 2011."

London Borough of Barking & Dagenham. 2010a. "General Election Results 2010."

London Borough of Barking & Dagenham. 2010b. "Joint Strategic Needs Assessment—Perceptions of Community Safety 2010."

London Borough of Barking & Dagenham. 2010c. "Local Election Returns—Thursday 6 May 2010."

London Borough of Barking & Dagenham. 2006. "Local Election Returns—Thursday 4 May 2006."

Lynd, Alice, and Staughton Lynd. 2000. "A Common Bond." In *Rank and File: Personal Histories by Working-Class Organizers,* edited by Alice Lynd and Staughton Lynd, 283–284. Chicago: Haymarket.

Maharidge, Dale. 1996. *The Coming White Minority: California's Eruptions and America's Future.* New York: Random House.

Maharidge, Dale. 1985. *Journey to Nowhere: The Saga of the New Underclass.* Garden City, NY: Doubleday.

Mahoning County Board of Elections. 2013. "General Election Results." http://www.mahoning-countyoh.gov.

Marx, Karl. 1975. "Letter Written 9 April 1870 to Sigfrid Meyer and August Vogt in New York." In *Selected Correspondence by Karl Marx and Friedrich Engels,* 220–224. Moscow: Progress Publishers.

Masaoka, Natalie, and Jane Junn. 2013. *The Politics of Belonging: Race, Public Opinion and Immigration*. Chicago: University of Chicago Press.

Massey, Douglas. 2007. Categorically Unequal: The American Stratification System. New York: Russell Sage Foundation.

Massey, Douglas S., and Nancy A. Denton. 1993. *American Apartheid: Segregation and the Making of the Underclass*. Cambridge, MA: Harvard University Press.

Maynes, Mary Jo, Jennifer L. Pierce, and Barbara Laslett. 2008. *Telling Stories: The Use of Personal Narratives in the Social Sciences and History*. Ithaca, NY: Cornell University Press.

Mazumder, Bhash. 2012. "Is Intergenerational Economic Mobility Lower Now than in the Past?" The Federal Reserve Bank of Chicago, 297.

McAdam, Doug. 1999. *Political Process and the Development of Black Insurgency, 1930–1970*. Chicago: University of Chicago Press.

McCall, Leslie. 2013. *The Undeserving Rich: American Beliefs about Inequality, Opportunity, and Redistribution*. Cambridge, UK: Cambridge University Press.

McDermott, Monica. 2006. *Working-Class White: The Making and Unmaking of Race Relations*. Berkeley: University of California Press.

Meyer, David S. 2004. "Protest and Political Opportunities." *Annual Review of Sociology* 30: 125–145.

Milbrath, Lester W. 1965. *Political Participation: How and Why Do People Get Involved in Politics?* Chicago: Rand McNally College Publishing Company.

Milliken, Peter H., and David Skolnick. 2012. "Documents Here: Oakhill Documents Reveal Web of Conspiracy." *The Vindicator*, July 27, http://www.vindy.com/news/2012/july/27/by-peter-h-milliken/.

Montopoli, Brian. 2012. "Charity President: Paul Ryan "Did Nothing" at Soup Kitchen Photo-Op." CBS News, October 16, http://www.cbsnews.com/news/charity-president-paul-ryan-did-nothing-at-soup-kitchen-photo-op/

Morgan, Edmund S. 1975. *American Slavery, American Freedom: The Ordeal of Colonial Virginia*. New York: W.W. Norton.

Mudde, Cas. 2015. "The Trump Phenomenon and the European Populist Radical Right." *Washington Post*, August 26, https://www.washingtonpost.com/blogs/monkey-cage/wp/2015/08/26/the-trump-phenomenon-and-the-european-populist-radical-right/.

Murray, Charles. 2012. *Coming Apart: The State of White America, 1960–2010*. New York: Random House.

National Equity Panel. 2010. "An Anatomy of Economic Inequality in the UK: Report of the National Equity Panel." http://news.bbc.co.uk/2/shared/bsp/hi/pdfs/27_01_10_inequalityfull.pdf.

Nelson, Bruce. 2001. *Divided We Stand: American Workers and the Struggle for Black Equality*. Princeton, NJ: Princeton University Press.

NEOSCC. 2013. "My Vibrant Daily Blog." Northeast Ohio Sustainable Communities Consortium Initiative, May 1, http://vibrantneo.org/.

Neville, John. 2009. "Ford Dagenham's 80 Year History." BBC Essex, October 6, http://news.bbc.co.uk/local/essex/hi/people_and_places/history/newsid_8292000/8292277.stm.

Newman, Benjamin J. 2013. "My Poor Friend: Financial Distress in One's Social Network, The Perceived Power of the Rich, and Support for Redistribution." *Journal of Politics* 76 (2): 126–138.

Newman, Benjamin J. 2012a. "Acculturating Contexts and Anglo Opposition to Immigration in the United States." *American Journal of Political Science* 57 (2): 374–390.

Newman, Benjamin J. 2012b. "Foreign Language Exposure, Cultural Threat, and Opposition to Immigration." *Political Psychology* 33 (5): 635–657.

OECD. 2010. *Economic Policy Reforms: Going for Growth*. Paris: OECD. http://www.keepeek.com/Digital-Asset-Management/oecd/economics/economic-policy-reforms-2010_growth-2010-en#page1.

Olsen, Henry. 2010. "GOP Heaven, West Virginia?" *National Review Online*, October 1, http://www.nationalreview.com/articles/248274/gop-heaven-west-virginia-henry-olsen.

Olson, Joel. 2002. "Whiteness and the Participation-Inclusion Dilemma." *Political Theory* 30 (3): 384–409.

Olson, Joel. 2008. "Whiteness and the Polarization of American Politics." *Political Research Quarterly* 61 (4): 704–718.

Packer, George. 2013. *The Unwinding: An Inner History of the New America*. New York: Farrar, Straus and Giroux.

Pakulski, Jan, and Malcolm Waters. 1996. *The Death of Class*. London: Sage.

Parker, Christopher S., and Matt A. Barreto. 2013. *Change They Can't Believe In: The Tea Party and Reactionary Politics in America*. Princeton, NJ: Princeton University Press.

Pettigrew, Thomas F., and Linda R. Tropp. 2006. "A Meta-Analytic Test of Intergroup Contact Theory." *Journal of Personality and Social Psychology* 90 (5): 751–783.

The Pew Charitable Trusts. 2013. "Moving On Up: Why Do Some Americans Leave the Bottom of the Economic Ladder, but Not Others?" http://www.pewstates.org/research/reports/moving-on-up-85899518104.

Peyko, Mark C., ed. 2009. *Remembering Youngstown: Tales from the Mahoning Valley*. Charleston, SC: The History Press.

Putnam, Robert D. 2007. "*E Pluribus Unum*: Diversity and Community in the Twenty-first Century." *Scandinavian Political Studies* 30 (2): 137–174.

Putnam, Robert D., Carl B. Frederick, and Kaisa Snellman. 2012. "Growing Class Gaps in Social Connectedness among American Youth." In *The Saguaro Seminar: Civic Engagement in America*. Cambridge, MA: Harvard Kennedy School of Government.

Reardon, Sean F. (2011). "The Widening Achievement Gap Between the Rich and the Poor: New Evidence and Possible Explanations." In *Whither Opportunity? Rising Inequality, Schools, and Children's Life Chances,* edited by Greg J. Duncan and Richard J. Murnane, 91–116. New York: Russell Sage Foundation.

Roediger, David R. 1991. *The Wages of Whiteness: Race and the Making of the American Working Class*. London: Verso.

Rotter, Julian B. 1990. "Internal Versus External Control of Reinforcement: A Case History of a Variable." *American Psychologist* 45 (4): 489–493.

Saffran, Dennis Jay. 1977. *Social Issues, Economic Issues and White Workers: The Effect of the Recession on White Working Class Political Behavior*. Cambridge, MA: Harvard University Press.

Savage, Mike. 2005. "Working-class Identities in the 1960s: Revisiting the Affluent Worker Study." *Sociology* 39 (5): 929–946.

Savage, Mike, Fiona Devine, Niall Cunningham, Mark Taylor, Yaojun Li, Johs Hjellbrekke, Brigitte Le Roux, Sam Friedman, and Andrew Miles. 2013. "A New Model of Social Class? Findings from the BBC's Great British Class Survey Experiment." *Sociology* 47 (2): 219–250.

Schlozman, Kay Lehman, Sidney Brady, and Henry E. Brady. 2013. *The Unheavenly Chorus: Unequal Political Voice and the Broken Promise of American Democracy*. Princeton, NJ: Princeton University Press.

Schneider, Jane, and Peter Schneider. 2005. "The Sack of Two Cities: Organized Crime and Political Corruption in Youngstown and Palermo." In *Corruption: Anthropological Perspectives*, edited by Dieter Haller and Cris Shore, 29–46. London: Pluto Press.

Schudson, Michael. 1999. *The Good Citizen: A History of American Civic Life*. Cambridge, MA: Harvard University Press.

Sennett, Richard, and Jonathan Cobb. 1972. *The Hidden Injuries of Class*. New York: Alfred A. Knopf, Inc.

Shefter, Martin. 1986. "Trade Unions and Political Machines: The Organization and Disorganization of the American Working Class in the Late Nineteenth Century." In *Working-Class Formation: Nineteenth-Century Patterns in Western Europe and the United States,* edited by Ira Katznelson and Aristide R. Zolberg. Princeton, NJ: Princeton University Press.

Sharone, Ofer. 2013. "Why do Unemployed Americans Blame Themselves while Israelis Blame the System?" *Social Forces* 91 (4): 1429–1450.

Silva, Jennifer M. 2013. *Coming Up Short: Working-Class Adulthood in an Age of Uncertainty.* New York: Oxford University Press.

Singer, Audrey. 2013. "Contemporary Immigrant Gateways in Historical Perspective." *Daedalus* 142 (3).

Skeggs, Beverly. 2004. *Class, Self, Culture.* New York: Routledge.

Skidelsky, Robert. 2013. "Meeting our Makers: Britain's Long Industrial Decline." *New Statesman,* January 24, http://www.newstatesman.com/culture/culture/2013/01/meeting-our-makers-britain%E2%80%99s-long-industrial-decline.

Skolnick, David. 2016. "Mahoning Co. Sees 1K Dems Defect to GOP." *The Vindicator.* 3 March 2016. Accessed via http://www.vindy.com/news/2016/mar/03/mahoning-co-sees-k-voters-defect-to-gop/.

Sniderman, Paul, and Louk Hagendoorn. 2007. *When Ways of Life Collide.* Princeton, NJ: Princeton University Press.

Sniderman, Paul, Louk Hagendoorn, and Markus Prior. 2004. "Predisposing Factors and Situational Triggers: Exclusionary Reactions to Immigrant Minorities." *American Political Science Review* 98 (1): 35–49.

Sniderman, Paul M., Pierangelo Peri, Rui de Pierangelo, Figuieredo, Jr., and Thomas Piazza. 2000. *The Outsider: Prejudice and Politics in Italy.* Princeton, NJ: Princeton University Press.

Standing, Guy. 2011. *The Precariat: The New Dangerous Class.* New York: Bloomsbury Academic.

Steele, Claude M. 1997. "A Threat in the Air: How Stereotypes Shape Intellectual Identity and Performance." *American Psychologist* 52 (6): 613–629.

Steensland, Brian. 2008. *The Failed Welfare Revolution: America's Struggle Over Guaranteed Income Policy.* Princeton, NJ: Princeton University Press.

Suddes, Thomas. 2016. "Donald Trump Won in Hurting Ohio Counties that Favor Political Outsiders: Thomas Suddes." *Cleveland Plain Dealer,* March 20, http://www.cleveland.com/opinion/index.ssf/2016/03/donald_trump_won_in_hurting_oh.html.

Sunak, Rishi, and Saratha Rajeswaran. 2014. "A Portrait of Modern Britain." London: *Policy Exchange.* http://www.policyexchange.org.uk/images/publications/a%20portrait%20of%20modern%20britain.pdf.

Sveinsson, Kjartan Páll, ed. 2009. *Who Cares About the White Working Class?* London: Runnymede Trust.

Tames, Richard. 2002. *Barking Past.* Chichester, UK: Phillimore and Company.

Tarrow, Sidney. 1998. *Power in Movement.* Cambridge, UK: Cambridge University Press.

Telegraph. 2015. "General Election Results." http://www.telegraph.co.uk/news/general-election-2015/parliamentary-constituencies/.

Templeton, Fredric. 1966. "Alienation and Political Participation: Some Research Findings." *The Public Opinion Quarterly* 30 (2): 249–261.

Thompson, E. P. 1963. *The Making of the English Working Class.* New York: Vintage Books.

UK Department for Business Innovation and Skills. 2015. "Trade Union Membership 2014." https://www.gov.uk/government/uploads/system/uploads/attachment_data/file/431564/Trade_Union_Membership_Statistics_2014.pdf.

UK Department of Education. 2012. "2012 School Census: Schools, Pupils and their Characteristics." http://www.education.gov.uk/researchandstatistics/statistics/allstatistics/a00209478/schl-pupil-charac-jan-2012.

UK Office for National Statistics. 2012. "Under 18 Conception Rate per 1,000 Women in Age Group (Barking and Dagenham Compared with England and Wales)." http://www.neighbourhood.statistics.gov.uk/HTMLDocs/dvc22/conception.html.

UK Parliament. 2000. "Select Committee on Trade and Industry-II Recent Events." http://www.publications.parliament.uk/pa/cm200001/cmselect/cmtrdind/128/12807.htm.

US Census Bureau. 1963. "Characteristics of the Population, for Standard Metropolitan Statistical Areas, Urbanized Areas, and Urban Places of 10,000 or More: 1960." *Census of the*

Population: 1960, Vol. 1 Characteristics of the Population, Part 37 Ohio. https://www.census. gov/prod/www/decennial.html.

US Census Bureau. 1973. "Race by Sex for Areas and Places: 1970." *1970 Census of the Population, Vol. 1 Characteristics of the Population, Part 37 Ohio.* https://www.census.gov/prod/www/ decennial.html.

US Census Bureau. 1983. "Race by Sex: 1980: Places of 2,500 or More." *1980 Census of the Population, Vol. 1 Characteristics of the Population, Chapter C General Social and Economic Characteristics, Part 37 Ohio.* http://www2.census.gov/prod2/decennial/documents/ 1980/1980censusofpopu80137un_bw.pdf.

US Census Bureau. 1990. "1990 Census of Population and Housing Public Law 94–171 Data (Official) Age by Race and Hispanic Origin." http://censtats.census.gov/cgi-bin/pl94/ pl94data.pl.

US Census Bureau. 2000. "Profile of General Demographics Characteristics 2000: Youngstown City, OH." http://factfinder2.census.gov/faces/tableservices/jsf/pages/productview.xhtml?src=CF

US Census Bureau. 2010. "Race and Hispanic or Latino Origin: 2010: Youngstown City, OH." http://factfinder2.census.gov/faces/tableservices/jsf/pages/productview.xhtml?src=CF.

US Census Bureau. 2015a. "Educational Attainment." *Current Population Survey.* https://www. census.gov/hhes/socdemo/education/data/cps/historical/.

US Census Bureau. 2015b. "Historical Incomes Table: People." *Current Population Survey.* https:// www.census.gov/hhes/www/income/data/historical/people/

US Census Bureau. 2015c. "Millennials Outnumber Baby Boomers and Are Far More Diverse, Census Bureau Reports." http://www.census.gov/newsroom/press-releases/2015/cb15- 113.html.

Usherwood, Bob. 2007. *Equity and Excellence in the Public Library: Why Ignorance is Not our Heritage.* Hampshire, UK: Ashgate.

Van der Waal, Jeroen, Peter Achterbergand, and Wim Van Oorschot. 2011. "Why Are in Some European Countries Immigrants Considered Less Entitled to Welfare?" Paper presented at the Norface Conference, London, April 6–9.

Vecoli, Rudolph. 1995. "Are Italian Americans Just White Folks?" *Italian Americana* 13 (2): 149–161.

Vedder, Richard, Matthew Denhart, and Jonathan Robe. 2012. "Ohio Right-to-Work: How the Economic Freedom of Workers Enhances Prosperity." Columbus, OH: The Buckeye Institute for Public Policy Solutions.

Verba, Sidney, and Norman H. Nie. 1972. *Participation in America: Political Democracy and Social Equality.* New York: Harper and Row.

Verba, Sidney, Norman H. Nie, and Jae-on Kim. 1978. *Participation and Political Equality: A Seven-Nation Comparison.* Chicago: University of Chicago Press.

Verba, Sidney, Kay Lehman Schlozman, and Henry E. Brady. 1995. *Voice and Equality: Civic Voluntarism in American Politics.* Cambridge, MA: Harvard University Press.

Vickers, Ian. 2012. "Barking and Dagenham Local History." http://www.barkingdagenhamlocal-history.net/index.html.

The Vindicator. 2013. "Youngstown Mayor's Race Leaves a Lot to be Desired." *The Vindicator,* October 27, http://www.vindy.com/news/2013/oct/27/youngstown-mayors-race-leaves-a-lot-to-b/?print.

The Vindicator. 2012. "A perversion of a system meant to promote good." The Vindicator, July 27. http://www.vindy.com/news/2012/jul/27/a-perversion-of-a-system-meant-to-promot/.

Wacquant, Loïc. 2008. *Urban Outcasts: A Comparative Sociology of Advanced Marginality.* Cambridge, UK: Polity Press.

Waters, Mary. 1990. *Ethnic Options: Choosing Identities in America.* Berkeley: University of California Press.

Welsh, Tom. 2009b. "Don Hanni: Remembering Mahoning County's Bombastic Democratic Party Boss." In *Remembering Youngstown: Tales from the Mahoning Valley,* edited by Mark C. Peyko, 78–84. Charleston, SC: The History Press.

Whoriskey, Peter. 2011. "Growing Wealth Widens Distance Between Lawmakers and Constituents." *The Washington Post*, December 26, http://www.washingtonpost.com/business/economy/growing-wealth-widens-distance-between-lawmakers-and-constituents/2011/12/05/gIQAR7D6IP_story.html.

Wilcox, W. Bradford. 2010. "When Marriage Disappears: The New Middle America." The State of Our Unions, http://stateofourunions.org/2010/when-marriage-disappears.php.

Willamson, Kevin. 2016. "The Father-Führer." *National Review*, March 28, https://www.national-review.com/nrd/articles/432569/father-f-hrer

Willis, Paul. 1977. *Learning to Labor: How Working Class Kids get Working Class Jobs.* New York: Columbia University Press.

Wilson, William Julius. 1987. *The Truly Disadvantaged: The Inner City, the Underclass, and Public Policy.* Chicago: University of Chicago Press.

Wirth, Louis. 1940. "The Problem of Minority Groups." In Ralph Linton, ed., *The Science of Man in the World Crisis.* New York: Columbia University Press.

Wray, Matt. 2006. *Not Quite White: White Trash and the Boundaries of Whiteness.* Durham, NC: Duke University Press.

Wright, Theodore P. 2004. "The Identity and Changing Status of Former Elite Minorities: The Contrasting Cases of North Indian Muslims and American WASPS." In *Rethinking Ethnicity: Majority Groups and Dominant Minorities,* edited by Eric P. Kaufmann, 31–38. New York: Routledge.

Yiftachel, Oren. 2000. "'Ethnocracy' and its Discontents: Minorities, Protest and the Israeli Polity." *Critical Inquiry* 26: 725–756.

Zaller, John. 1992. *The Nature and Origins of Mass Opinion.* Cambridge, UK: Cambridge University Press.

Zweig, Michael. 2000. *The Working Class Majority: America's Best Kept Secret.* Ithaca, NY: ILR Press.

INDEX